**Effective
Business
Relocation**

Effective Business Relocation

A Guide to Workable
Approaches for Relocating
Displaced Businesses

William N. Kinnard, Jr.
Stephen D. Messner

Center for Real Estate and
Urban Economic Studies
The University of Connecticut

Heath Lexington Books
D. C. Heath and Company
Lexington, Massachusetts

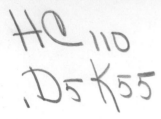

Portions of this book were made possible
through an Urban Renewal Demonstration
contract awarded by the Department of
Housing and Urban Development under provisions of Section 314(b) of the Housing
Act of 1954, as amended, to the University
of Connecticut.

Printed in the United States of America

Library of Congress Number: 78-113590

Contents

Preface

Public improvement and development programs frequently result in the forced displacement of business establishments lying in their path. With a combination of financial reimbursement for expenses and damages incurred in the process of relocating, and imaginative assistance in coping with the problems of finding and moving to a new location that permits the displaced businessman to continue to operate profitably, many local urban renewal agencies (whatever their official title) have benefited both the affected businesses and their communities by helping displacees relocate successfully. In this framework, a "successful" relocation is one in which a displaced firm is at least as well located and operating at least as profitably at the new site as in its former quarters.

The successful techniques and approaches of local urban renewal agencies and their business relocation staffs can serve as a guide to other groups confronted with similar business relocation problems. In addition, and potentially more important in the long run, these same techniques and approaches can be applied effectively to solve the problems of firms displaced by highway projects, public building projects, or any other type of public improvement program. The kinds of recurring problems encountered in business relocation are common to all such programs. So, too, are the workable solutions. Indeed, many of the techniques can be applied to entirely private relocations. The entire range of effective approaches discussed here includes some that are peculiar to public improvement programs, however. As a result, this volume focuses on what has proved effective and what can be done to keep *displaced* businesses operating profitably in acceptable locations.

In carrying out the research for this study and preparing the manuscript, the authors received assistance and advice from many sources. Each of the local public agencies discussed in this volume gave generously of its staff time and its records. Without this universally unfailing help, the study would not have been possible. To all these local agency staff members, and to the relocated businessmen who willingly submitted to lengthy interviews, we offer our sincere thanks.

Many staff members of the Department of Housing and Urban Development, both in Washington and in each of the HUD regional offices visited, helped us at two critical stages of the research. At the outset, they offered suggestions about research design and case studies to be included. They also made valuable critical comments about the finished manuscript. Financial support from HUD in the form of an Urban Renewal Demonstration Report Grant made the entire study possible.

Our colleagues and associates in the Center for Real Estate and Urban Economic Studies of the University of Connecticut gave us valuable support throughout the entire period of research and manuscript preparation. For nearly two years, our skilled and patient secretarial staff coped effectively with field notes and seemingly endless manuscript revisions. Particular thanks are due Sidney H. Seamans, the Center's editor, for his constant help in production, format design, style and proofreading.

We are confident that all this assistance has produced a factually accurate and usable document on effective approaches to business relocation. The opinions and conclusions are entirely our responsibility, as are any inaccuracies or misinterpretations that may remain.

Finally, we want to acknowledge the continuing and patient support of our wives for over two years. In partial recognition of their important but often unsung contribution, we gratefully dedicate this volume to Iris and Sue.

Storrs, Connecticut   William N. Kinnard, Jr.
October 1969   Stephen D. Messner

Key to Abbreviations

AHA	Atlanta Housing Authority
BDP	State-funded business displacement payment (Pennsylvania– Philadelphia)
BGF	Development Bank of Puerto Rico
BHURA	Baltimore Housing and Urban Renewal Authority (predecessor to the Department of Housing and Community Development)
CAC	Citizens' Action Committee (New Haven)
CBD	Central Business District
CCMO	Charles Center Management Offices (Baltimore)
CDC	Commercial Development Corporation of Puerto Rico
CPI	Community Progress, Inc. (New Haven)
CREUES	Center for Real Estate and Urban Economic Studies, University of Connecticut
CRP	Community Renewal Program
CRUV	Puerto Rico Urban Renewal and Housing Corporation
DARE	Downtown Area Renewal Effort (Greensboro)
DBL	Displaced Business Loan (Small Business Administration)
EDL	Economic Development Loan (Small Business Administration)
EOL	Economic Opportunity Loan (Small Business Administration)
FDC	Food Distribution Center (Philadelphia)
FHA	Federal Housing Administration
GNRP	General Neighborhood Renewal Plan
GSA	U. S. General Services Administration
HCD	Department of Housing and Community Development (Baltimore)

HUD	U. S. Department of Housing and Urban Development
IDC	Industrial Development Company (Little Rock)
IRS	U. S. Internal Revenue Service
LPA	Local Public Agency (responsible for execution of local urban renewal program)
LRHA	Little Rock Housing Authority
NHRA	New Haven Redevelopment Authority
OCU	Oklahoma City University
OCURA	Oklahoma City Urban Renewal Authority
OEO	U. S. Office of Economic Opportunity
PERT/CPM	Program Evaluation and Review Techniques/Critical Path Method (Little Rock)
PIDC	Philadelphia Industrial Development Corporation
PRA	Philadelphia Redevelopment Authority; Providence Redevelopment Authority
SBA	U. S. Small Business Administration
SBDC	Small Business Development Center (Detroit)
SBDP	Small Business Displacement Payment (Department of Housing and Urban Development)
SBOC	Small Business Opportunities Corporation (Chicago)
SCORE	Service Corps of Retired Executives (Small Business Administration)
SFRA	San Francisco Redevelopment Agency
TAP	Mayor's Committee for Total Action against Poverty (Detroit)
URA	U. S. Urban Renewal Administration, Department of Housing and Urban Development (now Renewal Assistance Administration)
VA	Veterans' Administration

Introduction

The Problem of Business Relocation

Urban renewal, highway development, the construction of public buildings and other programs involving public improvements typically require the acquisition of privately-owned real estate to provide space for public improvements. In addition, private developments frequently involve the reuse of land already occupied. In nearly all such cases, the existing occupants of the space planned for reuse must be displaced to make way for the new uses.

It has long been recognized that the involuntary displacement of private property owners places a special burden and hardship on them. Under the laws of eminent domain and condemnation, just compensation must be paid them for the property rights they are forced to relinquish. It is a relatively recent idea, however, that *occupants* of real estate who are displaced by public improvement programs, whatever their tenancy status, are entitled to compensation for the expenses and damages they experience when they are forced to move. Families displaced by urban redevelopment projects under the housing act of 1949 could receive moving expenses under special circumstances, notably when the legal costs involved in eviction were expected to exceed moving expenses plus one month's rent at the new location.[1] It was not until the Housing Act of 1956 amended the Housing Act of 1949 that all residential tenants (families and individuals) displaced by urban renewal projects were entitled to relocation payments. A 100% federal grant was made available to local public agencies for this purpose under the provisions of Section 106 (f) of the Housing Act of 1949, as amended in 1956.

The financial and other economic impacts on displaced businesses were also not formally recognized until 1956, when the Housing Act of 1949 was further amended to enable local public agencies to use federal grant funds to reimburse businesses displaced by urban renewal for moving expenses and/or personal property losses up to modest fixed limits.[2] In subsequent Congresses, the

[1] For a full discussion of the policies adapted from the United States Housing Administration for relocation payments to families, see Robert P. Groberg, *Centralized Relocation: A New Municiple Service* (Washington: National Association of Housing and Redevelopment Officials, 1969), pp. 2–4.

[2] See Section 304 of the "Housing Act of 1956" which amended Section 106 of the original Act to include subsection f(1–3).

amount and type of assistance that displaced businesses could receive were increased.[3]

The pattern of assistance has grown substantially in three directions. First, the kinds of loss or disruption for which compensation is paid have been expanded. Second, the amount of reimbursement or compensation for which a displaced firm may be eligible has generally increased. Third, both loans on terms favorable to the borrower and non-monetary assistance in the form of advice and consultation have become more widely available.

Studies of business relocation in urban renewal projects brought out the fact that financial reimbursement of expenses and losses dealt with only part of the problem, however.[4] The major objective is to *relocate* businesses successfully, and not simply to compensate them for direct out-of-pocket expenses occasioned by forced displacement, important as that compensation can be. Relocation involves both moving out of the firm's existing quarters and moving into a new location. Compensation or reimbursement is addressed primarily to moving out. For a relocation to be "successful" the firm must find and move into space at least as well located as its former quarters, and the firm must be operating at least as profitably as it was in the old location.

Thus, simply making more money available does not necessarily provide dislocated businesses with the means to relocate "successfully." Most displaced businesses are viable economic entities that can and should survive under "normal" market conditions. While most businesses have a high probability of survival and continued profitability in any reasonable location, the disruptive impact of forced relocation is frequently too severe a shock to withstand. This is particularly true for small businesses, or when displacement is coupled with an attendant reduction in business volume just before and just after the move.

Most dislocated businesses can and should be saved in the sense that they have a legitimate economic and financial reason to continue in operation. Yet many cannot do so without substantial outside assistance during the transitional period of relocation. This assistance takes both financial and non-financial forms. Still others do survive the move, but find it difficult to maintain a competitive level of profitability in the new location. Especially since the great majority of business firms affected by urban renewal projects in particular are

[3]Brian J. L. Berry, Sandra J. Parsons, and Rutherford H. Platt, *The Impact of Urban Renewal on Small Business* (Chicago: Center for Urban Studies, University of Chicago, 1968), pp. 197–210, especially Tables 6.1 and 6.2.

[4]This is a major point made in the following: *Ibid,* pp. xvi–xvii; William N. Kinnard, Jr. and Zenon S. Malinowski, *The Impact of Dislocation from Urban Renewal Areas on Small Business* (prepared for SBA; Storrs: School of Business Administration, University of Connecticut, 1960); William N. Kinnard, Jr., *Issues in Business Relocation and Property Acquisition Relating to Just Compensation* (Connecticut Urban Research Reports No. 2; Storrs: Institute of Urban Research, University of Connecticut, 1964); and Basil George Zimmer, *Rebuilding Cities: The Effects of Displacement and Relocation on Small Business* (Chicago: Quadrangle Books, 1964).

relatively small, it appears that outside assistance and skills must supplement the skills of owners and managers to bring about "successful" relocation.

Business displacement and the attendant problems of relocation are not restricted to urban renewal projects. Financial and advisory assistance to business displacees has the longest record of legislative authorization and application in practice in urban renewal, however. The results of business relocation efforts in urban renewal projects can serve as a guide to good practice in other public improvement programs confronted with similar problems.

Purpose of the Study

Because of earlier preoccupation with the nature and dimensions of the problems caused by business displacement, previous studies of business relocation have focused on the impact of forced dislocation on the affected businesses, and on the need for expanded and improved forms of assistance. There is now sufficient experience and exposure in business relocation activity (in urban renewal, at least) to consider the components and conditions for successful relocation in a variety of recurring problem situations. This study accepts the fact that achieving a successful relocation *is* a problem for every displaced business, as well as the public agency involved in the development program that causes the displacement. It thus uses demonstrated successes to develop a pattern of approach that can be employed effectively by both public agencies and private groups seeking to help displaced businesses relocate successfully.

Given the underlying assumption that most displaced businesses can and should continue in operation, the specific objectives are:

1. To identify those methods and techniques of business relocation which offer the greatest prospect for keeping displaced businesses in existence and operating profitably at their new locations;
2. To establish (for purposes of analysis and study) categories of business relocation problems and issues, especially those most likely to recur in other communities and other project areas;
3. To indicate which relocation efforts have proved most effective in dealing with the several types of problems specified, paying particular but not exclusive attention to efforts which are imaginative and innovative;
4. To report examples of successful experiences in business relocation which illustrate the application of those effective efforts;
5. To delineate the conditions under which the successful application of previous effective efforts can most probably be repeated;
6. To estimate and indicate the potential transferability of the reported techniques and procedures to other communities and projects, recognizing that what may appear unique in one situation may be a recurring problem from one community or project to another.

In summary, this volume may be used as a handbook or manual that offers guidelines to dealing with business relocation problems. It outlines methods and techniques whose effectiveness has been demonstrated in urban renewal projects under prescribed conditions. It should provide personnel concerned with business relocation in both public and private agencies with a sound basis for achieving good results as problems arise which are new to them. As a corollary, it can help them to avoid predictable pitfalls which may be anticipated from the cases and projects studied.

Scope and Coverage

The findings presented here are all based on business relocation experiences in urban renewal projects. Because similar sorts of business relocation problems occur in cities and urban renewal programs of all sizes, the communities studied range in 1960 population from 9,000 to 3,500,000. Most are in the medium-sized range, in appreciation of the fact that agencies in extremely large communities frequently have resources which are simply not available in smaller communities. The transferability of the findings could be seriously questioned if excessive emphasis were placed on what had been accomplished in major metropolitan centers only.

The cases and methods studied came from local public agencies in 24 cities. These cities, and the HUD regions in which they are located, are:

Region I:	Ansonia, Connecticut
	New Haven, Connecticut
	Pawtucket, Rhode Island
	Providence, Rhode Island
Region II:	Baltimore, Maryland
	Philadelphia, Pennsylvania
Region III:	Atlanta, Georgia
	Douglas, Georgia
	Greensboro, North Carolina
	Louisville, Kentucky
	Mobile, Alabama
	Nashville, Tennessee
Region IV:	Chicago, Illinois
	Fargo, North Dakota
	Detroit, Michigan
	Grand Rapids, Michigan
	St. Paul, Minnesota

Region V: Little Rock, Arkansas
                             Oklahoma City, Oklahoma

Region VI: Fresno, California
                             Sacramento, California
                             San Francisco, California
                             Santa Clara, California

Region VII: San Juan, Puerto Rico

It was quite apparent early in the investigations that organizational structures and legal frameworks within which business relocation activity takes place vary from one geographic area to another. In order to obtain information about business relocation processes under as many different sets of circumstances and patterns of enabling legislation as possible, there is a wide geographic spread among the cities studied. All seven Regions of the Department of Housing and Urban Development (HUD) are covered. In addition, the communities selected represent seventeen different states.

Preliminary investigations were made into business relocation experiences reported in existing literature on the subject. Supplemented with data from the relocation files of HUD in Washington, D.C., they served to identify a wide variety of relocation problems and issues for study. Moreover, a conscious effort was made to cover businesses of as many different types as possible, with respect to size, organizational structure, product or service, and tenancy status.

The problems selected for study represented the types of issues encountered in test communities, as well as in earlier studies. At the outset, specific groups of issues were consciously investigated. Others were added as they emerged in field interviews. The initial list included:

Small, owner-operated businesses;

Businesses with special locational or licensing requirements;

Businesses operated by minority group members;

Businesses operated by "elderly" businessmen;

Neighborhood-oriented businesses;

Non-retail, non-CBD business activities;

Churches and non-profit organizations;

Displacees seeking to return to the project area:

Temporary and/or interim relocations, whether on-site or off-site;

Cooperative groupings of related businesses, with or without joint ownership;

Unskilled owner-managers in non-specialized businesses;

Training of relocatees to become better businessmen;

Obtaining financing for working capital, leasehold improvements, and new business endeavors;

Qualification of small businesses for Small Business Displacement Payments;

Qualification for Small Business Administration loans, especially Displaced Business Loans and Economic Development Loans.

The standard for selecting cases to be studied in detail was the anticipated usefulness and/or transferability that the illustration would have for similar problems in other localities or project areas. Finally, the study attempted to utilize cases as recent as possible, so that current administrative procedures and regulations were applicable. In some instances, this standard was relaxed when the central issue was to illustrate a point or a procedure unrelated to the regulations or level of reimbursement.

Methodology

The study formally began in March 1967. The first step was to develop a preliminary list of local public agencies (LPA's) in which business relocation efforts might be studied most fruitfully. This was accomplished with the assistance of the business relocation staff of HUD in Washington. Supplementary information was obtained from the files of the Center for Real Estate and Urban Economic Studies on its earlier studies of business relocation, from the National Association of Housing and Redevelopment Officials, and from the Office of Consumer Relations of HUD. Forty LPA's were identified for further and more detailed investigation. Direct communication with each agency led to a final list of 24 LPA's in which case studies were obtained. This list is provided in the foregoing section on Scope and Coverage.

Between June and October 1967, each LPA was visited by one or both of the principal investigators. Detailed interviews were held with LPA officials and staff, and with each affected businessman in each relocation case included in this volume. These field visits also provided detailed information about the organization and operation of business relocation activities in each LPA, as well as specific data about each relocation studied. Over 125 individual cases were investigated, from which the final 86 included in this report were selected.

The information derived from all of these sources was compiled as individual case studies and organized for analytical purposes in terms of the issues and problems outlined in Part II. Draft copies of case studies developed in each LPA were submitted to the LPA staff for confirmation and/or correction of factual information.

Applications and Limitations

The findings of this study are applicable to the solution of business relocation problems under a wide range of public improvement programs. The approaches and techniques identified as effective are not restricted to urban renewal projects, or to application by public agency personnel. Some specific provisions of federal and/or state law may be specific to urban renewal projects. However, legislation can be and is being expanded to include similar provisions for relocation assistance (particularly reimbursement of moving expenses and/or property loss) in other public improvement programs. Much more importantly, however, non-financial assistance is frequently more effective in solving most business relocation problems. And this type of assistance can often be provided as easily and as effectively by private agencies, consultants or real estate advisors as by public agency personnel.

This report does not provide a statistically representative sample of business relocation efforts for the nation, specific regions, or even the individual LPA's covered. It offers case studies suggestive of effective approaches rather than either a statistical analysis or a generalized description of the process of business relocation.

Moreover, no attempt has been made to evaluate business relocation programs, either nationwide or in individual communities. The sole concern is with individual cases and organizational structures selected for their applicability as illustrations of effective techniques for dealing with specific relocation problems or issues.

Finally, this report is neither a comprehensive critique nor an evaluation of legislation, regulations, policies, or administrative procedures relating to business relocation. It emphasizes what can be and has been done while working within an existing regulatory framework. Policies and procedures are discussed only to the extent that they are relevant to the handling of a specific type of relocation problem.

Conclusions

Despite the large amount of information studied and reported in this sizable volume, the conclusions drawn from the data are relatively few and simple. They have ample detailed support in the analysis of business relocation problem-solving and in the individual relocation cases reported. The usefulness and meaning of this report do not depend upon the conclusions, significant though they may be. Its real contribution lies in the guidance and help that the problem analysis and individual case reports will provide to business relocation advisors and to displaced businessmen when they are confronted with the same or very similar problems.

Based on their intensive study of business relocation cases and procedures, the details of which are presented in Parts II and III, the authors conclude that:

1. Ample opportunities are available to business relocation personnel *within the existing legislative and regulatory framework* to deal effectively with virtually any business relocation problem that might arise. In most instances, alternative lines of action are open, allowing for flexible treatment in accordance with the specific requirements of the particular case. This conclusion is supported by evidence derived from over 80 business relocation cases in 24 LPA's throughout the United States. It is reached in full recognition of the fact that current regulations and statutes may occasionally inhibit the handling of specific relocation problems in accordance with the desires of business relocation personnel and of the affected businessmen. But as long as this regulatory framework permits adaptation in response to the needs of displacees, these specific limitations can usually be resolved on an individual case basis.

2. The successful application of currently available techniques and resources to individual business relocation cases in any urban renewal program (or public improvement program) depends upon the creation of an atmosphere of mutual understanding and trust between public officials on the one hand, and affected businessmen on the other. This is an essential precondition before attention can be focused on the real estate, financial and business management issues that are peculiar to the relocation of displaced businesses.

3. There is clearly a general procedure and approach common to the successful handling of all business relocation problems that should be applied by every public agency in each and every business relocation case. Systematic organization for relocation, careful advance planning, continuing information flows through open channels of communication, sound advice on planning the move, personalized assistance in the execution of the move, and prompt processing of relocation claims and other financial entitlements – these are all essential ingredients of this universally effective approach. Within this general framework, however, business relocation personnel must develop a high degree of sensitivity to the importance of different component issues in each business relocation case. They must approach every case with flexibility of thought and behavior. This flexibility should reflect willingness and ability to adjust actions to meet the

specific requirements of the particular business in question, within the framework of law, regulations and agency policies in force at the time.

4. A continuing flow of carefully detailed analyses of past experiences is needed, both within the public agency itself and among similar agencies throughout the United States. This would provide a continuing guide to *how* business relocation personnel can adapt and adjust to the specific requirements of each individual case. Significant savings in time, effort and money can be realized by regularly publishing these experiences and distributing them widely. Such information would provide the background knowledge necessary to identify workable alternative courses of action. It would also establish a foundation from which truly innovative efforts can be undertaken in new types of situations. It would help avoid attempting approaches that have already been demonstrated to be unworkable.

5. The techniques and approaches to business relocation that have proved effective in the context of urban renewal are generally transferable to other public improvement programs — and indeed to private relocations as well. The specific capabilities and resources available will vary from one legislative and regulatory framework to another, influencing the specific steps that can be taken in any given situation. Nevertheless, the process of finding a suitable new location and relocating the business successfully is basically the same. Both relocatees and those seeking to advise and assist them can follow the framework presented here to achieve the common objective of occupying new quarters at least as well located and operating at least as profitably as was the case at the firm's former location.

Summary Findings:
Effective Approaches
to Business Relocation
Problems

Summary Findings: Effective Approaches to Business Relocation Problems

Business relocation activities in urban renewal programs are carried out within a framework of federal legislation, HUD regulations, and state and local law. Moreover, the specifics of individual redevelopment plans vary from one project area to another. At any given given point in time, the business relocation staff of an LPA must operate within this framework of laws, regulations and plans.

The history of legislation and regulations relating to business relocation since 1956 demonstrates clearly that this is *not* an unchanging framework which LPA's and affected businessmen must necessarily accept as given. Indeed, most of the changes that have occurred have been the result of suggestions and pressures from LPA personnel and business groups, as well as from HUD staff. Nevertheless, it is not the function of the business relocation officer to question or attempt to alter laws or regulations that appear to inhibit successful solutions to relocation problems currently confronting him.

This report, therefore, concentrates on the methods and approaches developed by business relocation personnel in selected LPA's throughout the United States within the framework of then-existing laws and regulations. Whether changes or improvements in these constraining influences appear necessary or appropriate is irrelevant here (although in the professional opinions of the authors, there are several changes that they would recommend).

The findings indicate clearly that a great deal can be and has been accomplished. The potential negative impacts of displacement and relocation on affected businesses can be reduced. The selected experiences of particular LPA's can be used as an effective guide to business relocation personnel in other communities confronted with the same types of problems.

Nature of the Business Relocation Problem

When a particular business relocation case enters the work load of the business relocation staff, the fundamental issue to be resolved is: "How can this business be relocated in order to maintain its existence as a viable economic unit with the least negative impact on its operations or profitability?" A business relocation effort is "successful" when the operator remains in business (not necessarily the same line of business) with no diminution in the profitability of his operations. If, as a result of the relocation effort, the business is larger, more efficient, or more profitable, this is a dividend which is highly desirable but not essential to achieving the objectives of relocation.

In order to achieve this "success" in every case, the business relocation officer (whatever his or her precise title) must satisfy the conditions established by

HUD, by the LPA, and by the local municipality (in those cases in which the LPA is not an integral part of the municipal administration). Federal policies and requirements were first established in the Housing Act of 1956, which amended the Housing Act of 1949 by adding Section 106(f). It authorized LPA's to make payments to all dislocated families, individuals and *businesses* for "reasonable and necessary moving expenses and any actual direct losses of property."

This legislation constituted recognition of the responsibility of both the federal government and the LPA to assist displaced businesses in relocating successfully, as this term has been defined above. Because of questions over the constitutionality or legality of extending compensation in excess of acquisition awards in some states, the 1956 amendment provided for relocation payments to be financed by a 100 per cent federal grant. The specific types and amounts of relocation assistance and relocation payments for which displaced businesses are eligible have been expanded through subsequent Congressional amendments. Interpretations and regulations relating to the implementation of business relocation activities under these legislative authorizations have been issued periodically by HUD, through amendments to the *Urban Renewal Manual* and through numerous *LPA Letters.* These set the conditions which must be met by the LPA through its business relocation staff in order to satisfy HUD requirements.

The first major component of the business relocation "problem" confronting the local business relocation officer, then, is to operate within the limits established by federal legislation and regulations. This is necessary to ensure approval of reimbursement for the performance of service activities and the award of compensation to displaced businesses. Compliance with these statutory and regulatory requirements does not mean unthinking and slavish acceptance without appeal in specific "hardship" cases. However, they do provide constraints to the alternative solutions that can realistically be considered by the business relocation officer attempting to deal effectively with the needs of the specific business.

A second level of constraining influences on the pattern of behavior of business relocation officers is provided by the policies and objectives of the LPA. These are, in turn, a function of the social and economic goals of the municipality. Workable solutions to specific business relocation problems are conditioned and defined by the character and objectives of local renewal programs. A common goal in renewal programs is the maintenance or improvement of the employment, income and tax base of the community. Moreover, the planning of the business relocation work load may be seriously influenced by the staging and timing of project execution. The reuse plan and disposition policy of the LPA for specific project areas will also dictate the kinds of approaches which can be regarded as appropriate in handling specific relocation cases. These local policy and program considerations do not *determine* the precise treatment of each business displacee, but they do decidedly limit the feasibility and acceptability of the choices for action by the business relocation staff.

Business relocation officers do not make federal or local policy with respect to the business relocation program, nor do they effect changes in these regulations or policies to accommodate the needs of individual businesses in cases currently being handled. They can and must, however, recognize the wide range of alternatives available to them within the confines of these regulations and policies. Their task is to identify and apply the most appropriate and effective techniques for relocating the affected business as a profitable enterprise, within the limits of allowable action.

Conditions for Successful Relocation Efforts

The most inspired and imaginative ideas for handling a given relocation case cannot be effective unless they are carried out within an environment which contributes to their success. This observation may be obvious and unnecessary, but it can be and frequently is overlooked in the pressures of "getting the job done." Particularly in new programs or in those which have not previously involved business relocation, the sudden addition of a large number of business relocation cases can lead to *ad hoc* reactions and efforts which are self-defeating because they are not well planned or systematically organized.

The first important ingredient in any business relocation program is adequate staffing. Increasingly, LPA's have discovered that business relocation is an activity which requires a separate, specialized staff of its own. While successes have been recorded by agencies which assign family and business relocation cases to the same personnel, business relocation generally requires both undivided attention and highly specialized skills. The regulations and requirements related to business relocation are complex and differ from those applicable to family relocations. Business relocation specialists are required in all but the most simple and commonplace cases. Businessmen are also human beings who need sensitive understanding of their human problems in the disturbing and even traumatic experience of displacement. Nevertheless, their basic relocation problems are more directly related to real estate, site selection, financing, and business operational skills.

The volume of business relocation cases in most communities, when added to the need for continuing attention to the more troublesome and involved cases, means that both adequate numbers and necessary skills must be available on the business relocation staff to handle both the volume of routine cases and those cases the staff considers unusual or unique. For smaller communities or those with a very limited urban renewal program, temporary appointments of staff or consultants from outside frequently provide the personnel and skills required.

Coupled with the need for adequate staff is the requirement for a budget sufficient to permit the staff to perform its assignments satisfactorily. This involves a commitment on the part of the LPA to the proposition that effective business relocation is a major component of a successful renewal effort.

This leads to an intangible but critical point. Successful business relocation efforts are commonly found in programs where the *community* (represented by the municipal government and by action-oriented organizations of businessmen) has adopted maximum success in business relocation activities as a major objective of the renewal program. This must be manifested in more than mere words and expressions of concern. Communities with the best "track record" in business relocation, as well as those which have demonstrated the highest degree of innovative skill in handling unusual business relocation cases, have typically enjoyed direct personal involvement on the part of the mayor, municipal officials, business leaders, and the top executives of the LPA. Thus business relocation is not an activity which can be delegated to a specialized staff which is then left to its own devices outside the mainstream of the renewal program.

Even less tangible is the creation of an atmosphere in which displaced businessmen are confident that their problems are a matter of genuine concern to the LPA and to the community. Numerous cases of successful relocation efforts have hinged on mutual trust and cooperation between affected businessmen on the one hand, and local officials on the other. This is an extremely important consideration, because businessmen confronted with forced displacement and relocation frequently exhibit an inability to take positive action that borders on the paralysis of shock. Although it is a standard procedure in any renewal program, forced displacement is usually a unique experience to the businessman concerned. Demonstrations of genuine interest in his future by local officials, including business relocation officers, are typically necessary in order to overcome this tendency to inaction. The displacee can be conditioned to act in his own behalf, as well as in cooperation with the business relocation staff. This is achieved through early and periodic personal visits, individualized explanations of the relocation process and of the assistance and reimbursement to which he is entitled, personalized identification of his problems and needs, and participation by local officials other than business relocation personnel in the joint decisions about the most appropriate way to solve his problems.

Business relocation is a continuing process that requires an overall plan (quite apart from that stipulated in HUD regulations) to maximize the success of individual business relocation efforts. An essential ingredient in this plan is effective organization of files and procedures to handle commonplace, recurring cases as expeditiously as possible. This has two important effects. First, the individual businessmen involved are more likely to be satisfied with their treatment and to require less personal handling because of complaints or misunderstanding. Second, it will allow more time for the business relocation staff to devote to the really complex and demanding cases. The LPA's with the most efficient organization for expeditious processing of "normal" claims are typically those with the best record of imaginative and innovative solutions to the more knotty problems.

The best organized business relocation staffs have developed local manuals for the systematic processing of all cases on the business relocation work load, and have developed forms for internal use which provide a continuing check on the status of all active cases. Moreover, they have developed data forms for recording all of the pertinent information that experience has shown is necessary in order to work out the proper solution or approach to each type of case. This approach is particularly effective when it is combined with a program of continuing and systematic review of the status of active cases through personal contacts. This is one more illustration of the critical importance of recognizing that businessmen are people, with human fears and reactions at least as strong as those of displaced families.

The cases discussed in detail in Part III of this report indicate the kinds of activities that have proved successful in widely separated communities of different sizes, to cope with a great variety of business relocation problems. For these cases to be useful guides to other LPA's confronted with similar situations, there must be an appreciation of the reasons why these efforts have proved successful. Two basic categories of reasons have emerged from this study. First, there must be an atmosphere of total commitment to success in business relocation within the framework of an adequately staffed and well-organized business relocation office which is oriented to expeditious handling of every business relocation case on a systematic basis. Second, there must be sensitivity to the peculiar and individual requirements of displaced business, coupled with the ability to adapt available resources to each problem on the basis of the needs of the business and the demonstrated workability of similar efforts from prior experience — locally or elsewhere.

Transferability of Prior Experience

One of the major impressions to emerge from the field work involved in this study was the lack of effective communication of ideas and experiences from one LPA to another. No matter how well organized or how well staffed a business relocation office may be, its personnel are typically so deeply involved in carrying out *their* program that there is little time available to share experiences or problems with others. In many communities, the business relocation staff has drawn upon its own experience to apply and adapt the techniques employed in prior successful relocations to similar situations as they have arisen. The creation and maintenance of good working files contributes greatly to the ability of a business relocation staff to draw effectively on its own experience.

In the course of the field interviews, the authors were frequently able to relate details of cases in one city to other business relocation personnel currently perplexed by similar situations which they had encountered for the first time. The necessarily limited range of skills and experience in most LPA's, especially those with relatively new programs, argues strongly for a conscious program of continuing exchange of information and experiences in business relocation through conferences, case studies, and visitations from one business relocation staff to another. It is only when the details of each case (including the background and the motivations of the parties involved) are understood that their applicability in similar situations can be detected. For effective handling of business relocation problems that are new or unusual locally, a business relocation staff must remain continuously aware of what has worked and what has not worked in other communities confronted with similar problems. With this backlog of knowledge from the experience of others, variations and innovations to meet the current requirements are much more likely to be developed.

Recurring Issues in the
Relocation of Businesses

The examination of business relocation cases in widely separated communities with significant differences in the scope and character of their urban renewal programs, and of their business relocation activities, has yielded a large number of "success" stories. In case form, they describe and explain the techniques employed in the relocation of individual businesses and groups of businesses, as well as the handling of selected types of relocation problems.

This report offers a compendium of guidelines and suggestions for workable approaches which can be employed by LPA business relocation personnel and LPA executive administrators when they are confronted with similar challenges. For this presentation to be useful, the findings from the case studies must be classified and categorized in some systematic fashion. This section offers such a classification of business relocation problems, arranged in terms of what the authors consider the most significant recurring issues. Under each heading, the approaches and techniques which have proved effective in one or more communities are summarized. References to the specific cases in Part III which illustrate the successful handling of each issue or problem area discussed are provided in the topic index at the beginning of Part III.

Any such classification system is necessarily a matter of personal professional judgment. Although the headings have been chosen carefully on the basis of the evidence from the cases studied, as well as an extensive search of existing literature on business relocation, the overlapping nature of many problems and their effective solutions means that the categories are not necessarily mutually exclusive. There is inevitably some repetition of ideas and techniques under more than one heading. The justification for this admittedly somewhat artificial classification system is that it is designed to provide a meaningful working aid to LPA personnel seeking guidance in the resolution of their own business relocation problems.

The ideas and techniques listed here are reports of what has actually worked under specified conditions in individual localities. They are not suggestions by the authors or others for actions which have not been tested in the field. Moreover, it is obvious but worthy of mention that no one community has undertaken *all* of the efforts enumerated. Indeed, it is extremely doubtful whether any one LPA necessarily should have. However, the problems have recurred within and among urban renewal programs thoughout the United States, and in all probability will recur again and again.

In serving the relocation needs of business displacees effectively, the LPA business relocation staff also serves the objectives of the national and local program. The ultimate function of business relocation activity is to support the achievement of the goals of urban renewal.

Obtaining Cooperation and Support from the Displacee

In every business relocation case, the process is smoother and more efficient if there is effective cooperation between the business relocation staff and the displacee from the outset. In most cases, the relocation is involuntary in every sense of the word. Even when the displaced businessman is willing and anxious to cooperate, however, the responsibility for creating the proper attitudes and atmosphere that will be conducive to successful relocation rests with the LPA staff.

Early Notice of Displacement

Innumerable experiences demonstrate convincingly that early notice and contact with the businesses to be displaced are essential. Normally, this should occur as early in the planning stage of the project as possible. Even when little hard information can be given to the affected businessmen, it is important to scotch rumors and misimpressions as quickly as possible. Information about the business relocation process itself can be provided very early. Moreover, at least planned dates can be communicated, particularly to discourage precipitate and ill-advised action on the part of the displacee.

Forms of Notice
Personal visits. The most effective form of contact, when staff time and personnel permit, is a personal visit to each affected businessman. This may be carried out by the LPA staff, by a local business advisory group, or by a firm hired for this purpose. The important point is that the individual calling on the business should be sufficiently informed to be able to answer the predictable questions of the displacee, and to provide accurate information about the business relocation process and the known details of the project plan.
Personal letters. These are less effective than personal visits, primarily because they are not necessarily read, nor understood if they are read, by the businessman. They offer no opportunity for direct questioning by the businessman. However, such letters as have been reasonably effective have contained a strong invitation to call or visit the LPA business relocation staff for

the answers to any questions. In communities with relatively small business relocation staffs or with extremely heavy work loads, it is sometimes preferable to provide early notice through the mail than to wait for a personal visit to each business. Under these circumstances, a follow-up personal visit as soon after mailing the letter as possible has proved extremely effective.

General information bulletins. Many LPA's have distributed booklets explaining the business relocation process and the ingredients of the project plan, together with an invitation of the personnel to contact for further information. This has sometimes proved to be a useful supplement to be included with the personal letter distributed simultaneously to all affected businessmen. With the advent of mechanical equipment to perform the task, individually typed and personally addressed letters have proved to be much better received by displacees than obviously mimeographed or printed form letters.

Dissemination of information through news media. In communities in which there is good rapport between the LPA and local news media, news releases explaining the character of the project and the business relocation process have been successful as supplements to personal visits or letters. Interview programs on radio and TV have worked in a number of communities. LPA staff members have had an opportunity to answer in advance many of the most frequently asked questions. This helps create an atmosphere of understanding and appreciation. However, it should be regarded as a supplement to personal contacts, and not a substitute for them.

Meetings with groups of displacees. A number of LPA's have supplemented individual personal contacts by meeting with small groups of between 25 and 35 of the businessmen in the project area at a time. This is particularly effective if it is not possible to make the initial contact through a personal visit. The meetings are held very shortly after an informational letter has been mailed out. Frequently, the letter itself contains an invitation to a specific meeting on a particular date. This affords the businessmen an opportunity to raise questions, and to meet in person the LPA personnel with whom they will be dealing. One community has developed a slide presentation which is shown to displacees at such meetings. This is followed by a discussion period in which every businessman is introduced to the executive director of the agency and the director of the business relocation office. In addition, a representative of the SBA regional office is present, both to explain the SBA loan program for displacees and answer questions about it, and to become known to the businessmen for future contacts. In many communities, local business groups such as the chamber of commerce co-sponsor the group meetings.

Use of receipts. In at least two communities studied, displacees are requested to sign a receipt indicating that they have been provided with preliminary information, and have received a copy of the informational booklet on business relocation prepared by the LPA. This helps make the businessman conscious of the fact that he is being given information. It also serves as an extremely effective check on the status of the business relocation work load for internal review within the business relocation office.

Organizational Structures

The organization of the LPA and the relation of the relocation staff to other divisions are important determinants of the effectiveness of early contacts with displacees. The accuracy of the information transmitted to displacees is directly dependent on continuing communication of plans and other project data to the business relocation staff. Moreover, lack of effective planning and organization can lead to either duplication or contradiction in the information provided to the displacee. Either tends to result in confusion and concern on his part, and some loss of his cooperation and support.

Internal coordination. Particularly in large LPA's with a high degree of departmentalization there is a risk that business relocation activities enter the picture only after the property has been acquired — or at least after several contacts have been made by the acquisition staff. Many large LPA's have avoided this risk by coordinating the activities of acquisition and business relocation personnel. As a result, many of the fears and uncertainties of displacees are reduced because they are provided with information and know someone to contact for advice and assistance early in the redevelopment process. When urban renewal is handled by a city department, as it is in many states, coordination of effort with other departments not directly involved in urban renewal (e.g., public works, health, building inspection) has also reduced the risk of inaccurate or contradictory information being transmitted to displacees.

Joint visits. Some LPA's send both an acquisition staff member and a business relocation officer to visit businessmen being displaced. This initial contact provides information to the displacee about the timing and procedures involved in both acquisition and business relocation. Joint visits demonstrate to the businessman that there is real concern by the LPA, and that relocation is an integral part of the redevelopment process.

Use of planning programming charts. At least one LPA uses a "critical path chart" to identify the timing of business relocation activities in conjunction with the several stages of project execution. Staging of relocation is reviewed on a monthly basis, and personnel are reallocated to complete preliminary visits to all businessmen within the planning stage.

Early Identification of Problems

From the point of view of the business relocation officer, early contact with displacees helps identify the nature and magnitude of the problems likely to be encountered in handling the relocation work load in a given project. With this information, it is possible to plan more effectively for the treatment of the more difficult problems, as well as to identify the kinds of assistance that will probably have to be provided. For example, the number of firms likely to require and qualify for SBA loans, the amounts and types of loans likely to be sought, and the uses to which the loan proceeds will most probably be put all represent useful information which can be obtained through early contacts.

Contact with both business tenant and building owner. When the business to be displaced is a tenant, early discussions with both the businessman and his landlord can help to avoid subsequent conflicts over what are movable fixtures, and who is to receive compensation for damages to elements of personal property.

Revision of relocation plan. The early identification of special relocation problems not previously recognized in the project area has in several instances led to a modification of the relocation plan well in advance of its execution. This has reduced delays in approval and compensation, and has permitted the business relocation staff to plan appropriately for the treatment of the special problems unearthed in the early contact.

Staging of relocation. By early identification of the desires and needs of displacees, especially in terms of their need to remain on the site for specified periods, the staging of both relocation and demolition activity has been clarified in a number of communities. Possession of this information early in the planning stage has made it possible to reduce the number of temporary or interim relocations required, and has also made clear those specific situations in which interim moves have been necessary.

Business operational needs. In several communities, early visits and interviews with displacees have led to the discovery of weaknesses in their business skills. One LPA utilizes a university research organization whose representatives analyze the business problems (as opposed to the locational problems) of each affected businessman. In many instances, the specific skills required are identified, and recommendations are made for training which will aid and equip the businessman to accomplish a successful move and to do a better job in his new location.

Effect of Information on Displacee Attitudes

Better Cooperation through Full, Prompt Information

Rumors and misinformation are generally rampant as soon as renewal planning is announced for a project area. The experience of those LPA's with a systematic and comprehensive program of providing as much information as is available as early as possible indicates clearly that fewer suspicions or ill-advised actions by displacees are encountered when businessmen are provided with full information.

Awareness of alternatives. When the businessman is aware of his entitlements under business relocation and the procedures to be followed, his actions generally follow the lines prescribed under HUD and LPA regulations. This helps to minimize difficulties at a later time, when questions about reimbursement (or even refusals) might otherwise arise.

Personal contacts. Whether the initial contact with the business displacee is in person or in writing, an early interview has been demonstrated to be by far the most effective device for eliciting cooperation from the businessman. Given an opportunity to have his questions answered and his fears allayed, he frequently accepts the idea of relocation, whether he happens to support urban renewal and the attendant relocation of his business or not. Those LPA's with the greatest success along these lines are the ones which approach businessmen as human beings with human fears and uncertainties.

Overcoming communications difficulties. Many LPA's have encountered groups of businessmen who are not proficient in English. In such cases, it is extremely important to translate the pertinent regulations and other information into the language of the businessman. Moreover, many elderly businessmen in particular are illiterate. This emphasizes the critical importance of personal contacts, so that regulations and entitlements, as well as the redevelopment plan itself, can be explained orally in a face-to-face meeting. When the businessmen have little proficiency in English, it has proved effective to add (occasionally temporarily) a relocation officer who is bilingual to conduct the interviews with these businessmen. The incremental cost has been considerably more than offset by the reduction in difficulty and agitation encountered when the moves take place.

Continuous Flow of Information

Throughout the relocation process, but most especially during the period of waiting between the initial contact and the actual planning of the move, it is important to reassure displacees that the LPA is concerned with them and their problems. They should be kept informed about progress in the development of the project. This is particularly important if there are unscheduled delays in the execution of the project which will modify the timing of business moves.

Maintaining interest and enthusiasm on the part of displacees. Affected businessmen should not feel neglected, but as much a part of the project as possible. Several LPA's have accomplished this through follow-up visits on a systematic, periodic basis to keep track of the status of displacees before they move. A few LPA's have distributed monthly informational bulletins to businessmen not yet relocated, to keep them abreast of developments that will affect them in the project.

Information about program changes. Few LPA's have been able to carry out their business relocation programs entirely on schedule. Those which have followed a procedure of periodic flows of information to businessmen remaining on site, either through personal interviews or newsletters, have encountered substantially less resistance to changes. It has been possible to explain the reasons for changes or delays, while convincing the affected businessmen that the LPA still has their interests in mind.

Post-relocation interviews. A few LPA's interview relocatees after their moves, on a systematic basis. This is further evidence of the continuing concern of the LPA for the individual businessman, and is also a source of extremely useful information in planning and carrying out subsequent relocation programs. Reactions to the relocation process and suggestions for improving the services have in some instances resulted in changed procedures within the LPA.

Specialized or Separate Relocation Staff

Although effective business relocation efforts have, on occasion, been encountered among LPA's with relocation offices that handle both family and business relocations, the best experiences and the greatest opportunity for innovative and imaginative handling of "problem" cases were found among LPA's which had separate staffs specializing in business relocation. The size of the business relocation staff is largely a function of the work load to be handled. Whether this separate staff is large or small, however, there is a cumulative benefit to be derived from continuous handling of business relocation exclusively.

Specialized Business Relocation Staffs

Effective treatment of specialized problems. Business relocation problems and their solutions differ significantly from those encountered in relocating families. Efficiency and effectiveness are in part a function of experience. This experience can be gained considerably more rapidly by specialists in business relocation.

Utilization of specialized backgrounds. Business relocation problems involve special considerations of location analysis, market analysis, financing, and business operations. In a separate and specialized staff, it is possible to attract individuals with experience and skills in these critical areas. Except in the processing of claims and general procedures for relocation, family relocation personnel rarely have the necessary experience and skills to cope with these issues. They may become significant "problems" to the LPA primarily because the staff lacks the ability to handle them. By far the most successful efforts and the most imaginative treatments of special problems have occurred in LPA's that have in-house skills in real estate and business financing.

Better general assistance. By specializing in business relocation exclusively, a separate staff has the advantage of operational familiarity with regulations and procedures. This considerably increases the speed and accuracy of processing the routine cases that constitute the bulk of the work load.

Specially Designed Business Aids

A corollary result of having a separate business relocation staff is often the development of internal working materials that experience has shown to be successful in handling business relocation cases efficiently and well. Moreover, continuing exposure to recurring problems helps in identifying those cases in which highly specialized outside assistance is needed.

Internal manuals and forms. A number of LPA's have developed business relocation manuals for internal use. These manuals itemize the steps, procedures, and forms to be utilized in every business relocation case. In addition, some LPA's have developed local forms or checklists that are used to ensure that every step in the prescribed procedure is followed in the proper sequence, at the right time, and with no omissions. This considerably enhances the effectiveness of dealing with each individual businessman. It also helps provide for uniform treatment, which is essential to acceptance and cooperation from displacees.

Use of supplementary help. No matter how large or skilled a business relocation staff may be, situations arise in which outside technical assistance is both desirable and necessary. This has been particularly effective in non-recurring (for that locality, at least) problem cases, and for the performance of functions that would seriously interfere with the handling of the bulk of the relocation work load by the LPA staff. Several of the LPA's studied have utilized consultants to conduct relocation surveys and inventories, especially in the early planning of projects. In addition, market surveys have been successfully delegated to consultants, who have provided the LPA staff with necessary information about the resources expected to be available for relocation. In particularly difficult problem situations, such as machinery and equipment appraisals or the relocation of highly specialized manufacturing establishments, individual consultants have successfully supplemented the efforts and skills of the LPA staff. **Development of internal skills.** LPA's with large enough staffs to permit specialization of function have utilized individual staff members as specialists in difficult but recurring situations. For example, a number of those studied have assigned an individual staff member to work primarily with SBA in arranging financing for displacees. This time-consuming procedure has been carried out much more successfully when this type of specialization has been possible.

Liaison with the Business Community
In a number of communities, active cooperation and support from organized business groups has proved to be a very effective aid to the LPA in "selling" both urban renewal in general and the idea of relocation in particular to business displacees.
Effective cooperation with business groups. Relocation personnel with business experience can deal on a more nearly equal basis with the business leaders who generally make up the action committees of local business and development groups. Substantial success has been achieved in some instances by working through existing organizations such as the local chamber of commerce, a local development commission, and/or the local real estate board. One LPA has had particular success in working closely with the local chapter of the Society of Industrial Realtors. In other areas, *ad hoc* committees have been formed to supplement the LPA's program. Their primary function has been to work with businesses affected by urban renewal. Among other functions, they have demonstrated an ability to "sell" the potential gains from relocation to displacees.
Encouraging the creation of business advisory groups. Some LPA's have consciously and actively encouraged the formation of action committees to aid and advise business displacees, as a supplement to the activities of the LPA staff. This procedure has had the secondary effect of acquainting businessmen not directly affected by urban renewal with its implications and anticipated advantages. They, in turn, have helped convince displacees to cooperate with the LPA.

Use of Outside Groups and Individuals

LPA's with relatively few business relocation personnel and a limited range of skills (but not only in such cases) have found outside groups with specialized skills and abilities an important supplement to the LPA staff. They provide the necessary expertise to cope with unusual and/or time-consuming cases, as well as helping to create an environment of acceptance by business displacees.

Existing Groups and Agencies
The LPA business relocation staff must be aware of the resources that are potentially available to it, both locally and outside the community. Those which have exploited these resources consistently have domonstrated a higher propensity to "solve" their problem cases.

SCORE (the SBA volunteer program) is active in only a few communities. Where it is, however, it has proved to be a useful device both for aiding the businessman and for promoting better relations between the LPA and displacees. This is particularly true when the LPA staff serves as intermediary in bringing the displaced businessman and the representatives of SCORE together.

Local business organizations such as chambers of commerce, real estate boards, and industrial or commercial development corporations can be enlisted to provide advice and counsel to displacees. Once again, the favorable impact is greater when the LPA staff is the intermediary between the business and the organization.

Small Business Opportunity Centers, where they exist, have proved to be an important source of advice and training for displaced businessmen. Because they are independent of the urban renewal program, they can be quite effective in gaining acceptance and cooperation from displacees.

Colleges and universities represent an important potential source of assistance both to displaced businesses and to the LPA. In one community, the resources of a local university have been most effectively utilized on a continuing and integrated basis in the relocation program of the LPA staff. In this instance, representatives of the university who are skilled in market analysis and business operations make the initial contact with the displacee, analyze his potential problems or sources of difficulty, recommend appropriate courses of action to solve his problems, and offer training courses to improve his business skills. This assistance is provided on a long-term basis, through a third-party contract between the LPA and the university. The result has been widespread acceptance and cooperation from the affected businessmen in an area where considerable difficulty and opposition was initially encountered. The individual attention received and the recognition of businessmen as people which is demonstrated by this program have substantially reduced the problems and difficulties encountered by the LPA business relocation staff.

Other public agencies, most especially other LPA's and the HUD regional office, represent an important source of information and advice to the LPA which is commonly overlooked. In those few instances in which information and assistance have been sought, however, the process has worked extremely well. The most effective use of this approach has been through group meetings with business displacees at which HUD regional office business relocation personnel and those from other LPA's have explained the operation of the business relocation process on the basis of their own experiences elsewhere. The ability to cite specific cases to illustrate the major points being made has contributed greatly to displacee acceptance of the fact of relocation in their own cases.

Creation of Ad Hoc Groups

A number of LPA's have enlisted the aid of local business leaders to support and explain business relocation to displacees. The most effective groups are action-oriented, however, and not simply used for public relations purposes.

Advisory committees of successful businessmen in the community have been formed to offer counsel and individual assistance to displaced businessmen. In a number of communities, they have been particularly effective as intermediaries between the LPA and groups of displacees who are being encouraged to band together in a joint relocation effort. The advisory committee of businessmen is frequently helpful in overcoming the fierce individualism that characterizes many small businessmen, and in convincing them that it is in their own best interests to participate in a joint effort with their competitors.

Business liaison groups have helped in a number of cases in dealing with potential developers of sites designated for occupancy by displacees. These liaison groups have been especially helpful in explaining the implications and anticipated benefits of occupying such sites to the individual affected businessmen.

Neighborhood business associations have proved successful in a few communities as a channel of communication between member-displacees and the LPA. Information about project plans and timing can be disseminated to the affected businessmen more readily through this channel. The recurring problems and concerns of displacees can in turn be brought quickly to the attention of the LPA. Many displacees are more likely to complain or share their fears with their own representatives than to present them directly to the LPA staff. This device provides a significant opportunity to minimize friction and conflict between displacees and the LPA by identifying problems and acting promptly to alleviate them.

Providing Effective Guidance and
Counsel to Displacees

Most displaced businessmen have rarely relocated during their business careers. Only a few have ever gone through the experience of forced relocation before, and not all of them have been eligible for reimbursement of moving expenses and/or personal property losses. As a result, they need a great deal of information and advice, so that their decisions and actions can result in a successful relocation. Those LPA's demonstrating the most effective handling of business relocation problems are also the ones that recognize their responsibility to *initiate* advice and guidance to the displacee on all aspects of the business relocation process.

Development and/or Acquisition of
Specialized Skills to Support LPA Personnel

Successful business relocation requires skill in dealing with problems of location analysis and site selection, real estate markets, product and service markets, business financing, and business operations. In addition, arranging and managing the actual moves, and processing relocation payments efficiently, call for specialized experience and skill. These prerequisites must be available either within the business relocation staff of the LPA or from consultants and outside agencies. LPA's with a wide range of available internal skills and outside assistance have consistently demonstrated greater capability to deal successfully with the varied problems that arise in business relocation.

Use of LPA Staff for Specialized Problems
Within the LPA staff, individuals can be hired with specific skills, or they can be assigned to specialized tasks in which they develop the necessary expertise. Assigning individual staff members to frequently recurring activities, such as the evaluation of moving bids or arranging SBA loans for displacees, usually produces this expertise. A list of the specialized activities performed by LPA business relocation staff members encountered in this study is presented below.
Qualifying Displacees for Reimbursement and Compensation. This activity covers both moving expenses and property losses, and Small Business Displacement Payments (SBDP's). It requires familiarity with current regulations and procedures. In particular, questions of timing and documentation are most appropriate for a business relocation specialist to handle. This activity has generally proved more effective when included as part of the business relocation function, rather than as an activity of a separate division of claims.
Assistance in obtaining SBA loans. Here too, intimate working knowledge of the requirements and regulations applicable to displacees is essential. Larger LPA staffs in particular have found it most effective to assign one or more staff members to this activity as their primary responsibility.
Maintaining contact with the Financial Community. This function is frequently coupled with the handling of SBA loan applications. The requirements of private lenders are sufficiently varied and complex to necessitate having a staff member devote a large portion of his time to maintaining contact with those institutions operating regularly in the local market. This has proved particularly effective in cases involving larger displaced businesses and groups of displacees joining together for corporate ownership of their real estate.
Local real estate market contacts and analysis. Especially in larger communities, information on the availability of vacant space and sites must be continuously acquired and evaluated for transmittal to displacees. Off-site locations are a significant relocation resource which should be exploited effectively by the LPA staff. Those LPA's which have done this most successfully have assigned at least one staff member to make periodic surveys of vacancies and to work closely with organized real estate groups in the community.
Knowledge of the life style of displacees. Communities which have encountered concentrations of ethnic or socio-economic minorities among displaced businessmen have found it particularly helpful to assign specific staff members to handle

all such displacees. One LPA made special efforts to provide duplex units in public housing projects which had rental commercial space on the first floor and living units on the second. This was entirely in keeping with the traditional pattern of living of business displacees in several project areas. This type of sensitivity to the peculiar needs of certain business groups made the entire business relocation process much easier to handle. It was achieved through the concentrated activities of one business relocation officer assigned to this particular problem.

Use of Outside Specialists and Consultants
Some business relocation problems require an independent viewpoint that is best obtained from outside the LPA. Other problems involve highly technical skills that the LPA is not likely to have within its staff. Still others call for concentrated efforts within relatively short periods of time, during which temporary assistance is preferable and more efficient. Retaining outside specialists and consultants has proved to be the most effective way of dealing with all three groups of problems. This approach has enabled the LPA's to maintain a smaller permanent staff which has been able to concentrate its efforts on the continually recurring cases most responsive to staff treatment. The kinds of activities which have successfully been delegated to outside specialists and consultants include:

Special surveys. Studies of the business relocation work load, the relocation needs of displacees, relocation resources, and market analysis are frequently best carried out by outside consultants.

Advice on business operations. The objective here is to improve the displacee's abilities as a businessman. In one community, local university personnel work with individuals and small groups of displacees on a continuing basis, emphasizing the importance of keeping records and books of account. A corollary result is that the businessmen helped in this way are better equipped to qualify for relocation expense reimbursements and SBDP's.

Architectural and design advice. In one community, an architectural review board is utilized to maintain the integrity of the design of a reuse area. They work directly with displaced businesses planning to construct new buildings as redevelopers in a project area. While this board is occasionally regarded as a deterrent by some of the relocatees, the overall result has been to resolve a number of design problems that were beyond the capabilities of either the displaced businessmen or the LPA staff.

Legal skills. In a number of communities, outside legal assistance has been retained to advise and work with groups of displacees planning joint ownership of their relocation facilities. Particularly when the condominium form of ownership has been proposed, highly specialized legal skills not readily available within the LPA have been required.

Special financing arrangements. Although financing is a recurring problem that normally calls for in-house skills on the part of the LPA staff, there are situations in which specialized assistance and advice are required by displacees, or by the developers of facilities designed to house displaced businesses. For example, one LPA turned to a local non-profit industrial development corporation to make the financial arrangements for a major food terminal. The corporation served as an intermediary between the developer and the ultimate lenders. As a result, financing on terms more favorable to the borrower was obtained. This same industrial development corporation has served as a channel for loan funds in a number of other industrial relocations within the city. The credit standing and non-profit status of this corporation have enabled it to grant loans to displacees at less-than-market rates.

Use of Outside Agencies for Direct Advice and Counseling to Displaced Businessmen

Consultants and outside specialists have proved extremely effective in supplementing the activities of LPA staff by working directly with displacees on complex relocations. This approach has freed staff business relocation officers to deal with the more routine cases that constitute the bulk of their work load.

Specialized Consulting and Advisory Groups
Although not all have been employed in any one LPA, several types of arrangements between the LPA and outside groups have been devised to provide direct assistance and advice to displaced businesses. This assistance ranges from serving as an intermediary between displacees and lenders, property owners or developers — to assuming operational responsibility for a major portion of the entire business relocation process.

Third-party contracts. In at least two communities studied, the LPA has entered into a third-party contract with an outside agency to handle the bulk of business relocation activity in a project area and to provide advice and assistance to displaced businessmen. One LPA retained a local university to conduct all of the initial interviews and surveys. Supplementary market analyses and inventories of vacant business space are conducted periodically. This information is conveyed to each displacee to help him select an appropriate location, as well as to consider entering a new line of business activity. The university also provides advice on business operations, both individually and with small groups of businessmen in similar lines of activity. This program has resulted in many changes in lines of business, a high percentage of successful qualification for SBA Displaced Business Loans (DBL's), and expansions of several businesses.

An alternative effort has been to assign the entire business relocation function, with the exception of the processing of reimbursement claims, to a non-profit organization established for this purpose. It is financed with city funds under the third-party contract. This organization handles the moves as well as development of the project area. It provides an integrated service, especially for those firms seeking to relocate back into the project area.

Local and regional development corporations. In one instance, a local industrial development corporation has worked directly with industrial and wholesale displacees in arranging financing for them on favorable terms. All firms that appear eligible for assistance from this organization are referred to it by the LPA staff. In another instance, a regional development corporation has undertaken the responsibility for relocation of businesses displaced in urban renewal projects in which it is the redeveloper. The LPA is concerned only with reimbursement of relocation expenses as a result.

Small Business Administration and SCORE. In a few communities, business advisory services have been provided by SBA and SCORE, significantly reducing the necessity for the LPA to have staff personnel to perform these functions. SBA and SCORE facilities are available only to "small" businesses, however.

Business advisory groups. Several LPA's have encouraged the creation of local business advisory groups which have provided advice and counsel concerning business operations to displacees. In one instance, the advisory group has served as an intermediary in obtaining financing for several displacees, especially groups of displaced businessmen seeking to finance jointly-owned real estate. This particular agency also supplemented the LPA business relocation staff by arranging the developmental and legal plans for an industrial area occupied exclusively by displaced firms.

Real estate brokers' organizations. Several LPA's have developed a strong working relationship with the local real estate board and have obtained effective cooperation from its members. Finding sites or new locations for displaced businesses has been delegated almost entirely to cooperating brokers. In one community the local chapter of the Society of Industrial Realtors (SIR) works closely with the business relocation staff, particularly in finding rental space for industrial and heavy commercial operations. The LPA and the SIR chapter exchange lists periodically; the LPA supplies information about displacees and their space requirements, while the SIR chapter supplies the LPA with information on current vacancies and their prices or rentals. The business relocation staff recognizes the right of the brokers to receive a commission for their efforts, and protects the brokers' interests by not circumventing them.

Use of HUD Regional Staff in Special Problem Situations

Because of their exposure to the experiences of other LPA's in the Region, business relocation officers in HUD regional offices are in a position to offer suggestions and direct aid to LPA business relocation personnel. One regional office has assigned a staff member to work directly with groups of Negro businessmen to encourage them to become developers and owners. This effort supplements the activities of LPA staff in several communities in that HUD Region. Moreover, regional business relocation officers can help train LPA staff in the handling of specialized problems which are likely to recur. This is especially helpful to new LPA staff members and newly-organized LPA business relocation offices.

Organizing Community Action to
Aid Business Relocation

Because business relocation staff time and abilities are necessarily limited no matter how large the staff, community resources should be tapped to help carry out the relocation job. LPA's which have done this successfully have shown a much greater ability to resolve business relocation problems as they arise. They have a wider range of resources on which to draw. Creating these arrangements is the responsibility of the LPA administration rather than the business relocation staff.

Creating Public Awareness of the Problem

Business relocation efforts are more effective and generally better supported by the affected businessmen when there is community-wide understanding of the reasons for and procedures in business relocation. Publicizing and explaining the process have been undertaken with considerable success by several LPA's. Generally, the task has proved easier when the local municipal administration has cooperated with the LPA (if the two are separate) in supporting and explaining the nature of business relocation to the general public, and to the business community in particular.

General Informational Programs
Publicity efforts which have proved successful in many LPA's in enlisting public acceptance and support of the business relocation program include:

(1) *Public meetings*

(2) *Periodic special publications or newsletters*

(3) *Newspaper stories, radio and television programs* explaining the objectives, procedures and timing of both the project and the business relocation program.

Special Promotional Efforts
Individual LPA's have found specific promotional efforts helpful in enlisting public support of both proposed and on-going business relocation programs. These have included:

Creation of a "theme" for the project or the business relocation effort. This helps to stimulate general public acceptance of the urban renewal project and to solicit aid for business displacees.

Inclusion of schemes designed to attract public support and to help business displacees in the redevelopment plan. For example, a number of LPA's have concentrated on remaking the character of the CBD and have emphasized the role of retaining displacees in this revitalization. Identification of the project with a specific commercial mall has created public interest in several instances. Also, the development of a new facility important to the economic life of the community, not necessarily in the CBD, has helped enlist community support. A major new food wholesale distribution center, an industrial park designed primarily for displacees, or a facility for specialized types of wholesaler-distributors have stimulated support of relocation efforts.

Tours of completed projects and relocation facilities, and of project areas in both the planning and execution stages, have in several cases proved helpful. They have encouraged support of the business relocation program by business and civic leaders. In one instance, potential displacees from one project area were shown the results of several relocations from earlier projects. This answered a great many questions in advance. It also greatly increased the cooperation received from displacees when their own relocations occurred.

Many LPA's have provided preference or priority in occupying reuse sites to displacees, either as a matter of agency policy or through direct specification in the redevelopment plan. Special efforts are usually made to publicize the action widely, both among displacees and with the general public. It has usually received favorable reaction, especially from the displacees themselves.

One LPA has made a special effort to promote participation by local banks and other financial institutions in the financing of relocations. The local financial community has virtually been courted by this LPA. As a result, a number of relocations for which financing was originally thought to be questionable have been helped by local lenders.

Public Involvement in Relocation

Once the public, especially the local business community, has been made aware of the nature of business relocation and has accepted the basic idea of the relocation plan, it is most helpful to enlist active participation in the program. Many LPA's have recruited various civic and business groups to "sell" business relocation to the displacees involved, as well as to offer them encouragement and assistance. This kind of cooperation is an important adjunct to the direct efforts of the LPA business relocation staff.

Coordination with Local Development Groups
The LPA can channel the support of civic and business groups in meaningful directions by working closely with them, and coordinating their efforts at encouraging and supporting business relocation programs.

Promotional programs have been developed jointly with local civic groups such as the chamber of commerce.

The work and assistance of local development and real estate organizations have been widely publicized by a number of LPA's. Public acknowledgement of the efforts of private groups and expressions of appreciation have helped stimulate further support and assistance.

The LPA can perform an important function in its own behalf by coordinating public and private efforts to develop relocation sites. Directing displacees to a privately sponsored industrial park has proved quite effective in one community. Conscious efforts to protect the sales and leasing commissions of real estate brokers has resulted in wholehearted support from the brokers' organizations in another. Referring displacees to developments sponsored by utility companies and railroads has helped solve the relocation problems of individual firms. It has also created an atmosphere of working cooperation between the LPA and these organizations that has resulted in the resolution of subsequent problems involving utilities and rail lines.

Creation of Special Committees

Business and civic leaders can be enlisted to support business relocation efforts by appointing them to special advisory committees designed to offer advice and assistance to displaced businessmen. These committees have been most successful when their members have been brought into direct personal contact with the individual displacees, and when their efforts have received the widest possible publicity in local news media. The publicity has been initiated by the LPA.

Coordination and Cooperation with
Municipal Agencies

The solution to many business relocation problems lies with one or more municipal agencies. Whether the LPA is a city department or independent of the municipal administration, effective cooperation and understanding of the problems of urban renewal are essential in order to achieve desired results in business relocation. The record shows clearly that LPA's with a good working relationship with other public agencies can achieve solutions to many kinds of business relocation problems much more readily and effectively. The agencies from which the LPA is most likely to need help and cooperation are:

Office of the Mayor. Imaginative and innovative handling of business relocation problems is almost always associated with a community in which the mayor is a strong and active advocate of urban renewal. Conversely, when the municipal administration and the LPA or its executive director are at odds, routine problems frequently become major issues which are resolved only with difficulty and the expenditure of much time and effort.

Zoning authority. Whatever the agency or agencies with jurisdiction over zoning changes, variances, or exceptions may be titled, the LPA frequently needs cooperation in order to carry out a reuse plan, or to achieve success in a given relocation problem. Mutual understanding of each group's objectives is essential, together with an appreciation of the difficulties that each encounters in attempting to achieve those objectives. Numerous successful business relocations have depended upon an adjustment in zoning regulations. This underscores the critical importance of a cooperative attitude between zoning authorities and the LPA.

Public works department. Many business relocations require the closing or opening of streets, the provision of temporary access roads during construction, or the relocation of utility lines. Moreover, the timing of many improvements for reuse areas can be critical to the success of a particular relocation. Many cases uncovered in this study bring out the important point that effective solutions to business relocation problems would not have been possible without the cooperation and assistance of the local agency responsible for streets and utility lines.

Health department. Certain types of activities, such as food handling establishments and barbershops, require public health permits before they can engage in business. Several cases illustrate the importance of working closely with the local health department, especially in providing ample advance notice before the proposed move to permit inspection of the new premises. With a spirit of cooperation and understanding between the LPA and the health authorities, occasional difficulties can be resolved. One example is the case of the small barbershop that relocated without obtaining a health permit in advance. Because of a good working relationship established earlier, the LPA was able to obtain a health permit for the barber with a minimum of delay. Without this help, the barber would very probably have been forced out of business; he had no backlog of savings and could not afford any prolonged interruption of his business.

Building inspectors. Cooperation with the local department of building Inspection includes providing them with ample advance warning of an intention to move. In most cases this has created an atmosphere in which rapid approval can be obtained in emergency situations.

Licensing boards. Although many licensing boards are actually state rather than municipal agencies, the principle of LPA cooperation with their efforts remains valid. In many instances, a business relocation officer has petitioned a licensing board on behalf of a displacee, or has submitted evidence and documentation in support of the displacee's application. Moreover, it is important for the LPA staff to be aware of the policies and regulations of these licensing boards. Then appropriate advice can be given to displacees seeking to obtain or relocate a license. Careful advance explanation of the relocation plan and its role in the redevelopment plan has on occasion influenced a licensing board to exercise discretionary powers and permit an otherwise questionable relocation.

Creating New Business Organizations for Relocation

In many instances, the solution to a business relocation problem lies in a change in the form of business organization of the displacee. The LPA staff must be sensitive to this possibility, and to the circumstances under which it is likely to be effective. Two major types of situations have proved particularly susceptible to a change in the form of business organization: group ownership of real estate and incorporation of unincorporated businesses.

Associations of Several Displacee Firms

Many cases illustrate the fact that there are significant advantages, particularly but not exclusively to small firms, in banding together to own and occupy their business facilities. The actual form of organization may be as a partnership, a corporation, or a condominium, but the corporate form is most commonly used. Whatever the organizational form, however, there are substantial advantages to

the individual businesses which generally far outweigh any loss in individuality
and independence of action that is entailed.

Business Complementarity
Establishments in the same line of business frequently find it desirable and more
profitable to be located near one another. Despite the fact that they are
competitors there are real advantages in close physical proximity. Customers
seeking the particular product or service provided go to a central facility in
greater numbers than separate and isolated firms can hope to attract. Specialized
facilities can be provided more efficiently when they can be installed at the same
time, or shared in actual use. Service facilities and suppliers are more likely to
locate close to a concentration of businesses in the same line, with savings in
costs to the affected businesses.

Examples of successful groupings of displacees were found in a wide variety
of types of activity. They include wholesale meat establishments, wholesale
seafood establishments, wholesale produce establishments, wholesale dry goods
establishments, retail outlets in a shopping center, and manufacturing firms in an
industrial park. In every one of these situations, which occurred in a large
number of communities, the relocation needs of the individual businesses were
met through some form of group ownership or tenancy of the real estate.

Ownership by the displaced businesses. One alternative method widely used is
for the displaced businesses to band together and establish a new organization
(usually a corporation or condominium) to serve as a real estate holding
company. Each member business owns a *pro rata* share in the holding company,
which reflects his interest in the real estate he occupies. This technique has been
successful for both large and small firms in many lines of business. The
important point is that there must be (and often is) some logical business reason
for the several firms to be located in close physical proximity to one another.

Ownership by an investor or development group. Groups of businesses in similar
or complementary lines of activity have occasionally found it necessary to
accept tenant status in order to obtain occupancy in the kind of space they
need. In a number of communities, private or quasi-public corporations have
been formed, often at the instigation of the LPA, to own real estate and rent it
to displaced businesses. This is especially effective when the displacees are very
small firms.

Financing
Small businesses in particular are frequently unattractive as borrowers from
major financial institutions. Moreover, the resources of many small firms are
typically inadequate to permit them to occupy the most ideally situated
locations for their activities. Bringing together a number of complementary
displaced businesses and pooling their resources can make them attractive to
both private lenders and to SBA. A number of LPA's have recognized this fact,
and have encouraged displaced firms to join together as owners of their real
estate in order to obtain the financing necessary to permit them to acquire and
occupy needed and desired facilities. The LPA business relocation staff in each
of these instances played an important role in bringing to the attention of
lending agencies the economic and financial power of the businesses as a group.

Negotiating Advantages

A group of displacees seeking to acquire a site within a project area has considerably more influence on the disposition staff of the LPA than each of the individual firms would have independently. As a group, they frequently become an important resource which the community wishes to retain. This was true of wholesale food distributors in a number of cities, shoe wholesalers and dry goods wholesalers in some cities, and a group of Kosher food stores in one city. The business relocation officer can help these businesses most by making them recognize their potential power, and encouraging them to take advantage of it by pooling their resources in a joint effort.

Basic Considerations in
Organizing a Joint Effort

While the specific ingredients of a joint effort to acquire and own business facilities in a new location will vary widely from one case to another, the experiences of those LPA's in which such efforts have been successful point to some basic steps that should be taken in every case by the business relocation officer.

Identify the leader(s). Every joint ownership effort which has been successful has succeeded in large part because of the willingness of one individual businessman or a small group to assume the responsibility for leading the others. These are the organizers and the drivers. The first major task of the business relocation officer is to identify the leadership in the group as early as possible. Then the businessmen themselves can feel responsible for the determination of their own fate.

Organize the corporation as early as possible. Collective experience has shown that binding the members to a fixed organizational form as early as practical helps strengthen the commitment of the individual businessmen involved. It also offers them substantive evidence of progress.

Obtain top-quality legal advice in the early stages. The lawyer retained by the group should understand the process of redevelopment and business relocation. He should be well versed in the law of real estate organization and ownership. He should also understand fully the financing of real estate ownership through a corporate body. Talent of this caliber is expensive. The job of the business relocation officer is to convince the leadership of the group, at least, that this is the most important investment that the group will make throughout the entire relocation process.

Salesmanship is required. The most serious obstacle to overcome in a joint ownership effort is usually the fierce independence of the small businessman. Both LPA staff and the leadership of the group must work together to convince the displacees that it is in their own financial and economic interests to give up some of that independence, as far as real estate ownership is concerned. Cooperation among life-long competitors is often difficult to accept. Nevertheless, the record is clear that small complementary businesses banded together are almost invariably more successful than those which locate independently.

Arrange financing. Cooperation from the business relocation staff in finding potential sources of financing can be extremely important. However, in many instances the attorney and the officers of the corporation actually prefer to arrange their financing "without outside help." In a number of instances, the personal intervention of the mayor proved to be the most effective aid in arranging financing. This underscores the importance of having a commitment to business relocation from the municipal administration.

Long-term commitment. Joint ownership efforts usually require a number of years for completion. This means that at least one business relocation officer must continuously work on the project (although not full time) over that entire period. The really successful cases are those in which a business relocation officer has been involved and committed to the project over the entire process.

Changing from Proprietorship or Partnership to a Corporation

Many small businesses are operated as single proprietorships or partnerships because the owners are unaware of the advantages in the corporate form of ownership. In a large number of cases, LPA business relocation officers have convinced displaced businessmen to incorporate when they relocate. In some communities, businessmen are systematically referred to SBA for advice on the appropriate form of business organization. One LPA utilizes the services of a local university to advise individual displacees on the potential advantages of incorporation.

The basic advantages of the corporation are financial. Small, growing firms that require reinvestment of profits can achieve tax advantages when they operate as corporations. Financing of real estate acquisitions may be more readily obtained by a corporation, with its continuing existence independent of the life of the owners.

The important point is that LPA business relocation personnel should be in a position to advise individual displacees about the most appropriate form of business organization, or at least to refer the displaced businessmen to authoritative sources of information in the community. In addition to SBA and local universities, a business advisory group can perform this function extremely well.

Changing the Nature of the Business or its Method of Operation

Forced relocation or displacement is often the occasion for a fundamental reevaluation of the entire business operation. In numerous interviews, relocated businessmen reported that they were subconsciously aware that they were not operating as efficiently or as profitably as they might in the old location. However, because their business activities had been "satisfactory," they had little incentive to change their ways of doing business.

The necessity to relocate, or even to consider discontinuing operations as an alternative, forces most businessmen to analyze their basic approaches to their businesses. LPA business relocation personnel can help create a positive impact of relocation by encouraging a fundamental reexamination of the business operation. However, most business relocation staffs do not have skilled business management specialists in sufficient numbers to consult with all of the displacees who can benefit from such help. Frequently, the most effective assistance that the LPA staff can provide is to bring the displaced businessmen and outside consultants or advisors in touch with one another. This means that the LPA must make the advisory services available, on the one hand, and strongly urge affected businessmen to seek their advice, on the other.

Business Expansion

In a large number of cases studied, displaced businesses expanded their operations at the new location. This was often the result of advice from a consultant or business advisor provided through the LPA. In addition to benefiting the business and making the relocation successful by at least one standard, this approach also adds to the economic vitality of the community.

Enlarging Facilities

One form of business expansion is to increase the physical space occupied. This may offer an opportunity to relieve overcrowding. Most commonly it has resulted in increased business volume and accompanying increases in employment. The LPA business relocation staff can provide assistance in planning for the expansion, as well as directing the firm to sources of financing. In particular, the most frequent successes stemmed from advising the displaced businessman about the opportunities and requirements in the SBA loan program.

Arrangements can be made to supplement an SBA Displaced Business Loan with an Economic Development Loan. This has been achieved in several communities for the expansion of firms when they relocate.

The displacee can be encouraged and aided in becoming a real estate owner and landlord, so that his tenants in the new facility help to pay the increased occupancy costs associated with ownership.

For extremely small firms, the SBDP and relocation reimbursement payments can be combined to obtain increased equipment and inventory. At least one LPA has a definite policy of advising its small displacees about this opportunity.

Expansion of Product Lines or
Production Facilities

In addition to the possibility of acquiring larger quarters, a displaced firm has an opportunity to expand its product line or to increase its production facilities (or inventory). Much the same considerations apply here. It is important for the LPA business relocation officer to recognize the difference between the two alternative forms of business expansion, however, especially when financial resources are limited and a choice must be made between the two. This is a classic situation for the use of business advisors or consultants. Several communities call on members of their business advisory group in such cases. One community uses the business expertise of local university staff to provide this kind of advice.

The LPA staff can advise displacees about the availability of moving and personal property-loss reimbursements, and of SBDP's. In some instances, the decision to keep and move equipment or dispose of it at a "loss" has been conditioned by advice about new product lines or new equipment.

Several LPA's have encouraged small business displacees to use the SBDP to add to their inventory or to add new product lines. This advice worked well in one community for a small shoemaker who began to sell shoes at retail at his new location, a tire distributor who added a line of truck tires at his new location, and a metals fabricator who was able to attract additional customers for a new product line when he acquired two new machines at his relocated plant.

The LPA staff should encourage displacees to reevaluate the basic nature of their businesses, especially when they have been operating at the same location for many years without a change. In those communities in which the most successful cases of additions to production facilities or product lines have occurred, the LPA staff has been particularly active in referring displacees to available business advisory groups or consultants.

Improvement of Layout and Work Flow

A forced relocation should encourage the displacee to evaluate the layout and work flow of his operation. Since he will be occupying different space, the arrangement of production or sales facilities must necessarily be changed. This type of analysis requires the advice and assistance of an expert in this field. Many LPA's have utilized the services of SBA or SCORE, as well as members of business advisory groups or university specialists in layout and work flow planning, to improve the profitability of relocated firms.

It is important for the LPA to recognize, and to communicate to the displacee, that this type of improvement does not necessarily require an expansion in space occupied or an increase in production facilities. It simply involves changing the way in which work flows through the business. It is also an important consideration because many relocated firms actually occupy less space at higher rentals in their new locations. Greater efficiency in the use of that space can more than offset the increased occupancy costs.

Changing the Type of Business

Because forced relocation should require the businessman to rethink his entire operation, one alternative conclusion of that rethinking process is to go into an entirely different line of business. Another alternative is to attempt to serve a new or different market with essentially the same product or service. Finally, the businessman may decide to change his tenancy status to put more of his funds to work in the business. In each of these considerations and decisions, small businessmen in particular need advice and consultation from experts in the field.

The fundamental role of the LPA is to guide displacees to the most appropriate sources of information and advice for making these decisions.

Providing a New Product or Service

Many dislocated businessmen discover that they cannot obtain zoning or licensing permission to reopen their businesses in new locations. Others have been operating unprofitably or marginally in the old location. Still others are in businesses whose market is effectively destroyed as a result of redevelopment. Each of these situations offers an opportunity as well as a challenge to the LPA business relocation staff to find an alternative line of business for the displacee. In a number of communities, conscious efforts along these lines have resulted in "saving" many businesses originally considered to be doomed by redevelopment.

A few LPA's have directly encouraged displacees to change their line of business so that they might qualify as on-site relocatees in conformity with the redevelopment plan.

Some LPA's systematically refer apparently inappropriate or unprofitable businesses to SBA or to available private advisory groups for consultation. In many cases, an alternative line of business better suited to the skills and interests of the businessman has been discovered.

Displacees unable to obtain a suitable location consistent with their former line of business have been encouraged by some LPA's to utilize their relocation expense reimbursements and SBDP to purchase an existing business elsewhere. The acquisition of a profitable business in an established location is certainly a "successful" relocation from the point of view of the displaced businessman.

In at least two communities, the LPA refers marginal businessmen to local educational institutions for training in the skills required for management of a business enterprise. From these courses, the displacee frequently discovers he is better suited for a different line of business, and establishes a new business.

In one community, a university research group retained by the LPA conducts market analyses to identify the types of businesses which are needed or likely to succeed in different areas in the community. It then helps displacees make a choice based on the results of these studies.

A number of LPA's direct marginal businesses in particular to the Office of Economic Opportunity (OEO) or SBA for information about franchising. Several small displacees have been successfully placed in training programs for franchises, and are now providing services formerly unavailable in the areas in which they are operating.

Adjusting to New Market Conditions

Frequently, reasonably successful businesses discover that the market environment in which they have been successful in the past is effectively eliminated by redevelopment. Others discover that good locations which are available are situated in different types of markets. Their basic product or service lines do not change, but they must adjust to a new market environment. Once again, advice and consultation from specialists have proved to be the most successful device in preparing affected displacees to meet the demands and challenges of these different market conditions.

New locations frequently mean new markets. An Italian grocery centered in a predominantly Italian neighborhood moved to a good location in a non-Italian neighborhood. Although the owner continued to emphasize quality Italian foods, he found it necessary to add some products and drop others in order to meet the demands of his new situation. In this case, he was assisted by a representative of a local business advisory group in deciding which products to retain and which to substitute.

New locations in different markets frequently involve a change in clientele. A manufacturer who moved to a location with more convenient access to an interstate highway discovered that he was now attractive as a supplier to a major aircraft manufacturer. A Negro upholsterer who lived and worked in a predominantly Negro neighborhood moved to a racially mixed area with the advice and encouragement of a business advisor referred to him by the LPA. He made a conscious effort to attract white customers. By adding to his inventory of materials, he was able to adjust successfully to the new market and in fact expanded his business considerably.

Upgrading the Business
Relocation often provides the perfect opportunity to make improvements and generally upgrade the quality of goods and services provided by the business. Several instances were found where a small "gin mill" was, upon relocation, converted to a cocktail lounge. Other similar cases provide examples of small bars adding restaurant facilities as well as substantially improving the physical appearance of the operation.

The importance of upgrading through relocation was particularly well illustrated by a meat processing firm that was able to improve substantially its operation. The improvement in facilities was so significant that the firm was able to obtain federal inspection approval and licensing to sell its meat products beyond its own state boundaries — a right continually denied in the old location.

Changing Tenancy Status
Although relocation is frequently more dramatic when a displaced firm moves from tenant to owner status, a shift in the other direction is occasionally both desirable and profitable. This requires careful analysis of the nature of the business, which the LPA business relocation staff must provide directly or through a business advisor. In a few cases, displacees have been advised to use the proceeds from the sale of their real estate as working capital to expand inventory and the volume of their operations. This is a further example of changing the thinking of the businessman about his business operations. It is frequently difficult to overcome the instinct for ownership. However, when working capital is more important than real estate ownership, it can be extremely successful. This decision requires close analysis of the financial and operational status of the firm. Only an expert can engage successfully in this type of evaluation.

Obtaining Financing for Displaced Businesses

One of the most crucial ingredients in the success of any business relocation is ensuring that the business is adequately funded in its new location. This is especially true if the firm occupies real estate which costs more to own or rent than the previous location did, or if it moves from tenant to owner status. In addition, funds are needed for working capital purposes, to finance new inventory and/or equipment, and most especially to sustain the firm during the period of adjustment and reduced business volume that frequently precedes and often follows the actual move.

Because financing is a recurring, almost universal problem, it is a major responsibility of LPA business relocation personnel. This is one subject area in which staff expertise is virtually mandatory for all but the smallest LPA's. An extremely wide range of possibilities exists for handling the financing problem effectively. Many are applicable under special circumstances only. The LPA business relocation staff cannot be competent in dealing with all these circumstances. It should be able to handle the majority of cases, however. It should also recognize when its abilities are extended beyond their limits and a skilled consultant is required.

Organization for business relocation is most effective when it includes continuing contact and the development of rapport with the various institutional sources of financing. These should include at the least the Small Business Administration, local banks and other financial institutions, one or more life insurance companies active in the local real estate market, and local development banks or credit corporations.

Obtaining Displaced Business Loans

Small business firms displaced by urban renewal (among other programs) are eligible for Displaced Business Loans from SBA. The advantage of these loans is that they are available at less-than-market interest rates, and for longer maturities than regular SBA loans. The chief limitation that poses a problem for some applicants is that loan recipients are restricted in the extent to which they may expand their operations with the proceeds of a DBL. At the other end of the economic scale, extremely small firms with spotty profit records or insufficient financial records for documentation of their loan requests frequently encounter difficulties in qualifying. Moreover, the forms to be completed and the supporting documentation required are frequently regarded as formidable and even forbidding by potential loan applicants. Nevertheless, the DBL remains an important source of financing for small business displacees seeking the funds to improve, modernize, and/or modestly expand their operations.

Referral System
Most LPA's studied merely inform potentially eligible displacees about the existence of the DBL program and refer them to SBA for assistance. Even within this relatively simple and modest approach, however, several effective and workable techniques have emerged.

LPA business relocation personnel must be fully conversant with SBA standards and regulations, and must keep their own information up to date. This can be achieved by arranging for periodic meetings with local or regional SBA loan officers. These meetings also serve the purpose of establishing rapport with SBA staff members and informing them of local business relocation goals and problems.

The LPA business relocation officer should be aware of the alternative uses to which DBL proceeds may be put, and should transmit this information to the displacee. DBL's have been made to finance working capital and inventory, new construction, site acquisition, purchase of existing buildings, and leasehold improvements.

Business displacees should be informed fully about the alternatives and opportunities available through the DBL program. This information is best provided in an early meeting between the LPA business relocation officer and the displacee. It makes advance planning possible. In addition, it provides ample opportunity for the LPA to submit information about the displacee's interest to SBA, and thereby allow SBA to contact the displaced businessman directly.

Some LPA's periodically send lists of displacees and their apparent needs to the SBA regional office. This alerts SBA to the possibility of a loan application at a later date.

The LPA, in cooperation with SBA, should actively enlist support from the local financial community for SBA loan participations. This also requires advance planning.

Active Solicitation and Assistance

Displaced Business Loans have been obtained more regularly and with a higher degree of success in communities in which the LPA business relocation staff actively encourages displacees to apply, assists them in preparing the necessary application forms and supporting documentation, and follows the processing of the loan through to a final decision.

Many LPA's instruct business relocation officers to analyze carefully and in detail the past record and reasonable future expectations of the individual displaced firm. This information makes it possible to evaluate the probabilities of a successful application. It also helps to identify the gaps in documentation that must somehow be filled. Moreover, the LPA business relocation officer is better equipped as a result of this investigation to "sell" SBA on the soundness and appropriateness of the loan.

LPA's with the greatest success in obtaining DBL's for their displacees work closely with the individual businessman in working out his financial plan and identifying his specific needs. In a few communities, the LPA provides consulting advice and assistance (for example, from a university research group) in developing the necessary records for supporting and documenting the loan application.

The LPA's with the greatest success in obtaining DBL's for their displacees maintain a continuing check on the progress of the loan until a final decision is reached. Two LPA's utilize business relocation officers who literally walk DBL applications through the regional SBA office from one official to another, in order to expedite the processing of the loan application. In several instances, frequent and repeated visits to the SBA regional office were considered necessary and desirable by an LPA business relocation officer in order to expedite loan processing. Impressive results have been achieved. In one community, the LPA business relocation officer and the regional SBA loan officer agreed that no loan application had required more than 21 working days to be processed.

The LPA business relocation staff is in a position to assist SBA both during and after the processing of a loan application. In communities where the "take charge" approach has been employed for DBL's by LPA relocation personnel, SBA officials reported not one delinquent loan. This is partly the result of prior screening by LPA staff. It also reflects the critical importance of favorable financing to displacees and their generally positive response to the assistance provided them by the LPA.

Obtaining Other SBA Financial Assistance
for Displacees

Displaced Business Loans are not the only form of financial assistance available to displacees through SBA. Quite apart from business advice and counseling, SBA makes regular loans available, as well as Economic Development Loans (EDL's) and Economic Opportunity Loans (EOL's). Moreover, SBA has initiated a program of lease guarantee insurance designed to add to the competitive attractiveness of small businesses as tenants in shopping centers and industrial parks as well as other commercial space. The LPA business relocation officer must familiarize himself thoroughly with the regulations and standards applicable under each SBA financing program, and then transmit this information to interested or eligible displacees. In addition, the rapport between the LPA staff and SBA loan officers noted as essential for effective exploitation of DBL opportunities is just as important in arranging other types of SBA financial assistance.

SBA Loans to Supplement Displaced Business Loans
DBL's are often insufficient for the needs of the displaced business, particularly when significant expansion or improvement of its facilities is planned.

Regular SBA loans are available at higher interest rates than DBL's, but they have been utilized effectively to supplement a DBL. They are particularly appropriate when additional working capital or inventory is required, and when the firm is changing from tenant to owner status.

When a displaced firm is planning a significant expansion of its facilities in the new location, a supplementary EDL is particularly appropriate. These loans are designed specifically for the purpose of financing new construction and expansion. In several communities studied, combination DBL-EDL arrangements have been the key to successful relocations.

Particularly when a combination of a DBL and another type of SBA loan is sought by the displacee, the LPA business relocation staff should provide active support for the application. This requires thorough understanding of the firm's needs, resources and capabilities, as well as a preliminary evaluation of the probable feasibility of the proposed development. Where combination loan arrangements have been successfully obtained, the LPA staff typically participates actively in preparing the loan application and the supporting documentation.

Section 502 Development Loans

Displacees are rarely eligible for these loans, since an occupant of the structure(s) built under a Section 502 loan may not be an owner or participant in the development group that receives the loan. Therefore, these loans are appropriate in handling relocation problems only when group facilities are to be provided by a separate development organization that will house displacees as tenants. This financing has been employed successfully in a limited number of cases, however, and the LPA business relocation staff should be aware of the opportunities that Section 502 loans afford.

Lease Guarantee Insurance

SBA has embarked on a program of guaranteeing leases for qualified displaced small business firms, so that they may occupy space that would otherwise not be available to them. There is no rent supplement or subsidy of any kind. Developers of shopping centers and industrial parks in particular tend to utilize the credit standing of their tenants as a basis for arranging financing from private sources through an assignment of rents. The SBA lease guarantee, for which the small business tenant or landlord pays a modest annual premium based on a fixed percentage of the annual rent to be guaranteed, simply substitutes the credit of SBA or a participating private insurance company for that of the individual tenant. As a result, the developer can utilize this better credit rating as a basis for his own financing, and therefore is more willing to accept small business tenants. Owners of existing commercial space also find rental guarantees an attractive substitute for a high credit rating of tenants.

LPA business relocation personnel must develop familiarity with SBA standards and regulations in this program. In the one community studied in which a shopping center was being developed in part through the use of SBA lease guarantees, considerable delays were encountered while clarifications of regulations and standards were obtained.

The lease guarantee program is particularly applicable for displaced businesses that either do not desire or cannot afford ownership of their real estate. LPA business relocation personnel should investigate this possibility for firms oriented toward tenant occupancy.

In the few cases available for study, lease guarantees appear to be especially effective for displaced businessmen with brief or spotty profit records, and for members of minority groups not considered by normal financing channels to represent good credit risks. LPA staff must recognize that whether these businessmen are good credit risks or not is beside the point at this stage; the attitude of lenders determines whether a loan is made. Lease guarantee insurance can help to alter this attitude.

Obtaining Financing from Sources Other than SBA

SBA is not the only source of financing which has been exploited effectively by LPA's to relocate businesses. Many firms at both ends of the economic scale are not eligible for SBA financing. In addition, some LPA's have not been able to use SBA as an effective financing resource. Some displacees have required funds for purposes not eligible for SBA financing. Moreover, reports of delays in processing and complexities in documenting SBA loan applications have discouraged many business firms from applying for SBA loans.

In recognition of this, many LPA's have developed alternative avenues of financing for displacees. In some instances, the LPA has encouraged the creation of the financial resource; in others it has developed effective contacts and lines of communication with existing institutions so that displacees applying for financial assistance have had the prospect of a favorable hearing.

Public Sources

Both state and local governments have provided opportunities for financing real estate acquisition and/or occupancy by displaced firms. In many such instances, the LPA has not been directly involved, except when the municipality itself is also the LPA. Nevertheless, these experiences suggest the type of activity that can be encouraged by other LPA's in their own states and communities. Particularly with concerted support from the business community, similar opportunities can be created.

Lease-purchase of LPA-owned land. Some LPA's (especially when the city *is* the LPA) have offered displacees the opportunity to acquire project area reuse sites on a long-term lease basis, with a portion of the lease applied toward the purchase price. This arrangement involves substituting the credit of the LPA (or city) for that of private displacee firms. It is a form of subsidy in the sense that municipalities can borrow money at lower rates of interest. The city must generally raise the funds through a bond issue, which means that the financing is through public funds.

Long-term leases on LPA-owned property. The so-called *definitive lease* arrangement makes it possible for an LPA to lease a site for up to 40 years. This is a form of financing of the *occupancy* of the site with the use of public funds. Rentals can be and usually are at below-market rates because municipalities and local agencies can usually borrow money more cheaply than small, private business organizations can. In a few cases, the LPA or muncipality has constructed buildings on publicly owned sites and leased both building and site to the displacee firm.

Subordination of an LPA lease interest. When LPA-owned sites are leased to private firms which then construct their own facilities on the sites, institutional lenders on the structure usually require subordination of the lease interest of the LPA to the mortgage. This is commonplace in private financing, but represents a departure in thinking in some communities. It usually requires specific action by the local legislative body, through ordinance or other formal legislative action. By doing this, the LPA makes it possible for the displacee firm to acquire private financing for its building(s). Public funds are not directly involved, but public interests are. LPA business relocation personnel should be aware of this action when long-term leases on LPA-owned sites are being planned.

Tax concessions. Many local communities have provided tax abatement or a guaranteed level of property taxes for a specified period to encourage private development and private financing for displacees. This is an indirect use of public funds in the sense that revenue increases are foregone for a specified period to encourage private development and financing.

Local development corporations. In several communities, local development corporations have worked closely with the LPA in financing relocation facilities. They also provide relocation sites and/or buildings on terms favorable to displacees. This involves the use of public funds and the use of public credit to acquire funds at lower interest rates. In one instance, the local development corporation acts as a financial intermediary between private lenders and the displaced borrower. The development corporation borrows funds at low interest rates because its obligations are tax exempt. It then lends these funds to the displaced firm for site and building acquisition. Thus the credit of the local development corporation reduces financing expenses for the displacee firm.

State development corporations and banks. In some states, direct loans are available from a state development corporation or bank. In others, loan guarantee or insurance programs are available to supplement the credit of the displacee-borrower. In either case, the credit of the state organization is utilized to attract funds at relatively low interest rates. These savings are passed on to eligible firms, including displacees. The LPA business relocation staff plays an important role in informing displacees about these possibilities, and assisting them to qualify for a direct loan or loan guarantee.

Private Sources

Most private financing of relocation facilities has been obtained from local banks and savings and loan associations, or from life insurance companies. Only a very few cases of small business development corporation (SBDC) financing were encountered. There seems to be little direct advantage to the displacee firm in SBDC financing. Only a handful of instances were reported in which private development corporations were formed for the purpose of financing displacees. It appears that if local private investment funds are to be made available, they are much more likely to be channeled into equity investment in land and building development, with displacees becoming tenants. While this may serve as supplementary indirect financing of occupancy by displacees, the major attention of the LPA business relocation staff should be focused on utilizing private institutional lenders to finance directly the relocation needs of displaced businesses.

Exploitation of Private Loan Sources. Repeated cases of successful private financing of displaced firms emphasize the point that the LPA business relocation staff must have good working contacts and relationships with private financial sources. This is necessary both to understand lenders' loan standards and requirements, and to be able to explain them to displacees. Moreover, appreciation of these standards makes it possible for LPA personnel to screen displacee applications and advise displacees about the type of financing to seek, and the most appropriate sources to approach. In some LPA's, business advisory groups have played a strategic role as liaison with the local financial community. In at least one community, the mayor has directly intervened in some cases to convince local lenders to support the urban renewal program by lending funds to displacees for real estate acquisitions. The LPA, with the support of business advisory groups and the municipal administration, is most successful when it actively "sells" or promotes loan applications by displacees.

Assistance in loan applications. Just as in the case of SBA loan applications, LPA staff or their consultants can play a critical role in the success of private loan applications by helping displacees to prepare the applications and to assemble the necessary supporting documentation.

Lease subordination. As noted in the consideration of public financing sources, subordination of an LPA lease to the private mortgage is usually necessary to obtain private financing of building construction for the displacee. The LPA must be aware of this requirement and adopt a policy in advance that will permit such action. It offers one alternative avenue of financing if the conditions are established in advance.

Encouragement of joint ownership. Joint ownership of facilities to be occupied by several displacees, whether through a corporation or a condominium, enhances the financial attractiveness of the development to private lenders. LPA staff should be aware of this, and encourage joint ownership when it makes economic and financial sense as a further means of attracting private financing. This policy has been successfully carried out in many LPA's under a wide variety of circumstances.

Flexibility in the redevelopment plan. Land use requirements or zoning regulations, architectural requirements, building construction standards, and reuse patterns are all typically specified in detail in the redevelopment plan. In a number of cases studied, the requirements of private lenders have been at variance with the stipulations of the plan. The LPA should be prepared to consider amending or adjusting the requirements of the plan to allow for private financing, when it appears to offer a promise of successful completion of the project for displacees seeking to relocate within a project area.

Lease Insurance

One state department of commerce has initiated a program of lease insurance for small displacees who are tenants. This is designed to encourage private financing of the development for occupancy by displacees. Upon the payment of a small annual premium, the public agency guarantees the payment of rent under the terms of the lease. This makes it possible for the private developer to obtain private financing, using the guaranteed rent payment as a basis for obtaining favorable loan terms — or in some instances any financing at all. This is a potential line of activity that can be undertaken in other states, or even at the local level.

Finding an Appropriate Site for the Displacee

The central issue in the relocation process is identifying a satisfactory relocation site for the displacee. The basic problem of finding a new location is as ubiquitous as any in the business relocation process. It is therefore incumbent on LPA business relocation personnel to be familiar with the techniques of site search and selection, to maintain current information on the availability of vacant sites and space in the market area, and to develop continuing data on the requirements, needs and desires of displacees for new space. Most of these cases are relatively routine. LPA's with the greatest success in handling a heavy work load are those with highly organized and systematic procedures for the processing of site requirement and vacancy information, and the transmittal of that information to the displacees.

Aid in Selecting a New Site

Most LPA's studied provide some form of assistance to displacees to help them find a new location. The assistance generally falls under two major headings: (1) advice and counsel about what is appropriate and feasible for the displacee, and (2) direct assistance in the search process.

Matching Displacee Needs with Available Sites and Space
The first step in meeting the needs of displacees is to obtain detailed information about their locational and space requirements. In many LPA's this information is obtained in the first direct contact with the displacee during the early stages of project planning. Periodic checks are frequently necessary to discover whether any changes in plans or expectations have taken place. The LPA business relocation officer has a responsibility to advise the displacee about what he can reasonably afford, and what his tenancy status probably should be.

Many LPA's provide consulting advice to displaced businessmen to help them plan for more efficient use of the space in their new location. In a few instances, this advice is provided through an outside group such as a business advisory group, or a university research organization.

The LPA staff should conduct frequent surveys of available sites and vacancies in the community so as to be able to advise displacees about the prospects and possibilities that confront them. Some LPA's have developed direct working relationships with local real estate boards and/or SIR chapters to obtain this information directly on a continuing basis.

Many LPA's have operated successfully on a referral basis, bringing cooperating real estate brokers and displacees together, and then letting them work out the details of site selection independently of the LPA staff.

Matching the needs and capabilities of displacees with the space that is available on the market involves careful analysis and advice. Several LPA's have turned this function over to consultants, including a university research group.

Direct Participation in the
Site Selection Process

A few LPA business relocation staffs provide direct assistance to displacees by participating in the site search and selection process. However, this is so time-consuming that only a large staff or a diminutive business relocation work load permits direct involvement in *every* case as a routine matter. Many LPA's do provide direct assistance in "problem" cases — especially for extremely small businesses, minority group businessmen who may encounter difficulties in finding a new location through the private market, and displaced firms that the LPA is particularly anxious to keep in operation within the community.

Several LPA's maintain an active register of property information that is periodically distributed to all displacees. In turn, they supply lists of displacees and their space requirements to cooperating real estate brokers, property managers, and owners of rental property.

In communities in which more than one urban renewal project is in execution, reuse sites in other project areas or within the project area in question represent an important relocation resource for many displacees. Many LPA's regularly circulate information to displacees about the availability of sites and/or space in reuse areas.

Several LPA's actively encourage relocation within a redevelopment project area by specifying in the redevelopment plan that certain sites either are available only to displacees or are available to displacees on a priority preference basis.

A few of the larger LPA business relocation staffs inspect vacant sites and space that come to their attention. They do this regardless of who finds the vacancy in the first place, and advise displacees about the suitability of the vacancies.

An extremely important function of LPA business relocation personnel is to advise displacees *against* relocating in inappropriate or unsuitable locations. The pressure to "get the move over with" felt by many displacees can stimulate them to accept the first vacancy that comes to their attention. The LPA staff has a responsibility to ensure to the extent possible that the new location is appropriate to the type of business activity, and that it is consistent with the ability of the firm to carry occupancy costs.

Temporary relocations have been suggested and arranged, both within project areas and off-site, when the permanent new location is not ready at the time that the old location is to be vacated. In many cases, the LPA finds the temporary or interim relocation site, because displacees are usually reluctant to commit themselves to more than one move.

Assistance in Relocating in the
Same Project Area

For many displaced businesses, it makes economic sense to relocate in very close proximity to their current location. Retail establishments and CBD-oriented businesses in particular have found it "necessary" to relocate in essentially the same area. This process always requires close attention and direct participation by the LPA staff in site selection and relocation planning.

Maintaining the Business At or Near
Its Displacement Site
Possibilities for successful on-site relocation usually must be recognized early in project planning. The redevelopment plan should take this contingency into account, preferably by establishing priority for a displaced business in the site selected, and by specifying a use which is consistent with the activity of the displacee.

By establishing priority preference for displacees in the redevelopment plan, some LPA's have enabled the displaced businesses to acquire their new site by negotiation rather than through public bid or auction. This amounts to a virtual guarantee of a suitable new location for the displaced firm.

Staging of construction and redevelopment in the project area should take into account the needs of on-site relocatees. To the extent possible, construction of the new facility on the reuse site should be completed before demolition of the displacement site. This will eliminate the necessity for a temporary or interim relocation.

Construction can be planned around the old sites of displacees to enable them to remain on-site until they move into their new building. In one community, the new development was planned so that the old buildings were located on the parking lot of a new shopping center. When the new building was completed, the occupants moved into it and their old buildings were demolished to provide the parking area.

Temporary Relocation
Although most LPA's try to avoid temporary or interim relocations when possible, the device is frequently necessary. This is especially true when the permanent relocation site is in the same project area, or even on the same site as the old location. When temporary relocations are necessary or highly desirable to complete an on-site relocation successfully, several alternative approaches have been used with good effect.

LPA's with more than one project in execution can frequently utilize vacant space in one project area for displacees from another. This can have the effect of keeping the displacees in close proximity to both their former location and the ultimate new location. In addition, it minimizes management and security problems associated with LPA ownership of vacant structures. Many LPA's have, in effect, compensated displacees for the necessity of an interim move by charging minimum rentals in the temporary on-site relocations. A further consideration for project area properties not yet acquired by the LPA is that their vacancies can be kept to a minimum, and difficulties with property owners reduced as a result.

In a few instances, LPA's have been able to include the cost of preparing a temporary relocation site for a displacee as part of project costs. Each case has required prior approval from the HUD regional office. Such approval has been given only when the LPA has been able to demonstrate convincingly that the action was in the best interest of the redevelopment plan and of the program. Nevertheless, this does represent one alternative opportunity for effective action in a limited number of cases.

One possibility for housing displacees temporarily is to *create* a temporary relocation facility on LPA-owned land. This has worked extremely well in a few cases, when close proximity to the final relocation site was essential for the displaced businesses. One LPA financed construction of a temporary building through modest rentals charged the displacees, and in addition was able to keep a liquor store licensee in business by minimizing the distance of his move. In another case, a group of retail food merchants was moved to a temporary building erected by the LPA on the parking lot of their new site. The temporary structure was occupied during construction of the permanent building, and then demolished to make way for the parking area.

In one instance, state law has permitted the LPA to pay for moving expenses to a temporary relocation if it chooses to do so. This involves the use of non-federal funds. It has proved to be an effective device in handling relocations in the CBD of one community. It represents an idea which might be followed in other states.

Creating Sites for Displacees

Some LPA's have displaced so many businesses at one time that the currently available resources of the community were overburdened. In such situations, LPA's have provided space for displacees within urban renewal project areas, and have also encouraged both private and quasi-public developers to create off-site locations for displaced firms.

Providing Space for Displacees in
Urban Renewal Project Areas

Many LPA's have included specific provisions in redevelopment plans for individual sites to be available to displacees only, or to displacees on a priority basis.

In some communities, the redevelopment plan or the policy of the LPA has given priority to redevelopers who obligated themselves to give preference — or at least first refusal — to displacees as tenants in their new buildings.

Displacees have been successfully attracted and encouraged to relocate within project areas by specifying that they might acquire reuse sites by negotiation rather than through public bid or auction. This course of action usually requires prior approval from the HUD regional office, as well as HUD concurrence in the disposition price.

In some instances, LPA's have found it desirable either to develop a redevelopment plan or to amend an existing one to accommodate a specific displacee or group of displacees. A number of cities have provided space for food distribution centers on this basis.

Especially when the municipality is the LPA, it may be possible to relocate displacees on other city-owned land. In two notable instances, sites that were formerly city dumps were filled and developed for industrial park purposes, with displacees receiving priority preferences for locations in the new developments. In another case, a swampy salt marsh was filled and compacted to create sites for industrial and distribution displacees. In each of these cases, the city utilized its redevelopment powers to develop the new sites, but the projects were accomplished entirely *without* federal funds.

Encouraging Private and
Quasi-Public Developments
Several LPA's have encouraged and cooperated with developers of off-project sites to provide locations for displacees, among others. These efforts have been particularly successful in creating sites for industrial and wholesale-distribution firms in planned development or "parks."

The LPA business relocation staff can play an important role in referring suitable displacees to the developer, and in encouraging the developer to give priority preference to displacees for sites that are created.

In several cases, the LPA has enlisted the support of the municipal administration to encourage developers to give some form of priority preference to displacees. In those communities in which the effort has been most successful, the mayor has taken a strong public stand in favor of this course of action, as well as using his influence with the developer.

Moving the Business

Just as every relocatee must move *somewhere*, it is axiomatic that every relocatee must move. The physical process of moving is therefore a continuing "problem" for every LPA business relocation staff. Much of the success achieved in handling the moving work load has been the result of careful internal organization and systematic treatment of all moves according to a prescribed procedure. This has left more time for the LPA business relocation staff to devote to the really complex problems associated with physical moves.

Planning and Coordinating the Move

Most displacees have little experience with moving their businesses. As a result, the process is looked upon with apprehension. They are unaware of what procedures are involved, and what personal property should in fact be moved. Successful moves are almost invariably the result of carefully coordinated advance planning among the displacee, the mover, and the LPA staff.

Coordinating the Move with Redevelopment

Several LPA's attempt to stage project construction to conform with and accommodate the moving plans of displacees. This type of coordination requires careful advance planning, which must be based upon information obtained early in the planning stage in interviews with displacees. Moreover, it necessitates continuing contact with displacees so that any changes in project planning can be immediately reflected in the moving plans of the displaced businessman.

Staging of construction and demolition, and advising displacees about the timing of their moves, require careful consideration of the probable impact on business volume after construction starts in the area, but before the business moves. This "wet blanket" effect is particularly significant when the firm is dependent on surrounding area residents for the bulk of its business. Several LPA's have arranged for temporary access roads, relocation of utility lines, off-site parking facilities at LPA expense, and delays in street construction to permit remaining businesses to continue to operate before the move. This is a very critical time for the business in many instances. Sensitivity to this problem helps to avoid loss of the business before the planned move can occur.

Most LPA's keep displacees informed about the timing of acquisition of their properties by the LPA. This is extremely important, because a move prior to acquisition eliminates eligibility for relocation payments or an SBDP. The LPA staff must maintain constant contact with the businessmen, and strongly advise against moving prior to acquisition.

Several LPA's make arrangements for early acquisition in order to qualify displacees for relocation payments and SBDP's, as well as SBA financing. While they try to avoid early acquisition, it is preferable to the problems and unfavorable publicity that can result when a move prior to acquisition takes place.

Helping the Firm Plan for the Move

The LPA should supply displacees with complete information about acquisition plans, so that precise dates for the move can be established as early as possible.

Many LPA's make a point of advising displacees about the alternative benefits and advantages of moving property, as opposed to disposing of it and receiving reimbursement for damages.

Particularly among those LPA's that coordinate relocation and acquisition activities, owners are provided with advice to help determine which items of equipment should be included as fixtures and acquired as part of the real estate. This is not an easy determination in many cases, and the displacee generally benefits from LPA staff advice.

Several LPA's arrange visits or tours by groups of movers to inspect several premises and ascertain precisely what is to be moved. This aids considerably in the preparation and submission of bids. In a few LPA's, business relocation staff members ordinarily meet with movers and displacees to explain the nature of the move and the items to be moved.

LPA staff can be extremely helpful to the displacee by helping to prepare the inventory of items to be moved. This tends to encourage bids from movers, and also to avoid disagreements at a later date about what is to be moved and what remains as real estate or fixtures.

Some LPA staffs provide early advice to displacees about the layout and appropriate fixtures for their new location. This also assists the displacee in making his decision about what is to be moved and what should be included as personal property loss.

Many LPA's give detailed information and advice to displacees at an early meeting concerning their entitlements for reimbursement of relocation expenses. Understanding the regulations involved can help the displacee decide when, how, and what to move. It will also enable him to assemble the necessary documentation to support his subsequent claim.

Help During the Move

While many LPA's leave the physical process of moving to the displacee and the mover whose bid has been accepted, some remain active participants during the moving process. This is particularly helpful in the case of complex or lengthy moves, as well as self-moves. Continuing direct contact by the LPA staff tends to discourage inappropriate decisions that would later result in some or all of the claim for reimbursement being denied.

Promotional Help for the Move

A few LPA's distribute a booklet on the mechanics of packing and moving business equipment. These are usually made available by local movers. They make it possible for the displacee to stage his move with a minimum of damage or interruption of his business activity.

Some LPA's assist displacees in arranging inventory reduction sales, and in promoting them. This is particularly important at two levels of activity. First, small firms which are going to encounter substantial personal property losses are confronted with a $3,000 reimbursement maximum. Second, relatively large establishments sometimes find it difficult to keep moving expenses below the $25,000 reimbursement limit. In both types of situations, inventory reduction sales may help to keep the actual expenses of the displacee firm within the limits of reimbursement established by law. Few LPA's have participated in moving expenses in excess of $25,000.

The LPA can also help the displacee promote his move and attract the number of bids sufficient to satisfy federal regulations. Delays in reimbursement can be avoided if the minimum number of bids in prescribed form is received.

Coordination with Movers and Technicians

Some moves require considerable technical assistance; others involve a large amount of dismantling and assembly of equipment. In both types of situations, the LPA staff can and should serve as an intermediary between the displacee and the technicians required. This is necessary to expedite the move once it is begun, and to make sure that no actions or expenditures occur that would delay or jeopardize payment of the moving claim.

Some LPA's have been able to obtain authorization from HUD to arrange for partial payments to technicians. By serving as an intermediary, the LPA can help ensure that the work is done properly and that appropriate charges are made.

Arranging for Self-Moves

A self-move may be the most appropriate way to handle a relocation. Sometimes the amount of equipment and supplies to be moved is so small that it can be handled expeditiously by the displacee himself. At the other end of the scale, the move may be so complex and equipment so delicate or valuable that the displacee is reluctant to use commercial movers.

Whenever a self-move is suggested, the LPA staff must explain the regulations pertaining to self-moves carefully to the displacee. Failure to obtain necessary bids or to provide the required documentation can result in serious delays in reimbursement. This can usually be avoided by direct participation of LPA staff in the planning of the self-move.

Self-moves are frequently designed to allow for a move over a prolonged period, so as to minimize interruption of business work flow. This requires considerable advance planning between the displacee and the LPA staff, to allow sufficient time for the firm to carry out the move.

LPA staffs occasionally suggest a self-move when it appears that commercial moving costs would exceed the $25,000 limit. In a number of cases, displacees have elected to move themselves in order to recover all of their actual out-of-pocket expenditures.

Valuable and complex equipment which is not excessively heavy can frequently be moved with more care by the displacee, because he and his employees recognize the value of the items to be moved. Printers in particular find it preferable to move their own plates, set type, and type boxes.

Assistance After the Move

Relocation does not end when the physical move is completed. Several matters concerning the move must still be settled. These involve payments to the mover, occasional damage claims against the mover, and reimbursement of expenses incurred by the displacee. In all of these matters, LPA business relocation personnel can and should be effective aids to the business, in order to make the relocation a "success."

Encouraging Prompt Reimbursement of
Relocation Expenses

All relocatees who did not move prior to property acquisition are entitled to reimbursement of moving expenses, and many may claim reimbursement of personal property losses as well. A major responsibility of the LPA, whether through its business relocation staff or a claims department, is to ensure as prompt and as full payment of the reimbursement claim as possible.

Appropriate advance planning and coordination between the LPA and the displacee provide the basis for full documentation of the reimbursement claim.

Prior explanation of documentation requirements makes it more likely that the displacee will have the necessary information to complete the claim forms promptly and fully.

Most LPA's provide direct assistance to displacees in filling out claim forms and in documenting their claims.

Advance approval from the HUD regional office is essential for expeditious processing of claims in excess of $10,000. With careful planning and full documentation, approvals have been received within two working days by a number of LPA's.

Continuing close coordination and contact with the HUD regional office can expedite the processing of final payment approval. In some cases, LPA's have been able to issue a reimbursement check on the same day that the claim was prepared and submitted. The entire process sometimes takes place in the LPA office. Appropriate advance planning and good internal organization of the LPA normally permit reimbursement within two days.

For displacees with extremely limited funds, some LPA's arrange to pay the mover directly. This keeps the displacee from committing his own funds, even for a short period of time.

Supporting Damage Claims Against Movers

LPA's occasionally inspect items to be moved before and after the move, and verify any claims that displacees may have against the movers.

One device used by a few LPA's is to have the mover bill the LPA directly and make payment only after the relocatee reports that he is satisfied with the results of the move.

Creating a New Environment for Relocatees

Since business relocation is undertaken in the context of urban renewal, one objective is to revitalize the businesses in their new locations, as well as to stimulate the local economy. This frequently involves more than simply finding a new location, arranging financing, or planning a new layout for the firm. "Successful" relocation includes a new legal and economic environment, as well as a different physical environment. The LPA itself is frequently not in a position to change either the legal or the economic environment directly. In many communities, however, the LPA has been the primary moving force in stimulating such changes for the benefit of both the displaced firms and the community at large.

Creating a New Legal Environment

When the LPA is independent of the municipal administration, its role is necessarily that of suggesting and encouraging necessary changes to stimulate more effective business relocation activities. When the city is the LPA, the municipal administration can and frequently does coordinate changes in local ordinances with business relocation and other urban renewal activities.

Statutory Changes

LPA's, in conjunction with other state and local governmental authorities, have occasionally found the solution to relocation problems in changing existing state or local laws. Most frequently, new legislation or ordinances have been introduced to permit actions on which the law previously was silent.

State enabling legislation on redevelopment can be amended to provide for the availability of non-federal funds to carry out important types of redevelopment and relocation activities. In one state, authorization was provided for redevelopment of project areas which were predominantly non-residential in character, provided the reuse was for industrial and/or commercial purposes. A number of states have given LPA's the authority to utilize state and local funds for the development of open land for industrial purposes. In at least one state, municipalities (which are LPA's) have been given the authority to dispose of "excess" park lands for industrial development purposes.

Some LPA's have initiated legislation designed to cope with specific but recurring business relocation problems which were not susceptible to effective treatment under federal laws or regulations. In one state in which municipalities are the LPA's, municipalities were authorized to make direct relocation payments with local funds in cases of multiple moves involving temporary relocations. Another state statute specifies the method of compensation for church property acquired by LPA's: compensation is based upon replacement costs, rather than reproduction costs less accrued depreciation.

Exceptions to Local Regulations

LPA's have successfully sought zoning changes, as well as variances or exceptions to zoning regulations. The successful efforts are typically based on the argument that the contribution to the project and the community outweighs any gain realized by the displaced firm.

Both LPA's and municipal authorities must be sensitive to the changing economic and market conditions that often take place between the time that zoning regulations or redevelopment plans are formulated, and actual execution of the project begins. The major responsibility for reacting positively to these changes rests with the LPA.

Creating a New Economic Environment

A new location is appropriate only if it is served by necessary municipal facilities (especially utilities and access) and if it is appropriately situated for the firm to serve its market. The surrounding environment provided to the firm in its new location is frequently the ultimate determinant of whether the relocation is "successful." Both in its direct actions through urban renewal programs and in its encouragement of supportive municipal actions, the LPA plays an important role. These actions help create an economic environment that is conducive to profitable operations by displacees in their new locations.

Developing New Centers of Activity
LPA's have created new economic environments by developing industrial parks, food distribution centers, downtown malls, and wholesale distribution centers. The key to the success of these efforts has been the concentration of complementary business establishments. Together they have added more business and attracted more supporting activities than would have been possible if they had located separately and individually.

The successful new centers of activity have provided the necessary physical ingredients of a good economic environment: good access to markets and/or suppliers, adequate utilities, and appropriate transportation facilities.

The most effective centers have represented nearly ideal locations for the type of activity involved. By restricting the types of businesses permitted to locate in the area, they have encouraged greater efficiency in individual operations through carefully planned and integrated layouts.

Forestalling Business Relocation with
New Environments
Improving the surrounding area has occasionally resulted in the realization that many businesses scheduled for relocation need not move at all. Rather, conforming to the improved environment has resulted in a "successful relocation."

LPA's have occasionally concluded that businesses scheduled for relocation would serve both themselves and the community best by rehabilitating their properties instead.

Businesses scheduled to remain on-site may still occasionally have to be relocated temporarily. When this occurs, timing is essential to minimize the interruption of business activities.

It is usually necessary for the LPA to coordinate carefully the activities of the many business firms relocating, remaining on site, and moving into the new use area.

Handling "Special Problem" Displacees

The literature on business relocation is replete with illustrations and examples of business relocation problems that are regarded as "special," unusual or unique, especially difficult to solve, or even unsolvable. The interesting point is that essentially the same list of business types is repeated again and again when these contentions are made. Part of the motivation underlying this study was the belief that these "special" or "unusual" situations probably recur both within LPA's and among LPA's with notable regularity.

One important fact which emerged from this analysis of case studies and LPA business relocation operations is that many of the problems hitherto regarded as "special" are actually being encountered frequently and dealt with effectively in many communities. Moreover, patterns of treatment of such problems appear to be workable in other communities.

Firms with Negative Environmental Impacts

Many business activities are regarded as "unsuitable neighbors" both for residences and for other types of more "desirable" business activity. Finding such businesses locations which meet their requirements and also obtaining neighborhood acceptance is difficult and time-consuming for LPA business relocation personnel, but workable solutions have been found.

Industrial Firms

Firms using flammable materials have been successfully relocated in specially designated sections of project areas. Redevelopment frequently provides an opportunity to create relatively isolated sites that still meet the access and other locational requirements of the displaced businesses. Moreover, the creation of heavy industrial areas on former city dumps or on reclaimed harbor sites has proved effective, particularly when the development of the sites is planned in conjunction with adjacent major highway improvements.

Manufacturing firms, especially those with noise, odors or other "nuisances" associated with their operations, are equally regarded as bad neighbors. At the same time, most communities are anxious to retain the jobs and income, as well as the property taxes, generated by heavy manufacturing establishments. The creation of outlying "parks" or industrial districts on previously undeveloped and often "unusable" land has proved to be quite workable in a number of communities. With effective buffers provided by major highways in several instances, the nuisance aspect of the operations has been reduced while the economic and fiscal objectives of the community have simultaneously been served.

Retail and Wholesale Firms

Distribution centers generate a large volume of heavy traffic. They are regarded as particular nuisances in many communities because their historic locations have been in or near the heart of the downtown area. Several LPA's have accommodated major traffic generators on outlying sites created from land previously regarded as unusable or unbuildable. In several instances, they have been adjacent to major highway improvements. These provide the direct access to through-highways that is particularly important for the successful operation of distribution firms. This has been a particularly useful approach in relocating food distribution centers that have the added nuisance factor of unusual hours of operation (e.g., 2:00 a.m. until 6:00 p.m.)

Funeral Homes

Funeral homes often encounter difficulty in gaining neighborhood acceptance. Aside from the fact they they are frequently generators of heavy traffic, they are apparently unpleasant reminders of man's mortality. A number of LPA's have solved the problem of relocating funeral homes by providing space for them in the redevelopment plan. In some instances, the LPA staff has supported the displacee's application for zoning permission at public hearings, and has successfully presented factual information about the non-nuisance character of funeral parlors. Also, LPA staffs have given specific advice to a few displaced funeral home operators about screening their property and providing adequate on-site parking.

Firms Requiring Licenses and Permits

On many occasions, displacees requiring licenses and/or permits from public control authorities encounter difficulty when they attempt to relocate the business to a new site. State and local regulations vary widely in controlling mobility of licensees and permittees. Moreover, such firms are not eligible for reimbursement of the frequently substantial loss entailed in going out of business and losing the license or permit. They therefore have particular interest in maintaining operations at a new location.

Retail Liquor Stores
These displacees encounter special difficulty in obtaining permission to relocate their license, and in finding a new location which meets minimum distance specifications from certain types of activity (e.g., churches or schools) that are often included in licensing regulations. Some LPA's have provided for temporary on-site relocation and relocation back into the project area in order to keep the firm in business. With careful planning, the maximum distance permitted for a relocation has been honored, and the reuse plan has ensured no conflicting use within prescribed distances. A few LPA's have helped liquor store operators take advantage of the SBA Displaced Business Loan program, under which retail liquor stores can be eligible for SBA financing.

Intervention with the Licensing Authority
Several LPA's have discovered that licensing authorities have discretionary powers. By supporting the application for relocation of a license and explaining to the authority the nature of redevelopment, it has been possible in a number of instances to obtain allowable exceptions for the displacee. On other occasions, licensees have unwittingly jeopardized their licenses by moving without proper notification to the licensing authority. In such cases, intervention by the LPA on behalf of the displacee has usually resulted in renewal of the license at the new location.

Structure Design
Neighborhood acceptance of an "undesirable" property use has occasionally been overcome by changing the design of the structure so that it blends with existing structures in the area. This is important because licenses and permits are frequently denied if there is strong neighborhood objection.

Promotional Efforts
A number of LPA's have actively solicited neighborhood acceptance by publicizing the relocation and the construction or remodeling plans of the

displacee. They have recognized the fact that anticipation of change is frequently a more negative influence on surrounding neighbors than is the accomplished fact. By explaining and reassuring neighbors in advance, the LPA has helped the displacee gain neighborhood acceptance.

Acquisition of a Going Concern

In some instances, the loss of an existing license is not a major financial disaster, or a license is transferable but no suitable new location can be found. Then the LPA may advise displacees to utilize their relocation payments and SBDP to acquire a going concern already operating at an off-site location. The result has been to keep the displacee in business in an acceptable location, and in the same line of business as before.

Economically Marginal Firms

Extremely small businesses are particularly fragile, financially and economically. Every LPA encounters a large number of firms whose economic justification is questionable. Several LPA's studied have taken the approach that such businesses are salvable and relocatable, and have consciously sought to bring them into a competitive posture.

Improving the Business Enterprise

A number of LPA's offer direct advice and assistance to small and/or marginal businessmen to help make them better businessmen. Most important is training in bookkeeping and keeping records. In one community, a local university business research center offers both individual assistance and small group seminars to all displacees on the LPA work load.

Many LPA's refer marginal business operators to outside agencies for advice and assistance. In some cases, they are sent to local technical schools for counseling and training in the rudiments of business management. Other LPA's utilize business advisory groups created for this purpose. Still others refer displacees to SBA, SCORE, or the local Small Business Opportunities Center. In every instance, a common ingredient is the utilization of available local resources to supplement the skills of the LPA business relocation staff. In this way, personal advice and service can be provided directly to each displacee in need of help.

Changing the Nature of the Business

Without regard to the efficiency of their operations, many displacees ("Mom and Pop" stores, for example) have been confronted with a declining demand for their goods or services. Others have found their markets effectively eliminated by redevelopment. Sometimes the best solution to this problem is to enter an entirely new line of business.

One workable solution is to find another going concern for purchase by the displacee, using his relocation reimbursement and SBDP for the equity payment.

An alternative approach is to re-train the displacee to work for others. In some cases, LPA's have enlisted the services of local technical schools to provide this training. In others, the technical skills already possessed by the displacee have made it possible for him to find employment. This was the case in at least two wholesale food market relocations, for example.

At least two LPA's studied refer many marginal business operators to franchising organizations, from which they receive training for their new line of business. The relocation reimbursement and SBDP are frequently sufficient to finance acquisition of the franchise at the end of the training period.

Effective Liquidation

In some instances, marginal operators (especially elderly businessmen) do not have the desire to continue in business on their own. In these circumstances, when all other efforts for relocation and upgrading management skills have failed, the LPA should recognize the inevitability of the decision and advise them to liquidate their businesses.

Elderly businessmen in particular are frequently reluctant to go through what they regard as the agonies of relocation. It is sometimes possible to arrange for the sale of their business rather than to have the owners simply discontinue operations. In a few cases, LPA staff have sought and located purchasers of the businesses. The amounts have been modest, but greater than what would have been realized if the elderly businessman had simply liquidated his stock.

Elderly displacees eligible for retirement benefits are frequently assisted by LPA business relocation staff members in making application to the Social Security Administration.

In the case of liquidations, special efforts to process reimbursement claims and SBDP's rapidly are initiated by several LPA's. The reason for this is that the funds are often particularly critical for the businessman who suddenly finds himself with no income at all for a period of time.

When displacees who liquidate with or without the advice of the LPA are not elderly and not eligible for retirement benefits, several LPA's direct them to job training programs. In a number of instances cited in the interviews for this study, former business operators were able to continue as productive members of the work force after completing such training.

Other "Problem" Businesses

The following types of businesses defy easy classification. Nevertheless, they are encountered and mentioned by LPA business relocation staff members frequently as recurring problems that are difficult to solve. Some LPA's, at least, have developed workable approaches to these situations.

Elderly Businessmen

When elderly displacees wish to continue in business, the major problem confronting them and the LPA business relocation officer attempting to help them is obtaining financing. Some solutions which have worked in individual LPA's are:

Incorporate the business and obtain a loan in the name of the corporation. This is feasible only when the business is sufficiently large and stable to be independent of the life of the owner-operator.

SBA Displaced Business Loans have been obtained in at least one community through the efforts of the LPA for displaced businessmen over age 65. In these cases, the business has not been marginal, and the DBL has been used to finance real estate acquisition. The real estate itself has been the fundamental security for the loan, but the important point is that borrowers over 65 have been accommodated through SBA.

In one instance, an SBA lease guarantee was arranged for an elderly businessman.

Minority Group Businessmen

Negro businessmen in particular meet, or believe they will meet, opposition to moving into certain neighborhoods. They also occasionally encounter difficulty in obtaining financing. A number of LPA's have worked out programs that consciously assist Negro displacees.

Two LPA's in the study conduct special surveys of commercial vacancies in and near Negro neighborhoods. Negro displacees that serve an essentially Negro market are taken directly to these sites as they are discovered.

In some communities, shopping centers and groupings of businesses have been sponsored by Negro developers for occupancy by Negro businessmen. The LPA's involved have given them special encouragement and assistance, particularly in arranging financing. In a few cases, the centers have been developed on land leased on a long-term basis to the development by the LPA. In another community, the lease guarantee is being used to aid in the financing of a Negro shopping center.

One LPA has contracted with a university group to work directly with Negro displacees in an effort to equip them with necessary business skills and knowledge to compete in the local market. Particular emphasis is placed on bookkeeping and record keeping, as well as merchandising to serve a racially mixed clientele. The university advisors also recommend training for the acquisition of franchises, some of which have been successfully obtained by Negro displacees.

In the experience of many LPA's, the most effective approach is to treat Negroes simply as businessmen and people without regard to race, and to offer them every encouragement and necessary bit of advice that any displacee should receive. Some success has been achieved in convincing Negro businessmen that they can compete in a market outside the project area. Special care is taken to make follow-up visits periodically for at least a year after the move.

Churches

Because churches are not eligible for an SBDP, the funds available to them for relocation are frequently very limited. This is especially true of small, independent congregations that rent their quarters. The most effective device in handling church relocations is to work closely with the church leaders, and actively search out locations most convenient to the new residences of most of the congregation. Prompt handling of relocation claims is especially important here, coupled with encouragement of self-moves by members of the congregation. In a number of cases, individual members of the congregation have moved the church equipment for the amount of the low bid, and then donated the fee to the church.

The redevelopment plan has also been used to aid churches in relocation by designating an area or areas for use as church sites. One city was able to relocate several churches in public housing developments that were located in redevelopment project areas.

Topical Key to Case Studies

Topical Key to Case Studies

The individual descriptions of successful business relocations contained in Part III illustrate the application in practice of the principles and generalizations presented in Part II. Many successful and imaginative efforts depend on the organizational structure of the LPA business relocation staff, its standardized policies and procedures, and its working relationships with other public and private groups. Because of this, some discussion of the organization and operation of business relocation activities in each LPA covered in the study is included, together with brief commentary on the business relocation efforts in each HUD regional office.

For purposes of presentation only, the case studies are arranged by HUD Regions I through VII, and alphabetically by city within each HUD Region. There is no other significance implied in this organizational scheme.

Nearly all of the case examples cover more than one of the issues and problems considered in Part II. The descriptions of LPA business relocation programs also frequently point up several effective arrangements for successful handling of business displacees. As a result, the reader might encounter difficulty, and waste time and effort trying to identify which case examples or LPA operational descriptions offer workable alternative approaches to the resolution of the particular problem in which he is interested.

To counter this difficulty, the following index is provided. Business relocation problems and issues are listed according to the same format used in Part II. Under each heading, the individual cases and LPA descriptions that best illustrate effective approaches to the problem or issue are listed by title, city and page number. This should provide a useful guide to the reader seeking to learn how others have coped successfully with a particular business relocation problem.

Topical Key

**Obtaining Cooperation and
Support from the Displacee**

Effect of Information on Displacee Attitudes

Specialized or Separate Relocation Staff

Specialized Business Relocation Staffs

Liaison with the Business Community

Use of Outside Groups and Individuals

Existing Groups and Agencies

**Providing Effective Guidance and
Counsel to Displacees**

*Development and/or Acquisition of
Specialized Skills*

*Use of Outside Agencies for
Direct Advice and Counseling to
Displaced Businessmen*

**Organizing Community Action to
Aid Business Relocation**

Creating New Business Organizations for Relocation

Basic Considerations in
Organizing a Joint Effort

Changing from Proprietorship or
Partnership to a Corporation

**Changing the Nature of the
Business or Its Method of Operation**

Business Expansion

Enlarging Facilities

Changing the Type of Business

Providing a New Product or Service

Upgrading the Business

Obtaining Financing for Displaced Businesses

**Finding an Appropriate Site
for the Displacee**

*Assistance in Relocating in the
Same Project Area*

*Maintaining the Business At or
Near Its Displacement Site*

Creating Sites for Displacees

Providing Space for Displacees in
Urban Renewal Project Areas

*Encouraging Private and
Quasi-Public Developments*

Moving the Business

Planning and Coordinating the Move

Coordinating the Move with Redevelopment

Helping the Firm Plan for the
Actual Move

Help During the Move

Promotional Help for the Move

Assistance After the Move

Creating a New Environment for Relocatees

Creating a New Economic Environment

Handling "Special Problem" Displacees

Case Studies

Region I

The Relocation Branch of the Program Coordination Service Division, located in New York City, is responsible for business relocation assistance activities in HUD Region I.

The business relocation case load and the available staff to handle it are secondary in this HUD Region to those of family relocation. Nevertheless, the Relocation Branch has initiated training workshops for LPA relocation personnel in such matters as interpretation of regulations. This office has also attempted to process both Small Business Displacement Payment authorizations and moving claims expeditiously, in order to put the money in the hands of the displaced businessman as soon as possible.

This office was instrumental in introducing a plan for partial payment of moving costs when the moving claim would otherwise be delayed. This situation occasionally arises because of the lack of some minor substantiation (receipts) for costs incurred for a single part of the total move.

Based upon suggestions from the Relocation Branch staff, the LPA's from Region I selected for inclusion in this study were those in Ansonia, Connecticut; New Haven, Connecticut; Pawtucket, Rhode Island; and Providence, Rhode Island.

Ansonia, Connecticut

The town of Ansonia is located in southern Connecticut. With a population of 20,000, it is one of the smaller communities selected for study. The volume of business relocation activity, including a group move and a shopping center development that was designed for relocatees, has been large relative to the number of urban renewal projects. By summer 1967, Ansonia had one completed project (Broad Street Renewal Project), a second project nearing completion (Downtown Renewal Project), and a third project in the planning stage. The city is the LPA.

The business relocation staff of the Ansonia Redevelopment Agency includes one full-time business relocation claims officer and a relocation property management officer. These two men, together with the executive director, provide all the assistance to displaced businessmen. Because of the small size of this town and the limited drawing power of its commercial facilities, it is basic policy to encourage every displacee to relocate within the town. The redevelopment staff has incorporated the following elements in their relocation program to achieve this objective.

Staging. As an integral part of each project, relocations are staged so that no business is displaced prior to the completion of the new structure in which the business is to relocate. To date, no business has been forced to leave a project area before it was offered a suitable relocation site by the relocation staff. In addition, the movement of a business from the project area to the new location has been staged so that the interruption time to the business is minimal. This technique is particularly well-illustrated in the case of the West Side Shopping Center.

Business moves. As a matter of policy, the relocation staff handles the move from the planning phase, if necessary, to assistance in obtaining and receiving bids for the business firm. They also accompany potential bidders to each site to examine the physical problems involved in the move. Prior to this meeting, staff members furnish the movers with a complete inventory of items to be moved and answer questions concerning the move.

Advice and counsel. The business relocation staff provides advice and counsel to displacees. This includes aiding in the identification of alternative business sites, helping to obtain financing for both working capital and the purchase of new business property, stimulating shopping center developments for displacees, and assisting in the lease negotiations to the benefit of the displacee.

Priority Claims for Displacees. Businesses displaced by urban renewal are given first priority in obtaining sites in the redeveloped project areas that could appropriately house such businesses. One of the more important features of this program is that project design is intended to provide select locations for displacees. This is an extension of the recognized need to retain, in almost every case, the displaced businesses. For example, when project land was being subdivided, potential relocatees were consulted about their preferences and requirements at the new location. The land was subsequently subdivided so that it could meet the needs of these displacees should they elect to bid on the sites. The result has been that most redeveloped land is occupied by displacees.

The relocation staff devotes considerable time to each business displacee. Often as many as one hundred contacts and/or visits are made to a businessman to inform him of his rights under the program, the payments that will be made available to him, and to perform other counseling and direct services. Because of the size of the community and its deep involvement in redevelopment, the redevelopment staff is aware of most potential relocation sites and can provide displaced businesses with this information. The relocation staff maintains a detailed record on all businesses handled throughout the many visits and transactions. Each firm's file contains a running memorandum with a synopsis of all visits, the content of dealings, and problems that were dealt with in the move and in subsequent contacts.

Ansonia Plaza

Jerry DePalma and Melo Sampieri, both businessmen displaced by the Downtown Renewal Project, were the developers of a reuse parcel in this same project area. The developers organized under the name of SamPalma, Incorporated, and constructed a new downtown shopping center with a value of nearly $300,000. The center contains sixteen stores. Before completion of construction, eight stores and a bank had signed leases. The shopping center site covers an area of approximately 53,000 square feet, with a total building area of 18,000 square feet and approximately fifty-six parking spaces for customers.

Originally, the Ansonia Redevelopment Agency expected a larger group of small business displacees to develop this site. However, because of disagreement about the design of the center and the method of ownership, the responsibility fell to Messrs. DePalma and Sampieri. Both men had previously owned real estate in the project area and had the necessary capital and experience to promote and develop the venture. Of particular interest is the fact that these two displacees were able not only to provide better business sites for themselves, but also to furnish space for several other displacees from the same project.

For example, Mr. Arthur Silberberg, a tenant in a downtown business that was displaced by the same project, was most disturbed at the prospect of being forced to relocate. Mr. Silberberg made it clear during an interview that he was dissatisfied with the urban renewal process because he anticipated much higher rental costs upon relocation as well as the concomitant difficulties of the physical move. What Mr. Silberberg did *not* anticipate was that a marked increase in sales would result from his move, which more than compensated for the higher rents at the new location. He admitted that the real key to the success of his particular business relocation was the simple act of forcing him to relocate from the lower-cost but deteriorating surroundings in which he had operated for many years. The LPA encouraged him to move into the new plaza, and in fact promoted lease negotiations.

Mr. Silberberg was given adequate time to move to his new space in the plaza. He was also allowed to carry out a self-move; he occupied both his old location and the new one for a period of several weeks. He was able to take a portion of his stock to the new location each day. Within a period of approximately one month the total move was completed, with little if any interruption of business. Thus, he was never really out of business, and his sales volume never declined during the entire period of the move.

An interesting sidelight of this case was the manner in which sales were affected by the move. In Mr. Silberberg's old location, the area was such that women seldom visited his retail men's clothing store. Now, apparently as a result of the more pleasant and convenient surroundings, he estimates that 40 per cent of his business is accounted for by women who shop in the plaza. His volume of business has increased nearly 50 per cent. He is quite pleased with the results of the move in spite of the fact that he now must work somewhat longer hours and has more responsibilities.

Mr. Melo Sampieri, one of the two displacee developers of Ansonia Plaza, operated a beauty shop in a structure he owned in the downtown project area prior to being displaced. At first, Mr. Sampieri had not seriously considered sponsoring such a large investment venture. However, by combining his capital and efforts with Mr. DePalma, he was able to develop this plaza. The developers found the LPA very cooperative in approving their plans. They were given not only encouragement but design and layout ideas as well. Financing was obtained from a financial institution outside the community.

In Mr. Sampieri's opinion, the end result of this business venture was well beyond his wildest expectations. The volume of business in his beauty shop increased nearly three times after the move to the new plaza. The plaza has had no vacancies since it opened. The two developers have already been asked by some of their tenants to provide additional adjacent space if it should become available.

The second member of the development corporation, Mr. Jerry DePalma, was also a property owner in the downtown project, in which he operated a fruit and produce market. Without the encouragement of the LPA, Mr. DePalma would probably have simply constructed another building for himself elsewhere; he had no thoughts of a development venture of the size and nature that ultimately materialized. As in the case of his partner and the other businessmen in the plaza who were interviewed, Mr. DePalma's business is considerably improved over that in the previous location.

A total of five displaced businesses relocated in this shopping plaza. In addition to the two developers and the men's clothing store, a restaurant and drugstore also found relocation space here. All of these businesses had been in the project area for over eight years before being displaced, and thus had an established clientele. Judging from the increased sales of all of these displacees, few of their customers were lost.

A final noteworthy element in this development effort is the foresight used by both the LPA and the developers. The construction of the plaza building consists of steel frame on piles so that an upper story is possible if future expansion is needed. The higher initial construction costs would then be more than offset by the cost savings of this addition.

There are at least four key elements to be noted in the Ansonia Plaza case. First is the encouragement and assistance provided by the LPA to the displacees to develop a shopping center within the same project area. Secondly, the shopping center developed by two displacees provided rental space for other displacees who had neither the capital nor the desire to become equity partners in this venture. The third point is the contrast of sales volume and profits before and after the move. The higher rents charged all relocatees in this plaza was one of the basic problems associated with the move. Yet each relocated businessman found that the increased volume of sales and more efficient operations generated in the much improved environment resulted in higher profits. Finally, there is the basic policy adopted by the LPA of giving business displacees first priority to project land. This policy includes project planning to meet the specific requirements of the displacees so that they may qualify in most instances as bidders for the sites.

B & J Electric Motor Repair Company

Mr. Frank Johns, owner and manager of B & J Electric Motor Repair Company, constructed a new plant in a redevelopment project area before all demolition on the new site had been completed. Final sale of the site to B & J was not possible until all demolition work had been completed and approved by the Redevelopment Agency. In order to begin early construction of the new B & J plant, a special provision was made in the redevelopment plan to permit construction as soon as there was room in which to work. This unusual arrangement also made possible the completion of the new structure prior to the displacement of the business from another project area. It greatly reduced the interruption of business that would have occurred had the firm been required to wait until all demolition was completed in the project area.

Under an agreement between the Ansonia Redevelopment Agency and the Riverside Development Corporation (a corporation formed by Mr. Johns and Mr. John Preston, another business owner who would construct and occupy a second new structure on the light-industrial site), the company was given permission to begin construction prior to the actual sale of the site. Title did not pass until demolition work in the project was completed. However, the company was guaranteed ultimate ownership of the site under a legal arrangement that illustrates the inventiveness of this LPA in developing ideas to aid business displacees.

By granting this special dispensation to the displacee and his business associates, Ansonia was able to ensure retention of a firm within the town when relocation elsewhere was a strong possibility. In addition, Mr. Johns, who was a tenant in the Downtown Renewal Project Area, now owns the property in which his business is located. He was also able to acquire approximately 50 per cent more space for his operation. Further, he has approximately fifteen off-street parking spaces for customers and employees, whereas there was only on-street parking space at his old location. During his first year at the new site, Mr. Johns doubled the number of his employees (sixteen in the new location as opposed to eight at the old) and realized a much higher level of business activity.

As a final element in this case, it is interesting that this new light-industrial structure was the first to be built in Ansonia for many years.

Ralph Mann and Sons, Inc.

This move is another example of relocation within the same project area. The firm moved from the 400 block to the 500 block of Main Street, in the Downtown Renewal Project. The firm also changed its tenancy status from renter to owner through business relocation. In certain other respects, this case represents a unique illustration of the efficiency gained from relocation. Ralph Mann and Sons deals in both the sale and service of plumbing fixtures, as well as the sale of fuel oil in connection with furnace sales and service. Because of restrictive state and local regulations concerning the location and storage of flammable fuels, the business faced a difficult task in finding a centrally located

Service Auto Parts before relocation (above). Note the inefficient dispersion of this operation in several buildings prior to displacement. After relocation (below), the new structure permits the business to operate under a single roof. (Photos courtesy Ansonia Redevelopment Agency.)

site that was within the zoning and code regulations. In order to meet this requirement, the redevelopment plan was adapted so that the firm could find a suitable site within the project area.

Also, the manager reported that the business was now experiencing some walk-in trade because of the central location and improved environment. In response to this new market the firm constructed a large display of model bathrooms and other plumbing fixtures to attract more of such business.

A final element in this move was the increased efficiency gained through construction of a building specifically suited to the business' needs and operations. In the location from which it was displaced, the business had been housed in four separate buildings which were acquired during a history of rather sporadic growth. Increasing storage requirements dictated the acquisition of additional structures, which could be accomplished only by utilizing separate and somewhat inefficient structures adjacent to the main building. Now, the entire operation is under one roof with adequate off-street parking for fuel trucks and for employee and customer cars. The new building also has loading docks to overcome a handling problem that was acute at the old location. Comparison of the "before" and "after" photographs clearly shows the advantages of the new location.

The new structure represents an investment of nearly $150,000 and provides approximately six times more square-footage of usable space than the old location. Although this move required a considerable investment by the firm, sales rose more than 10 per cent in less than a year after the move.

Service Auto Parts

This firm located adjacent to Ralph Mann and Sons, Inc., in the newly developed light-industrial section of the Downtown Renewal Project. It is a retail and service auto supply store. It was displaced from a site directly adjacent to the location which it subsequently acquired for relocation. In this instance, relocation involved only a move from one corner of the street to the adjacent corner. This business was previously housed in several structures, used mainly for storage, which contained some 7,000 square feet actually occupied by the firm. The new site has over 20,000 square feet and represents an investment of approximately twice the proceeds received by the business owner for his condemned property.

One critical problem at the old location involved the inventory of millions of auto parts and accessories in three separate buildings. Effective inventory control was simply impossible. The LPA encouraged the owner of the business to remain in the project area even though he had already purchased an alternative site. Several distinct advantages are apparent in the redevelopment site.

The closeness of the new site offered easy access for moving, and a self-move was possible. Service Auto Parts was given nearly five months to complete the self-move because of its special inventory problems. The schedule of demolition and acquisition was coordinated to allow this time for a move. The cost of the move (under $10,000) was much less because of these special arrangements. With more space, improved layout and single-structure operation, Service Auto Parts has greatly improved the efficiency of inventory management. In addition, the greater amount of space has enabled the firm to expand its lines; it now sells tires and a greater variety of other auto accessories.

Another basic improvement at the new location is the amount of off-street parking available for employees and customers. A significant portion of the increased sales at the new location is attributed to this factor alone.

A final ingredient in this case is the manner in which moving costs were handled. Because of code restrictions, this business was forced to convert from a 220-volt to a 440-volt electrical system which involved more than $1,200 in conversion charges. The LPA assembled all cost data relating to this conversion and presented its case to the Region I office for approval, which was subsequently granted.

New Haven, Connecticut

Although New Haven is a city of only approximately 155,000 population, in 1967 it was engaged in one of the nation's most extensive and ambitious renewal programs. In addition to a city-wide Community Renewal Program and two major General Neighborhood Renewal Plan projects, there were eleven federally-aided redevelopment projects underway. Eight of these were in the execution stage. Moreover, one major state-aided project was in the final stages of execution. Taken together, these projects involve over one-third of the city's total land area.

In New Haven, special emphasis has been placed on revitalization of the industrial and commercial base of the city. This resulted in the displacement of over 1,500 business establishments of all types and sizes by 1967. A wide range of relocation efforts and techniques has evolved. There has been a business relocation office within the New Haven Redevelopment Agency (NHRA) since 1956. The three-man staff possesses real estate skills as well as good working contacts with the local financial community. As a result, particular sensitivity to the real estate and locational requirements of displaced firms has been evident in New Haven, as well as an imaginative and innovative approach to financing.

One of the most important features of urban redevelopment in New Haven is that, in common with all other communities in Connecticut, the City of New Haven is the LPA. NHRA is the administrative and action agency, but all contracts and official policy actions must be approved by the city's governing body — the board of aldermen.

In New Haven, the significance of the city's being the LPA goes much further. Mayor Richard C. Lee, in office continuously since 1954, made urban renewal one of his major programs from the outset of his administration. One of his objectives, reflected in the programs of NHRA, was to retain and expand local employment and incomes. Moreover, the administrative staff of NHRA is responsible to the development coordinator, who in turn reports directly to the mayor. In many instances, the mayor has lent his personal prestige and official influence to negotiations and programs designed to achieve successful business relocations. In New Haven, "successful" business relocations are those that are entirely *intra*-city, preferably to a new site in a redevelopment project area. As a matter of policy, the business relocation staff has actively encouraged joint and cooperative efforts among business displacees wherever and whenever this has appeared feasible. In many of these instances, the mayor has proved to be the determining influence.

This commitment of the municipal administration to urban renewal in general, and to successful business relocation in particular, has led both the Greater New Haven Chamber of Commerce and a privately financed citizens' action committee to lend support, advice and assistance to several relocation efforts. Another private organization, Community Progress Incorporated (CPI), has attempted to supplement NHRA's physical redevelopment of the city with human renewal on a major scale. CPI has encouraged widespread participation by neighborhood residents in many activities, including a manpower and employment program. This has been a useful supplement to the efforts of the business relocation staff.

Business relocation in New Haven is a highly systematized and organized part of a central relocation office which handles all family and business displacements caused by any public activity. Within this organized framework, however, a highly personalized and individualized approach to business relocation has developed. The NHRA staff can provide direct advice and assistance on many business matters: legal, financial, real estate, and even business operations. The result is widespread favorable reaction by relocated businessmen, reported in a number of independent surveys, as well as the interviews in this study.

From the variety of activities encountered in New Haven, five case studies have been chosen to represent the kind of innovative approach that is taken even in the absence of federal funds or assistance.

South Boulevard Industrial Park

Although this relocation case was initiated in 1955 and was accomplished without benefit of any federally supported relocation assistance or compensation to the affected businesses, it is a significant guide to what can be accomplished with imagination, effort and cooperation. It also illustrates New Haven's efforts to have laws and/or regulations amended when they represent barriers to successful relocation of business firms *within the city*. Finally, it demonstrates the willingness of New Haven to commit municipal resources (not necessarily monetary) to private business relocations when it appears to be in the interests of the city to do so.

The South Boulevard Industrial Park was developed entirely with relocatees from the Oak Street Project. Some 15 light industrial and wholesale firms were scheduled for displacement. No appropriate relocation sites appeared to be available. Many of the businessmen feared that they would have to cease operations. They were approached as a group by the business relocation officer and an official of the Citizens' Action Committee, with the encouragement of the mayor, to investigate what might be done to retain them in the city's industrial base.

Because there was no apparent financial or legal advantage in doing so at that time, no corporation was formed and the businesses had no formal organization. They simply worked together as cooperating individuals with the two local officials.

After preliminary discussions, it was decided to attempt to reclaim 21 acres of salt marsh between The Boulevard and West River which were then used as a city dump. In 1953, the city submitted a bill to the Connecticut State Legislature to permit New Haven to dispose of "surplus" park land for non-public use. The area in question was technically a park, although it was regarded by planners and builders as "unusable" except as a city dump. Following passage of the 1953 legislation, an aldermanic order was passed in 1955 to convert the area to a wholesale and light-industrial park. Priority in site acquisition was given to dislocatees from the Oak Street Project. NHRA was authorized to sell (but not to lease) the land at its fair market value. Private firms purchasing the land were required to construct improvements, and not speculate with the land.

Each industrial firm involved bought its own site. Each paid cash in advance to enable NHRA to proceed with site preparation. No public funds were made available for this development. Six of the firms put up "front money" in the amount of $60,000. This was used for "de-dumping, mucking out, and compacting." This was necessary to stabilize the land area so that spread footings could be utilized in building construction. Proceeds from the sales of the sites were also used by the city for site improvements, water and sewer lines, and streets.

The total site area was 21 acres, but only 14 acres were developed initially. The proceeds from the sale of the prepared sites made it possible to prepare the rear seven acres later. The sites were sold at approximately $.50 per square foot.

Displacement of the fifteen businesses was delayed until the site could be prepared and their buildings constructed. All of the firms in the South Boulevard Industrial Park reported great satisfaction with their new location, and with their handling by NHRA. They especially commended the mayor for his assistance and encouragement. The only complaint registered by the relocatees was that they were not "forced" to buy more land. Most of them have attempted subsequently to expand their operations, and have not been able to obtain the necessary land.

In addition to retaining fifteen industrial and wholesale firms within the city, the development also permitted utilization of land which was regarded as "unusable." Moreover, the development has served as a stimulus to further commercial construction in the vicinity, although prior to development the location was regarded by planners and developers alike as a poor one for commercial activities.

An interesting sidelight to this development is the fact that, although it was not intended to be profitable, approximately $50,000 in net proceeds reverted to the New Haven Park Department.

The essential requirements in this situation were first imagination, and then money. The talents required included salesmanship, real estate expertise, and legal skills. These had to be coupled with a group of individuals willing to expend time and money (expecially time) in order to bring the development to fruition.

Libby's Italian Pastry Shop

Libby's was located at 142 Wooster Street in the Wooster Square Project Area. This family-operated business had been at this location since 1922 in an old and dilapidated building which it owned. The property was scheduled to be acquired as part of the Wooster Square Project.

NHRA approached Mr. Dell'Amura, the owner of both the business and the building, to relocate his business in April 1962. After considerable investigation and discussion, he was offered a parcel of land directly across the street that was planned as a neighborhood shopping complex with off-street parking facilities for each business. The plot contained approximately 14,000 square feet, and was sold for $1.00 per square foot.

Mr. Dell'Amura requested permission to construct a two and one-half story building with living quarters for his family on the second floor. NHRA supported his application for a modification of the reuse specifications for the area to permit proprietor residency. The proposal was approved in April 1965.

With the assistance and support of NHRA, a DBL was obtained from SBA to help finance construction of the new building. The new structure contains a total of 15,000 square feet and provides over 10,000 square feet for off-street parking and loading. An eight-room apartment for the Dell'Amura family is located on the upper floors. The architectural style of the building conforms with that of many of the older residences surrounding Wooster Square Park, which were retained in the reuse plan. The considerably increased floor area of the new establishment permitted Libby's to add an indoor-outdoor sidewalk cafe.

Timing of the move was delayed to permit completion of the new structure. The move occurred in December 1966. The mayor officiated at the ribbon-cutting ceremonies on December 11.

In helping Libby's achieve this successful relocation, NHRA was instrumental in having local specifications altered to meet the needs of the business, providing assistance in obtaining the SBA Displaced Business Loan, and arranging the timing of the move to accommodate the needs of the business.

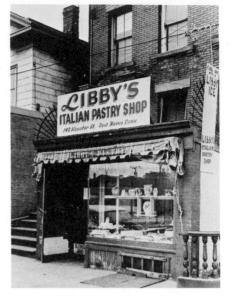

Libby's Italian Pastry Shop before relocation was a converted residential structure
located in a multi-use neighborhood.

Libby's new site directly across the street provides living quarters in the upper floor of a
basically commercial structure designed to conform with the redeveloped neighborhood.
(Photos courtesy New Haven Redevelopment Agency.)

Downtown Shopping Triangle
(Temporary Relocation)

In 1958, a group of nine retail merchants scheduled to be displaced from the Church Street Project Area formed the G & M Realty Corporation at the suggestion of NHRA and the Citizens' Action Committee (CAC). Seven of these firms were tenants in their old locations and two were owners. All expressed a strong desire to relocate permanently in the redeveloped Church Street Project, because of the CBD orientation of their businesses. They included a restaurant, a liquor store, three clothing stores, a shoe store, a bar and grill, a luncheonette, and a newsstand.

The nine merchants agreed to occupy a temporary prefabricated metal building (68' X 164') on a triangular parcel of city-owned land at the intersection of George and Meadow streets. The city had previously acquired the site through earlier redevelopment.

The nine displaced firms paid a total of $53,000 for the erection of the shell of the building, including ceiling, flooring and air conditioning. Construction started in December 1958, and was completed in February 1959. When the building was completed, it was sold to the city for $25,000. The capitol outlay of the nine businesses was therefore $28,000. This consisted of cash in advance in the amount of $1.00 per square foot of building area occupied (which was applied to the last month's rent), with the remainder financed by a loan from a local bank.

Rent was set at $2.00 per square foot per year. This was applied first to pay off the bank loan, and second to cover maintenance costs borne by NHRA. The loan was completely paid off in 18 months. Rentals were then reduced to a maximum of $50 per month to cover maintenance costs only. Although the bank loan was made to the city, the individual merchants personally endorsed the note.

Because of development and financing delays, several other potential occupants decided to move elsewhere. More could have been served in this facility. Any relocatee from the Church Street Project Area was potentially eligible to participate in the Triangle development.

Parking for 130 cars was available on the site. The city made this available free to the merchants. The nine tenants in turn were permitted to lease the parking rights. They did so, and a commercial operator ran the lot for them. Free parking privileges were arranged for customers of the Triangle stores.

The original plan called for occupancy of this building for a maximum of 30 months. However, serious delays were encountered in the major commercial section of the Church Street Project. The Triangle building was actually occupied for eight years. It provided a location closely approximating that which the merchants had occupied before relocation, and which they would also have when they moved to their permanent locations in the new development. This was especially important for the liquor store, since Connecticut State Law permits a liquor licensee to move a maximum of 1,500 feet and still retain its license.

Downtown Shopping Triangle is an example of a temporary relocation facility made available by the LPA in close proximity to the final locations of the tenants. (Photo courtesy New Haven Redevelopment Agency.)

All of the businesses survived during the lengthy period of "temporary" relocation, although a number reported a decline in their business. Nevertheless, all but one relocated permanently during March and April 1967. One merchant died a few months before the building was vacated, and his business was not continued.

Seven of the nine firms eventually located back in the original Church Street Project Area. In addition to the one merchant who died, the luncheonette operator went into business elsewhere. Seven of the firms became tenants in their final locations, while the newsstand became an owner directly across the street from the Triangle. Three of the firms relocated in the new Chapel Mall, at substantially higher rents than had been paid in their original locations. All but one of the firms occupied substantially larger space in their final locations, and all reported a considerable increase in business.

This case illustrates one technique for retaining CBD-oriented businesses in close proximity to their ultimate locations, to permit them to serve essentially the same clientele while construction is proceeding. Moreover, it indicates the potential for utilizing city resources and facilities at little expense to retain businesses in the CBD.

Sargent & Company

The architectural and residential hardware divisions of Sargent & Company were located in a complex of over 30 buildings of varying height ranging in age from 40 to 100 years on 25 acres of land on both sides of Water Street. This long-time New Haven firm employed over 1,000 persons. Because of crowded conditions and increasingly inefficient work flows, the firm began planning for a new location in 1956. Since major industrial sites were then nonexistent within New Haven, tentative plans were made to relocate the plant at an undetermined site outside the city.

A major objective of the mayor was to retain existing business and industry within New Haven, utilizing redevelopment powers and programs as fully as possible to realize this goal. The mayor and NHRA approached Sargent with the proposal that its old plant be acquired through redevelopment (since it was essentially a blighted area) and that the firm relocate to a new site to be provided through redevelopment. In 1957, it was proposed that the old Sargent plant be included in the Wooster Square Project, so that the firm could receive fair market value for its old plant and site. This was rejected by HUD (then URA) because the project area would then no longer have been primarily residential. Following this, New Haven initiated legislation in the 1958 session of the Connecticut General Assembly to make state funds available for the redevelopment of predominantly commercial and industrial areas for commercial and/or industrial reuse.

Public Act 8 was the result. This provides that municipalities with project areas not eligible for federal funding may receive state assistance for the purpose of industrial and commercial development. The state will contribute up to 50 per cent of net project cost, with a maximum contribution of $5,000,000. As soon as this legislation was passed, the Long Wharf Project Area was identified, and the redevelopment plan approved by the board of aldermen in September 1958. The Sargent plant was included within the boundaries of this project, and identified for acquisition.

The bulk of the Long Wharf Project Area was swamp and salt marsh. However, it was adjacent to the right of way of the Connecticut Turnpike, and divided by the terminal interchange of Interstate Route 91 with the Connecticut Turnpike. This represented an ideal location for industrial and wholesale-distribution firms, if appropriate sites could be found. The city determined to fill the area and stabilize the land through the time-consuming but effective surcharge process. The effect was to permit building construction with spread footings rather than piles, representing a cost saving of approximately $3.50 per square foot of building area. In addition, the city, operating through NHRA, provided necessary utilities and access roads to serve the project area.

When Sargent was informed of these plans, they agreed to move their Water Street operations to a 30-acre site developed through the surcharge process. Thus, redevelopment actually *created* industrial sites in a location formerly regarded as unusable.

Architectural planning began in January 1959. At the same time, Sargent began to develop a detailed relocation and moving plan. Sargent's management decided that the move should be accomplished with no interruption of work in process.

Site preparation was begun in the spring of 1960, and completed in May 1963. Total land preparation costs were approximately $5,000,000. They were financed under the terms of Public Act 8.

Construction of the Sargent plant started in July 1963. The 342,000-square-foot building was completed one year later. Because redevelopment powers were used to acquire the old property, Sargent was paid fair market value for the land and buildings: $2,800,000. The agreement between Sargent and NHRA stipulated that there would be no relocation payments.

Because of the importance of retaining Sargent in the city, no plans for demolition of the old plant were made until after the move was entirely completed. As a result of the detailed planning begun in 1959, the entire move of Sargent's operations was completed in eight weeks — between June 8 and August 8, 1964. In a lengthy article published in the *Hardware Consultant* in October 1964, the company claimed that there was less interruption of production than is usual during the normal summer vacation shutdown. The move was timed to coincide with this annual shutdown.

Sargent paid fair market value for the 30 acres in the new site, as well as $35,000 for off-site improvements. No tax concessions were made.

This case demonstrates how a municipality, operating through its redevelopment powers, can be coordinated effort save a major source of employment and income for the community. New Haven sought and obtained necessary enabling legislation from the state legislature. It devised a technique for reclaiming "unusable" land otherwise ideally situated for an industrial plant in terms of access. It utilized a method of land reclamation which significantly reduced the construction costs of the new plant, thereby adding to the attractiveness of the transaction for Sargent & Company. It acquired the former Sargent location at a price sufficient to help finance the new development. It also allowed the firm sufficient time to plan and carry out its move most effectively and efficiently. Throughout the entire process, the relocation effort received the personal attention of the mayor and the chief administrative officers of NHRA.

New Haven Food Terminal, Inc.

The wholesale produce, fruit and meat market of New Haven, which served much of Connecticut, was concentrated within a few blocks on Hill and State streets, in the Church Street Project Area. Most of the businesses were operated from old, dilapidated, crowded quarters in congested and frequently unsanitary conditions. Many of the meat wholesalers were under orders from public authorities to improve their sanitary control. Confusion and traffic congestion were rife. Many produce merchants sold their wares directly from trucks or the sidewalk. A number of firms had subsidiary facilities outside the area, because space was not available within it. This added to the inefficiencies and confusion of the operation. Most of the firms were tenants in their Hill and State Street locations.

As early as 1940, a small group of wholesalers attempted to convince the others to form an association and develop a modern food terminal facility in another location. Despite recognition of the need for improved conditions if the food market area was to remain economically viable, no agreements could be reached. In the middle and late 1950's plans for the redevelopment of the area were formally announced. This led to renewed efforts to convince the merchants that a new location was now not only financially necessary, but also legally required. The merchants themselves agreed almost unanimously that there were compelling economic reasons for them to remain in close proximity to one another. A small group studied food terminal facilities which had recently been constructed in other cities. Nevertheless, most of the affected businessmen remained extremely reluctant to consider moving seriously. In addition, a new element emerged. Virtually all of the wholesalers decided that they had to be owners in any new location (which they still resisted), although most of them were currently tenants.

Organization. Following the death of the original promoter of group action, Mayor Lee convinced Mr. James Lamberty to assume leadership of the effort to find a new location for the wholesale food merchants. Mr. Lamberty was himself a meat wholesaler, and also had several relatives in the wholesale produce business. As a result, he had direct personal contacts with both groups. It seemed necessary to keep the two groups together to create an economically viable new facility. A considerable amount of salesmanship was required to convince the affected businessmen that they really needed to stay together because of the linkages and economies involved in a central facility. They also had to be sold on the idea of pooling their resources, and changing their attitudes toward ownership and independence.

With the advice and assistance of city officials and CAC, the wholesalers retained a knowledgeable attorney who understood both redevelopment law, and corporate organization and financing. As the development proceeded, this emerged as a critical move on their part.

In 1954, with the preliminary agreement of the merchants, the city petitioned the Connecticut Market Authority for assistance in constructing a publicly-owned market facility in New Haven. In 1955, at the request of the city, the Connecticut General Assembly passed legislation authorizing the construction of a new market and earmarked $2,000,000 for this purpose. It was to be located in the Long Wharf Project Area. After considerable negotiation, the proposal was abandoned in 1957. The merchants raised objections about the level of rents to be charged and the fact that they would still be tenants in a public facility.

At this point, the mayor, with the assistance of NHRA and CAC officials, reopened negotiations with the group in terms of a privately-owned and privately-financed facility. Although this struck a much more responsive chord with the merchants, many of them still held out for individual ownership. A search for sources of financing, however, led to the conclusion that this approach was infeasible. The New Haven area is relatively unendowed with equity funds available for real estate investment. Moreover, the merchants themselves did not have sufficient capital to support their proposals. It was their attempt to utilize city resources to provide an appropriate site. In 1958, enabling legislation was introduced and passed in a special session of the Connecticut General Assembly to permit state assistance of predominantly non-residential redevelopment projects for industrial and commercial reuse. This was Public Act 8, which was discussed in more detail in the Sargent & Company relocation case.

Following passage of Public Act 8, it was agreed to form a corporation among the affected food wholesalers to enable them to obtain financing and ownership of a new market facility. A 35-acre site was selected in the Long Wharf Project Area to accommodate the new facility. The corporation was formed in 1960 as a profit-seeking organization. In that same year, the city started compacting and consolidating the fill in the Long Wharf Project through the surcharge process. With the availability of a site guaranteed, the corporation proceeded to raise equity funds as a basis for financing construction of the necessary buildings.

At this point, there were 45 potential stockholders in the corporation. Each stockholder was required to be a business scheduled for displacement, and each was required to invest $5,000 per unit of the terminal facility that it planned to occupy. Ownership and operation of the market facility are in the hands of the corporation.

Several potential stockholder-tenants dropped out at this point, partly because of a lack of funds, and partly because a few meat wholesalers felt that they could not wait for redevelopment to progress. A total of $350,000 in equity funds was raised.

Site preparation and financing. The original 35-acre site was selected because of its excellent location for a wholesaling and terminal facility. A food terminal is a noisy operation that works at odd hours (2:00 a.m. to 6:00 p.m.), and generates a great deal of heavy truck traffic. It was necessary to find a site removed from residential areas and which had truck access without traveling over residential streets. Quick and easy access to the area served by the terminal facility was essential. This is provided via access roads to nearby interchanges of both the Connecticut Turnpike and Interstate Route 91. In addition to filling the land and compacting it via the surcharge process, the city installed necessary utilities and access roads. Fifty per cent of the cost of site preparation was provided through state funds under the provisions of Public Act 8.

New Haven Food Terminal, Inc. obtained an option on the 35-acre site at a price of $20,000 per acre. The initial area acquired for construction of the first phases of the terminal facility was 15.5 acres. A lease-purchase arrangement was developed, whereby the corporation pays an annual rental to the city, equal to 6 per cent of the option price. This is on a 40-year lease, with options to renew for an additional 18 years. The corporation may apply part of the rental to the purchase price. The price of $20,000 per acre will be paid off in 26 years and one month. At that time, the corporation may exercise its option to purchase by the payment of $1.00 and receive title to the land. The remaining 19.5 acres are still under option, but not yet leased.

The corporation pays taxes on the land, which is assessed on the basis of $30,000 per acre.

Building financing. Following formation of the corporation, financing of the terminal facilities was sought from a number of private institutions. In this process, both the city and CAC provided a number of contacts and leads. One insurance company agreed to lend $1,250,000, but the terms of the loan were regarded as too stringent by the stockholders of the corporation.

Public officials then suggested that the corporation seek a Section 502 Development Corporation Loan from SBA. After months of negotiation, this possibility evaporated when it was learned that incorporators could not have more than a 25 per cent interest in the development being financed through a Section 502 loan.

Public officials assisted the corporation in reopening negotiations with the life insurance company contacted earlier. The results achieved in developing the Long Wharf Project Area and the apparent stability of the corporation made it possible for a loan to be granted on terms more agreeable to the corporation. The city subordinated its lease claim to the mortgage. This was essential in order to obtain the financing. The most significant change was that the life insurance company was willing to grant a 20-year mortgage, even though the leases were for only 10 years, with 10-year renewal options.

Building construction. With financing arranged, ground-breaking for the first two market buildings, a bank-office building and a gasoline service station took place in June, 1963. The corporation had retained an outstanding architect to design the facility. Investigation of a large number of food terminals constructed during the previous five years led to the conclusion that appropriate design was absolutely essential to successful operation of the terminal.

Because of the compacting of the site through the surcharge process, it was possible to construct the buildings on spread footings rather than on more expensive piles. The two terminal buildings contain 62 units of 2,160 square feet each (18' X 120'). The architect designed shallower loading docks than are usually provided in food terminals: 10 feet in depth, as opposed to the usual 25 feet. This was considered an advantage, particularly by the produce wholesalers. It meant that there would be no outside display or sales of the produce, and that the frequency of handling would be significantly reduced. This is an important consideration in minimizing spoilage.

One additional cost factor was added at the insistence of the lender. Higher ceiling heights than required or desired by the food merchants had to be provided, so that the buildings might be more readily marketable in the event of default.

Improvements to the individual units or groups of units were made by each merchant as required by the nature of his business. The meat wholesalers in particular had to add refrigeration and overhead tracks, frequently at consider-

The Standard Beef Company before relocation represents conditions typical of many
businesses involved in the total relocation
of the wholesale produce, fruit and meat
market of New Haven.

The specially designed loading dock is one of the many advantages gained by the Standard
Beef Company in its new quarters at the food terminal. (Photos courtesy New Haven
Redevelopment Agency.)

able expense. These improvements were financed by each firm individually. However, city and CAC officials helped bring the businessmen into contact with local lenders, and in turn encouraged local lenders to grant the loans. A refrigeration consultant was brought in by a number of the meat wholesalers, and savings were achieved by working through one supplier on a master plan.

Although the meat wholesalers use truck transportation exclusively, the produce wholesalers require rail facilities. A rail spur was brought in adjacent to the produce building at a cost of between $40,000 and $50,000. Produce merchants require quick handling of their merchandise, and as infrequent handling as possible. As a result, rail loading and docking has priority over trucks in the produce building. The merchants must share the loading dock because of the size of rail cars.

No garage facilities were provided for the trucks owned by the individual businesses. Each unit in the two structures has plug-in heating facilities to keep truck engines warm in cold weather. Several merchants indicated that garaging is not necessary for their trucks, and that outdoor parking saves approximately $50.00 per truck per month.

The produce building was completed and first occupied in May 1964; the meat wholesaler building was completed and first occupied in August 1964.

Relocation and occupancy. The actual moves of firms from their former locations into the food terminal occurred between May 1964 and June 1965. Twenty-six displaced businesses relocated into the terminal facilities. Of these, 19 were stockholders in the corporation. All 26 displacees were eligible for moving and/or property-loss reimbursement. As of June 1967, 15 moving claims and three property-loss claims had been settled. Four were still pending. Through careful planning, only one move involved the maximum reimbursement of $25,000.

NHRA allowed all the relocatees to remain in their old locations in the Church Street Project Area until their units in the new food terminal were ready. Following the advice of NHRA, all of the affected firms waited until the city condemned their properties, so that they were eligible for reimbursement. Acquisitions had to be timed so that firms with space in more than one project area were able to qualify as displacees. It was agreed between the corporation and NHRA that displacees would have a priority claim on space in the food terminal facility before any "outside" tenants were permitted.

A number of the very small food merchants went out of business when they were displaced. The president of the corporation reported that nearly all of the former businessmen had obtained employment with relocated firms in the new terminal facility.

Seven of the 26 relocatees in the food terminal received Small Business Displacement Payments. NHRA helped them document their claims.

The two major terminal buildings contain a total of 62 units, of which 50 are occupied by stockholder-tenants, and 12 are rented by non-stockholders. The two tenants which are not displacees include one meat packer who occupies half a space, and the Long Wharf Repertory Theatre (which rents six units and expended $150,000 on interior improvements). Six of the tenants rent less than one full unit, while 14 occupy more than one unit. The maximum occupied by any firm is six and one-half units.

All occupants must sign ten-year leases with ten-year renewal options. Stockholders pay $1.30 per square foot per year, or $234 per month, per space. Non-stockholders pay $400 per month per space.

The two-story bank-office building owned by the corporation contains 3,500 square feet of rentable space. A branch of a local bank occupies the first floor, while offices on the second floor are rented to businesses related to the terminal's activities: a trucking firm office, and a food broker. Rents in this building range from $3.50 to $4.00 per square foot annually. The bank has adjusted its hours to conform to the needs of the food merchants in the terminal.

The gasoline service station provides a major convenience to truckers serving the terminal as well as to merchant-tenants with their own trucks. It is also a significant source of revenue to the corporation. The lease was awarded on a bid basis to a major oil company. In addition to a minimum $25,000 per year rental, a gallonage fee is paid beyond a specified volume. The oil company also pays the taxes on the property it occupies.

There are several non-food tenants in the terminal facility. All but the theatre are somehow related to the food distribution industry, however. For example, there is a cutlery firm which specializes in meat-cutting equipment, a restaurant supply firm, a printing establishment, and a restaurant. All are dislocatees from the Church Street Project, and are stockholders.

Results of the move. Interviews with the president of the corporation (who is himself a tenant) and four other stockholder-tenants provided unanimous impressions on several significant points. Operating efficiency has increased greatly in the new terminal facility. Both pilferage and spoilage (especially for the produce merchants) have dropped substantially. Although the merchants discovered they could handle the same volume of business with fewer employees, total employment among all the firms has increased substantially over that in the Church Street area. Business volume and profits have increased for virtually all of the firms.

Ownership of stock in the corporation has become a profitable investment. The corporation operates on extremely low overhead, with only three employees. As of 1967, approximately one-sixth of its outstanding stock had already been retired by purchase from individual stockholders.

The terminal development has stimulated further expansion of food-related industry in the Long Wharf Project Area. The New Haven Cold Storage Corporation began construction of a major food freezer warehouse adjacent to the terminal property in December 1966. It is now in full operation.

Despite the time lag of approximately six years from the organization of the corporation to the final moves, the development is enthusiastically endorsed by both occupants of the terminal and public officials. The only regret expressed by several merchants was that they had not contracted for more units at the outset, because they wanted and could use more space effectively. As of June 1967, plans were underway for a third major terminal building. The inclusion of non-terminal tenants (bank-office building and gasoline service station) has proved extremely valuable both from a service and a revenue point of view.

Both public officials and members of the corporation agreed that condemnation of the Church Street properties was the key to the success of the entire development. No one firm felt capable of leaving the old location without a guarantee that the others would accompany it. Although most of the relocatees recognized that they really should move, none wanted to do so. Being forced to relocate by redevelopment also forced them to examine their problems and work out an effective solution.

One important lesson from this case is that bringing together a group of fiercely independent small businessmen requires a high degree of selling skill. Moreover, salesmanship of the highest order was necessary to arrange the financing. Beyond this, it is essential to have one individual who will serve as the coordinator and the driving force in carrying the project through to completion. He should be identified early in the development. Public officials should work through him and give him their fullest support when dealing with the rest of the group.

One measure of the success of this relocation is found in the frequent inquiries received from groups in other cities, seeking advice and assistance in planning a similar facility for their community. Finally, the New Haven Food Terminal could not have been developed and completed without extremely effective cooperation and mutual assistance between public officials and the organized merchants. The mayor wanted to retain the wholesale meat and produce market in New Haven. It was made possible through the help of NHRA and CAC. As the president of the corporation expressed it, "without city help, you're licked before you start."

Pawtucket, Rhode Island

Pawtucket lies just north of Providence. It is a medium-sized city with a population of approximately 81,000. The Pawtucket Redevelopment Agency had initiated only one urban renewal project by 1967, but the 55-acre project area encompassed most of the downtown shopping area. It displaced over 150 business firms during its three-year life. The Slater Urban Renewal Project was initiated in an effort to revitalize the declining downtown area.

Pawtucket faced competition from growing peripheral shopping center developments and associated population decreases. The city met this challenge by improving and modernizing its CBD shopping facilities. The relocation assistance provided the many displaced businesses has complemented the goals of this program.

The success of Pawtucket's business relocation efforts may best be illustrated by their ability to retain displaced businesses, not only within the city limits but within its downtown shopping core. Over 90 per cent of the businesses displaced have relocated within Pawtucket, and over two-thirds have remained in the CBD. The business environment in Pawtucket has been not only stabilized but enhanced by spot rehabilitation and new construction.

Several elements may be attributed to the success of this business relocation program. These elements, taken together, exemplify the full-scale attack on both a deteriorating downtown area and the exodus of business firms that had been going on for over ten years.

Early business contacts. Good rapport has been established with the business community through early contacts by the business relocation staff of the Pawtucket Redevelopment Agency. These contacts have been made both formally and informally. Staff members have "dropped by" each of the businesses slated for displacement long before such action is scheduled in order to establish communication between the agency and the business firm. Even while the project was in the planning stage, staff members of the LPA talked with most of the potential displacees. They were informed about the plans and assured that help would be provided them by the agency. Constant liaison and personal relationships between the staff and all displacees contributed immensely to the success of relocation efforts.

In addition, periodic newsletters were published by the LPA to inform businesses and other interested parties of progress in the Slater Urban Renewal Project and in providing aid to displacees. Formal meetings were also held to inform affected businessmen about the plans for downtown redevelopment, as well as the various services and assistance to which they were entitled. All of these actions brought about a generally congenial spirit of cooperation between the agency, other public bodies of the city, and the affected businesses.

"Matching" needs with available space. Urban renewal involved not only demolition and rebuilding but also rehabilitation and conservation in the downtown area. Available space was carefully appraised and inventoried so that the needs of displacees could be matched with existing vacant space. A significant amount of vacant space was available in the downtown area at the time that the Slater Project was initiated. This stemmed from the fact that many businesses had left downtown to move to peripheral shopping centers and to other towns. One case presented below illustrates this matching technique particularly well in that a department store, vacant for many years, was obtained and utilized for relocation.

SBA and SCORE. Close liaison was maintained with the SBA to provide financing, and with the nearby SCORE chapter to provide consulting help for displacees. In this city, the "referral system" is used to good advantage. That is, the LPA informs the displacee of the existence of SBA assistance and generally outlines the nature of its program and the associated services of SCORE.

Total community involvement. One of the most striking features of the Pawtucket relocation effort is the complete community involvement that the LPA has been able to generate and sustain throughout the execution of its urban renewal project. A special urban renewal committee was established within the local chamber of commerce to provide a coordinating body for the redevelopment agency, local political groups, and the business community. The local press has also contributed much to the efforts of the redevelopment agency. The periodic newsletters also helped convey information concerning plans, actions, and proposals regarding the downtown area.

Another helpful device that has been used under this general category is the "demonstration effect" of successful business relocations. By citing the efforts of the staff in specific cases and the subsequent success of the business after relocation, the LPA has been able to convince other businesses of the advantages of remaining in the local area on another site.

H. Cohen Furniture Company

This case illustrates imaginative matching of the available supply of retail space with the needs of displacees. Available space was found directly adjacent to the building to be demolished. In this instance, the business rented approximately 7,500 square feet in the structure from which it was displaced. The move was accomplished with few problems because the bulky inventory had only to be moved from one building directly into the adjacent building. Here, the business owner received both moving costs and direct property-loss payments. In addition, the business was eligible and received an SBDP.

Cohen's Furniture.   The sign "Cohen's moved next door" provides mute evidence of the efforts in this city to match displacees' needs with available space. (Photo courtesy Pawtucket Redevelopment Agency.)

In the new structure, the business obtained nearly double the square-footage that it previously occupied at an increase of only 30 per cent in monthly rent.

Major Electric and Supply Company

This case, like that of H. Cohen Furniture, involved a move to an adjacent building. However, circumstances here were quite different. In this instance, a business that rented a property for a number of years became the owner of the land that its business occupied. In the process it became the owner of a much improved structure that is ideally suited to the needs of the business.

The owners of this business were contacted long before displacement was scheduled. Specifically, they were first contacted in October 1962, while the contractual date of demolition was in early 1967. This early contact and the subsequent negotiations led to the ingenious arrangement that materialized. The land was sold to the owner of Major Electric. He was then granted permission to proceed with the construction of a building approximately three times the size of the structure from which he was being displaced. The new building was constructed directly adjacent to the fire wall of the old building. Upon completion, the fire wall of the old building was removed and the sizable inventory of the firm transferred directly over a few feet of space into the new building. The old building was then razed and a parking lot constructed on its former location.

This firm received an SBA loan of $300,000 that included participation by a local bank. This source of financing was a central factor in facilitating the relocation and the change in tenancy status of the business. As is the general policy of the LPA in Pawtucket, the SBA loan was obtained on a referral basis. The redevelopment staff informed the business owners of their possible eligibility for a Displaced Business Loan. The owners were then referred to the local SBA office for further information and action.

Presco's Department Store

Presco's Department Store has been located in downtown Pawtucket since the turn of the century. The relocation of Presco's represents a truly "city-wide" effort that involved not only the redevelopment agency staff but also the mayor and chamber of commerce members. The LPA staff was particularly anxious to relocate this business within the CBD. They were also concerned with promoting the use of several large retail buildings in the downtown area which had been vacant for several years. These vacant buildings gave evidence of the decline in the downtown area and the concomitant exodus of business firms to outlying locations.

In this specific case, one of the largest department stores in the city vacated the space they were renting in the face of declining sales. Because this national firm had a sizable tax write-off from the long-term lease on the property, it found certain financial advantages in simply allowing the store to remain vacant. Subtenants were also difficult to find and this undoubtedly reinforced the decision simply to "write off" this enterprise.

Through the efforts of the mayor, the executive director and staff members of the redevelopment agency, as well as other key businessmen in the city, the owner of Presco's was persuaded to bid on this department store property for use as a relocation site. Through many weeks of negotiations, local business leaders and public officials spoke on behalf of this local businessman and the interests of the city in reopening this store. Only after considerable effort was the property obtained for the Presco firm on a lease basis.

In addition to help in finding a suitable site for relocation, the displacee firm also required financing for improvements in the new location, as well as advice on how best to accomplish the move and reestablish the business at the new location. This financial and consulting help was provided through SBA in the form of a DBL and the aid of a SCORE representative. The firm obtained the services of a retired Sears & Roebuck executive on the staff of the nearby SCORE chapter of SBA. The actual move to the new location required considerable planning and rethinking in terms of layout, inventory levels, and other similar problems.

In the midst of this crucial planning period, the owner-manager of Presco's became critically ill. The SCORE representative literally took over this phase of the move to the point of selecting fixtures, overseeing installations, and making other important decisions for the business. Without this help, it is likely that the business would not have survived the move.

It is very likely that without the determined efforts of many individuals both in the redevelopment agency and outside, this business would have either discontinued operations or relocated in a peripheral area outside the CBD. Without the aid of the SBA loan, the payment of large moving expenses (over $20,000), and the efforts of a highly qualified SCORE expert in overseeing the business while the owner was ill, this success story could well have ended instead in failure.

Saltzman's Men's Store

This case received considerable local publicity because a well-known business firm relocated within the downtown area. By doing so it registered a significant vote of confidence in the future of the CBD as well as the redevelopment agency.

The Saltzman operation has a history in Pawtucket dating back nearly fifty years. The retail operations of the firm were conducted from two locations: one owned by the firm and another that was rented. The business owners recognized the problems of the dual location but could not expand on their original business site because of physical limitations. So they rented another structure in the CBD. Because the firm was notified well in advance of actual displacement, the owners, with the help of the redevelopment agency, began negotiations for the lease of a large downtown structure which had been vacant for nearly twelve years. With the combined efforts of the business owners and the redevelopment agency, several lease concessions with respect to refurbishing the interior were obtained. The owner of the structure invested $50,000 and Saltzman's matched this amount in renovating and improving the structure. It is now considered one of the "model" retail establishments in the downtown area and has provided an excellent example to other business firms facing the prospects of moving.

By combining the two operations under one roof, the firm has been able to lower costs and increase efficiency noticeably. In addition, sales increased more than 10 per cent during the first four months of operation at the new location. Many new features were incorporated in the new location; the firm was able to install a freight elevator, clothing chutes, and other modern devices not available at the old stores. In addition, they have entrances in both the front and rear of the store and off-street parking which serves the rear entrance.

Initially, the firm's owners admitted that they were very much opposed to the move and the entire idea of being displaced. The early notification and subsequent help provided by the redevelopment staff, in addition to receiving over $20,000 in moving costs, convinced them that the move was in their best interest. As a result, the business owners became solid supporters of the redevelopment agency in advancing the cause of downtown renewal and business relocation.

Scriven Advertising

This case involves business owners who were elderly and had highly specialized site requirements for their business firm. Although both elements generally present problems in business relocation, the Pawtucket relocation staff not only found a suitable location but provided complete planning service throughout this relocation effort.

Because of the nature of the business and the fact that it served a downtown clientele, the owners felt that a central location was critical. They also specified a second-floor location served by a freight elevator because of the cost factor associated with first-floor locations. Heavy paper stock and other equipment dictated the need for a freight elevator. Adequate stress and load-bearing characteristics were also necessary because of the printing press and other heavy equipment used in the business. A comprehensive inventory of available downtown business sites enabled the redevelopment staff to identify appropriate alternatives. The staff was also able to obtain suitable lease terms for the firm in a location which exactly met the needs of the business.

In addition to the help provided the business owners in finding a new location, other planning advice and aid was provided them. The redevelopment staff encouraged the business owners to take advantage of the move by obtaining a new printing press. Initially, the owners intended to move the old press to the new location. However, they were advised by the relocation staff to buy a newer machine and install it at the new location in advance of the move.

Since this situation involved elderly business owners, the staff members of the redevelopment agency handled nearly all the arrangements, including the purchase of the new press. They contacted several printers and equipment suppliers and arranged group meetings with the business owners to negotiate for the purchase. In the end, the firm purchased a machine that was slightly used, and their old machine was used in trade. Much of the other older machinery used in connection with the press was declared for direct property-loss settlement and the proceeds applied to acquisition of the new machine. The result of these efforts was that no outlay of cash other than the proceeds from the direct property-loss payments and the sale of the old printing press was required to acquire the new press. The firm also received an SBDP plus moving costs for the equipment moved to the new location.

In this case, as in nearly all others in Pawtucket, much advance warning was given to the business. The first LPA contact with the business owners was in October 1963; the actual move took place in April 1966. The entire move was accomplished without one day of interruption of the business.

Providence, Rhode Island

The Providence Redevelopment Agency (PRA) is the LPA for the city of Providence. Business relocation is carried out under the auspices of the Family and Business Relocation Service. This is a central relocation office for all public improvement programs within the city of Providence. This office has 14 full-time relocation personnel, but their primary concern is with residential relocation. At the time of this study, PRA had completed four projects and had five in the execution stage. These had involved the displacement of approximately 327 businesses, of which 277 were reported as successfully relocated. The current population of Providence is approximately 175,000.

In the planning stage in each project, PRA conducts a survey to identify all businesses in properties scheduled for demolition. An informational brochure is sent to each potential relocatee, explaining the process of relocation and the entitlements of displaced businessmen. A commercial staff representative is assigned to the businesses in each project area. Personal contacts are made to identify the relocation needs of business firms, as well as to initiate an inventory of equipment and stock in each firm. When the project goes into execution, an active and current list of available business properties both for sale and for rent is given to each business. A detailed record form is maintained for each business. In addition, advisory and informational services concerning zoning, licensing and taxes are provided on request.

A routine visit is made to each firm scheduled for displacement at least once a month, to ascertain progress in relocation. Assistance is provided in preparing documents to ensure elegibility for reimbursement of relocation expenses and qualifying for an SBDP.

Because PRA has several projects in execution simultaneously, particular attention is paid to staging in order to utilize reuse areas designated for commercial or industrial use as relocation resources. This requires special attention to timing, to avoid temporary relocations if at all possible. The fundamental policy of PRA is: "There is no such thing as a temporary relocation." The primary objective of the PRA business relocation staff is to find an appropriate location for the displaced business the first time. The only exceptions involving temporary relocations are firms planning to return to the project area following redevelopment.

For those firms remaining in the project area during redevelopment, particular attention is paid to maintaining access, especially while construction is underway.

PRA has built upon the initially successful results of the Willard Avenue Center, and consciously encouraged groups of businesses in similar lines of activity to form associations for joint ownership of new facilities in reuse areas.

Willard Avenue Center

The Willard Center-2 Project Area contained an L-shaped strip of some 30 commercial establishments in predominantly dilapidated structures which comprised the largest Kosher food center in Providence. Not all of the stores were Kosher food establishments, but nearly all of the stores focused on serving the predominantly Jewish population of the surrounding neighborhood.

Survey and planning work began in the project area in July 1950. The redevelopment plan was approved in the spring of 1954, following a two-year delay while the constitutionality of the Rhode Island Slum Clearance and Redevelopment Act was tested and affirmed. The merchants in the area organized informally and approached PRA with a strong request that they be allowed to remain in the project area, and together. PRA agreed with this basic idea. This concentration of Kosher food stores and related activities was felt to represent both a commercial and a cultural asset to South Providence. The businessmen, for their part, recognized the disadvantages of dispersion and the attractions of continuing to operate in one location in close proximity to one another.

After several meetings, it was decided that a corporation should be formed to buy the land. Several problems arose at this point, in part because of then-existing regulations. First, SBA financing was not available for tenant firms to become owners. Several of the firms in the corporation were in fact owners. In addition, the SBDP had not yet been authorized, and the maximum reimbursement for relocation expenses was $2,000.

An even more significant obstacle, however, was the fierce independence of the individual small businessmen making up the corporation. They would not agree to corporate ownership of the real estate. Instead, each insisted on separate fee title to his own building area, as well as to the land in the rear (loading) and in the front (parking). At the same time, PRA insisted on one building for the entire development, and the transfer of a single parcel to the redeveloper (the corporation).

It was finally agreed that the Willard Realty Company, Inc. would acquire the 4.5-acre tract for approximately $135,000. (Condominium ownership was not at that time legal in Rhode Island.) The building was erected by Willard Realty Company, in accordance with specifications approved by PRA. The building contained 22 stores. The original plans called for more, in two wings and a second story, but these plans were abandoned when several of the original participants dropped out along the way. Some were impatient with the delays, and others lost heart as anticipated costs mounted.

Serious difficulties were encountered when efforts were made to finance the development. Several financial institutions refused to consider the loan because of the individual ownership of building space and land, with no separate and distinct partitioning of store sections within the building. The common-wall and connecting-beam construction was a serious deterrent. Finally, mortgage financing was obtained from a federal savings and loan association in the amount of 60 per cent of the total cost of the project. On completion of the building, title was passed from Willard Realty Company to the individual store owners, and 20-year mortgages were placed on 20 of the 22 stores. Two of the owners paid cash.

Forty per cent of total development cost, therefore, had to be raised by the individual businesses. This was a further discouraging feature to some who were originally interested in the project. One of the reasons that the project was able to continue was that the building contractor accepted ownership in three of the proposed stores. In addition, financing was possible only when six members of the Willard Realty Company guaranteed the lending institution that any property that went into default would be acquired by them. By 1967, this had become a problem in two of the stores.

The land was sold to Willard Realty Company in October 1956. Some temporary relocations were necessary, contrary to the general policy of PRA, in order to keep affected businesses in the area while construction of the Center progressed.

One very important aspect of this relocation case is the fact that the Center was designed with a substantial setback from the street. The old buildings in which most of the members of Willard Realty Company were located fronted on the street in what eventually became the parking area for the Center. Because of the setback, they were able to remain in their former locations until the new building was completed. As each store was finished, the new owner was able to move his inventory through the back door and into the Center. Then demolition could begin on his building. As soon as the Center building was completed and formally opened in December 1957, the entire block of former locations in front of it was razed, and the land area cleared and surfaced for parking.

Willard Avenue Center.   This aerial view shows the new shopping center under construction (foreground) with many of the old buildings still standing on what became the parking lot of the center. (Photo courtesy Providence Department of Planning and Urban Development.)

During the construction period, PRA and the City of Providence cooperated by providing a temporary access road and low-rent parking space across the street from the old locations. This was essential to keep the firms operating and in business during the construction period. In addition, as PRA acquired title to the properties, rents were substantially reduced to cover only taxes and maintenance costs. This was a further aid to the remaining businesses, since the volume of sales fell off sharply during this period.

A total of 18 relocatees finally moved into the Willard Avenue Center. Four tenants of the building contractor and one other owner also moved in. An association was formed to provide for maintenance of the parking area and other common facilities.

For several years after the relocation, the businesses did at least as well in the new center as they had in their former locations. Most reported increased profits. By 1967, however, the essential character of the surrounding neighborhood had changed drastically. The predominantly Jewish population of former years had moved away. As a result, the demand for Kosher foods dropped significantly. By June 1967, there had been turnover in eight of the stores, and two were vacant. Nevertheless, careful investigation revealed that the relocation itself had been successful. It was further deterioration of the surrounding neighborhood over the intervening years that undermined much of the effectiveness of the relocation effort.

One of the major features of the Willard Street Center relocation was the individual leadership in organizing the corporation and forwarding its plans provided by one of the displacees. It was critically important to identify and work closely with leadership from within the group of affected businesses which is willing to devote the time and energy to see the development through to completion.

Based on this experience, PRA has used essentially the same format and approach in dealing with two other groups of related, complementary businesses in the East Side Project. More effective use of SBA loans and other aids developed between 1957 and 1967 were employed, but the fundamental nature of the plan in each case was essentially the same. An association of dry goods wholesalers has formed a corporation to acquire land and develop a center in Randall Square. In addition, 12 meat packers (processors rather than slaughterers) have associated to develop a common facility in the East Side Project on a site which has been re-zoned to permit this use. Neither relocation had been completed by June 1967. Nevertheless, the experience and knowledge gained by PRA in the Willard Avenue Center provided the guidelines for undertaking these efforts. Thus the transferability of the basic idea has already been demonstrated within Providence itself.

Region II

The HUD Region II office is located in Philadelphia. The relocation staff consists of three professionals, all with prior relocation experience as LPA staff members.

The chief concern of the Region II relocation staff, with respect to business relocation, is to work for the expeditious and proper processing of relocation payment claims. This occupies approximately 90 per cent of the staff time devoted to business relocation.

The staff is especially anxious to ensure that all requests for action and all claims for payment are made with sufficient lead time, and appropriately documented with necessary facts and figures, to allow for prompt processing and payment.

The Region II relocation staff has actively encouraged LPA's to develop lists of available business locations, both for rental and for purchase, in advance of the actual execution of relocation programs. They suggest periodic distribution of this information to affected businessmen. The Region II relocation staff has also placed special emphasis on providing LPA advice and assistance to extremely small businesses. They further argue that an effective program of internal procedures to expedite routine cases will allow more time for dealing with the more knotty problems in business relocation.

Attempts have been made by the Region II relocation staff to stimulate better working relationships between the regional SBA staff and LPA relocation officers. They feel responsible to stimulate more effective utilization of SBA programs of financial assistance.

The Region II relocation staff has actively encouraged groups of affected businessmen to organize and work with LPA relocation officers to develop group quarters which are suitable for their needs and which would qualify them for further SBA financial assistance. This effort has borne fruit in a number of specific cases in Philadelphia in particular. In addition, the regional relocation staff has worked directly with organized groups of relocatees to provide them with information about the regulations under which they will have to operate, plus the opportunities for financial and other assistance that are available to them. They have further encouraged the development of local business groups concerned with small business opportunities for non-whites, whether they have been operating within the framework of the urban renewal program or not. The Region II relocation staff has developed especially close ties with several such organizations in Philadelphia. This is a supplement to the relocation efforts of the LPA involved.

A pilot program has been initiated in Morristown, New Jersey, aimed at expediting the processing of both relocation payment claims and property loss payments. This program involves having formal appraisals and estimates made of both the value of machinery and equipment and the probable costs of moving, in advance of any specific actions by the affected businessmen. These appraisals and estimates provide the affected businessmen with a basis for determining what shall be included in acquisition and what shall be moved. The financial implications of these decisions are better known and appreciated by displacees.

Baltimore, Maryland

Baltimore is a city of approximately 1,000,000 persons (1960 population: 939,000). In Maryland, the municipality is the LPA. Renewal projects are authorized by an ordinance of the city council and administered by the Baltimore Department of Housing and Community Development (HCD) under the jurisdiction of the board of estimates. This board is composed of the mayor, the president of the city council, the city comptroller, the city solicitor, and the commissioner of public works.

As of September 1967, the Baltimore Urban Renewal and Housing Agency (BURHA, the predecessor agency to the Department of Housing and Community Development) had completed seven renewal projects, and had twelve in execution. At that time the relocation work load was in excess of 1,000 firms. Many were concentrated in the Charles Center Project, which involved 33 acres in the central business district.

Until 1964, the housing management division of BURHA handled all relocation. Thereafter, to provide better control and meet the increasing relocation work load, a relocation division was established with a staff of approximately 140. This division is a central relocation activity which provides assistance to all families and businesses displaced by public improvement programs within the city of Baltimore. It also processes all claims for relocation payments, including moving expense, additional payments to residential displacees, personal property loss, and Small Business Displacement Payments.

The services provided by the business relocation staff include: advice on all aspects of relocation; assistance in arranging financing; and finding new locations for consideration by the displacee. In addition, a list of Realtors who have agreed to cooperate with urban renewal by helping in finding new locations is provided to all affected businessmen. The staff seeks to enlist the cooperation of all public agencies which might be able to provide a relocation service.

During the planning phase of each project, an informational booklet is distributed in person to each business identified as a potential displacee. For the record, a receipt is sought from the businessman, indicating that he has received, read and had the information in the booklet explained to him.

In addition to the specific relocation cases developed in field interviews, a number of general operating programs and arrangements are in effect in Baltimore which provide guides to the handling of certain types of relocation problems.

Priority to displaced businesses. In generating the redevelopment plan for many projects, HCD has inserted stipulations that in specific parcels scheduled for commercial and/or industrial reuse, formal priority shall be given to displaced businesses seeking to become developers. In other cases, the project disposition program recognizes the department's prerogative to grant priorities to displacees. HCD has worked with groups of small businesses displaced by urban renewal to form corporations to enable them to remain in the general vicinity of their former locations.

Payment for temporary or interim relocations. Under certain circumstances, in accordance with the city's interpretation of Maryland law, the city can make payments for moving expenses of displaced firms to other locations within a project. This payment for a temporary on-site move, coupled with a payment under federal regulations for the permanent move, can entitle a displacee to reimbursement for two moves. This is illustrated in the Vermont Federal Savings and Loan Association case.

Relocation of churches. Maryland law specifies that church properties acquired for public improvement programs (including urban renewal) shall be compensated at their replacement cost — not appraised market value or reproduction cost new less depreciation.

Charles Center Management Office (CCMO). In 1959, HCD (through the city) entered into a third-party contract with a private party to carry out the management and development activities for the Charles Center Project. The city paid all operating expenses of the Charles Center staff under the terms of this contract. In turn, the organization coordinated the activities of both private and public groups and agencies in the execution of the project. It represented the city and HCD in land disposition, relocation assistance, property management (until demolition commenced), design of public improvements, and general administration. The office utilized the services of city departments as supplementary staff. The handling of relocation claims remained with HCD.

In 1965, the city requested the Charles Center organization to expand their work into Baltimore's Inner Harbor renewal program. The Charles Center Management Office was converted into a non-profit corporation, Charles Center-Inner Harbor Management, Inc. The corporation reports to HCD and is responsible for the continued administration of the Charles Center Project, as well as the planning and execution of the first projects in the Inner Harbor program.

The Charles Center Project had a total work load of 350 businesses. Most relocated within the city of Baltimore. Although the basic orientation of the Charles Center Management Office was toward development, a business relocation specialist was assigned full time to assist the displaced businesses in their relocation planning.

Hamburgers (Isaac Hamburger and Sons Co.).

This men's and women's clothing store was located in a multistory building on a corner site within the Charles Center Project Area. The building was old and obsolete (built in 1906) but was in good physical condition. Approximately $1,000,000 had been spent on remodeling with the five years previous to the project.

The redevelopment plan for Charles Center originally called for office facilities to be constructed for the Baltimore and Ohio Railroad in air rights spanning Fayette Street. This idea was developed because the B & O did not pay local taxes on its land. The city wanted to accommodate the B & O, and yet not reduce the tax base of the project.

When the merger of the B & O and the C & O (Chesapeake and Ohio Railroad) was announced, the B & O decided to defer new office construction in Baltimore and withdrew its plans to build and occupy this space.

In 1960, the site was offered to Hamburgers. Because it was very close to their former location and offered some intriguing possibilities, Hamburgers accepted the opportunity. As a business displacee, it was granted exclusive negotiating privileges by the city, in accordance with the Charles Center disposition policy.

The first problem encountered was to create usable air rights, since local and state law made it impossible to have private property on a public right of way. The city solicitor's office developed a procedure whereby the street was condemned and closed by city council ordinance. After the air rights were conveyed to Hamburgers, the street could then be rededicated to right-of-way use, subject to the fee interest of Hamburgers in the air rights.

It was specified that the new building must span the 100-foot width of Fayette Street without intermediate columns. The architect designed the building so that the top floor spanning the street was constructed like a bridge. It utilized Vierendeel trusses instead of standard trusses to maximize the usable space on the top floor. The second floor was suspended below. This design was a source of much publicity for Hamburgers, but it was extremely costly as well. In order to obtain the necessary financing, Hamburgers leased the development rights to a developer, who then built the structure for them in accordance with the plans and specifications approved by the Charles Center Architectural Review Board. The building was then leased back to Hamburgers on a long-term lease. They are therefore owners of the land and air rights, and tenants of the building. Full property taxes are paid on the building and on the land and air rights.

HCD acquired the old Hamburgers building in August of 1961. That building contained slightly over 34,000 square feet. The actual move was delayed until the new building was ready, to avoid interruption of business or a temporary relocation. The move occurred in October 1963. Moving expenses in excess of $18,000 were paid in November 1963.

Hamburgers now occupies 40,000 square feet of building area. Since the move, growth in business in the downtown store has exceeded the growth in their suburban stores. This reversal of a previous trend is the best indicator of the success of the move, as far as Hamburgers is concerned.

Through this relocation, Baltimore was able to retain a major retail outlet in its CBD. In addition, otherwise "unproductive" space was utilized effectively and added to the tax rolls. Imaginative legal actions were necessary to make this possible, and leasing was used extensively to create a package for appropriate financing. The status of Hamburgers as a displaced business permitted the city to dispose of the site through an exclusive negotiating priority, rather than through public bid. The integrity of the overall design of Charles Center Project was preserved; Hamburgers provides a pedestrian bridge between 1 Charles Center and the Vermont Federal Savings and Loan Association building.

Stamper's Barber Shop

The Reverend Benjamin Stamper ran a two-chair barber shop in the McCulloh Homes Extension Project. Mr. Stamper was an elderly Negro who had difficulty in communicating with the HCD staff because of a recent operation for the removal of his larynx. This is important to note, because of the additional effort and care that had to be taken to make sure that information was understood by Mr. Stamper.

The first interview with Mr. Stamper was held at the project office in July 1966. He approached HCD for assistance in moving to a location that he had found three blocks away. The difficulty was that the area was zoned for residential use only, and he required a zoning board permit for a non-conforming use. When neighbors in the area objected, this request was denied.

The HCD staff then undertook an intensive search of available stores in the area in an effort to find a suitable location for Mr. Stamper. Meanwhile, the old location was acquired by the city in November 1966. Mr. Stamper indicated he needed financial help to acquire new equipment. HCD contacted SBA, and assisted Mr. Stamper in applying for an SBA Displaced Business Loan. In December 1966, HCD found a vacant store nearby. Mr. Stamper saw it, liked it, and signed a lease. His rent was $1,040 per year, which was the same that he had been paying in his old location since 1958.

HCD staff told Mr. Stamper to remain in his old location until the necessary permits could be obtained to allow him to move. He required the approval of the

Maryland Board of Barber Examiners, the Baltimore Health Department, and the City Bureau of Building Inspection. Nevertheless, Mr. Stamper moved on his own on January 1, 1967, and HCD discovered it a few days later. This created a problem in terms of licensing. Technically, Mr. Stamper's operation could have been closed down.

HCD made direct contact with the public agencies involved, requesting approval and permits on behalf of Mr. Stamper. Approval was received from the State Board of Barber Examiners on January 30, and from the City Health Department and Bureau of Business Inspection on February 8.

Through the assistance of HCD, Mr. Stamper sold his used barber chairs and other equipment. Despite the fact that he had moved without formal approval, moving expenses of $45 and reimbursement of property loss of $1,085, less rent owed the city of $20, were paid to him on March 6. He also received an SBDP of $2,500. With these funds, he was able to pay for his new equipment, and the SBA loan application was cancelled.

The shop is still a two-chair shop. Mr. Stamper's assistant is a Negro woman barber. Mr. Stamper reported that his business has increased substantially in the new location. He expressed considerable satisfaction with his treatment at the hands of HCD.

This case indicates the kind of individual and custom service that is frequently necessary to accomplish a successful relocation of a small business, especially one operated by a minority-group member. HCD went to work on his behalf to save him from a potentially difficult situation with respect to his licenses and permits. Prompt handling of reimbursement for his expenses and property loss, and of the SBDP, eliminated the necessity to borrow funds to finance equipment in the new location.

Vermont Federal Savings and Loan Association.

Vermont Federal occupied its own building at the corner of Fayette and Hanover streets in the Charles Center Project Area. The building had been built in 1925. Vermont Federal occupied 4,200 square feet of area, and leased out the remaining 57,400 square feet. The building had been remodeled in 1959.

CCMO approached the Vermont Federal management with the proposal that they remain in the project area as redevelopers. Since the Vermont Federal management regarded their location as an important competitive advantage, they were anxious to remain as close as possible to the old site. CCMO offered them a site which was approximately the same as that which they formerly occupied. As a result, it was necessary for Vermont Federal to relocate temporarily, while their old building was demolished, the new site was assembled and prepared, and a new building constructed.

For this purpose, the city and Vermont Federal made arrangements for Vermont Federal to move into a vacant building owned by the *Baltimore Sun* which had formerly contained the offices of the newspaper. From April 1962 until September 1964, Vermont Federal occupied this building, first as tenants of the *Sun*, and then as tenants of the city after the property had been acquired by the city. The building was located within the Charles Center Project. Vermont Federal made approximately $30,000 worth of leasehold improvements.

Vermont Federal did well in the temporary location. Its growth continued uninterruptedly during the two and one-half years in the *Sun* building. Because Vermont Federal was granted exclusive negotiating privileges for the site, it was enabled to acquire the site non-competitively as a displaced business, rather than at public bid.

New construction was financed entirely with Association funds. The design of the building conformed to the Charles Center plan, and was subject to review by the Charles Center Architectural Review Board. Moreover, because of the second-floor-level pedestrian mall and plaza, Vermont Federal operated lobby and teller facilities both at ground level and on the second floor until it was able to find a tenant for the second-floor space.

Vermont Federal wanted to build room for expansion. The original plans called for a five-story building. This was changed first to six and finally to seven stories, with the approval of both the city council and HUD. These approvals were necessary because the increased height represented a change in the redevelopment plan. CCMO helped to facilitate these approvals. In addition, time extensions were given because of delays in obtaining architectural and planning approval. Vermont Federal was allowed to remain in the *Sun* building until the problems could be worked out.

The city paid $350,000 for the old property. The site for the new building was purchased for $145,000.

Construction went on between April 1962 and September 1964. Vermont Federal occupies the basement and the first and third floors of the new building. The balance of the building is tenant occupied. The building cost approximately $2,250,000. During this relocation, Vermont received relocation payments for both the temporary and permanent moves. A non-federal reimbursement for the temporary move amounted to $3,700. The final move in September 1964 received a federal relocation payment of $3,000 for moving and loss of personal property.

Throughout this process, Vermont Federal was able to remain at essentially the same location, which was critical to continuing profitable operations.

Philadelphia, Pennsylvania

Philadelphia has a long-standing urban renewal program of major proportions. As of July 1967, Philadelphia had initiated fifty-five Title I projects, of which ten were completed and twenty-four were in execution. In addition, there were three federally funded General Neighborhood Renewal Plan projects with a total of twelve General Neighborhood Renewal Areas. Four of these were in the planning stage. Finally, eleven projects were in process without federal aid. Seven of these were city-aided: two completed and two in the execution stage. The remaining four projects involved city-owned industrial land in thirteen tracts. Of these, six were completed and seven were in execution.

These figures indicate the magnitude and scope of urban renewal in Philadelphia. They also bring out the important point that *staging* and *timing* are particularly important aspects of urban renewal activities, including business and industrial relocation. Although detailed data are not complete prior to 1963, the best estimate of the business relocation work load through December 1966 was a total of 1,658 displacements from 20 project areas. Projected business relocations between 1967 and 1972 were 1,188.

To handle this volume of activity, the Redevelopment Authority of the City of Philadelphia (PRA) has a business and industrial relocation staff of nine. This division is separate from residential relocation activities. During the summer of 1967, when the interviews were held, a student from the University of North Carolina was temporarily attached to the business and industrial relocation staff. His responsibility was to conduct a follow-up study of relocatees to ascertain their sales and profit experiences in their new locations.

This study exemplifies a continuing research and evaluation program in which the business and industrial relocation staff of PRA is engaged. The proximity of the University of Pennsylvania and Temple University, both of which have active programs in community development, makes it possible to carry out an essentially internal evaluation of the relocation program without serious diversion of resources from the major task of handling the business relocation work load. In handling this major work load in a diverse and large program, the business and industrial relocation staff of PRA has employed a number of major approaches which are discussed here under separate headings. Each of these is illustrated in the case examples of successful business relocation which follow.

Organization for relocation. The nine-man business and industrial relocation staff make personal visits to every business firm to ascertain their relocation desires and requirements at the time the property is acquired. Detailed information is kept in well-organized files from which data can easily be retrieved. This information is utilized to prepare periodic lists of businesses seeking new locations, together with their indicated space and locational requirements. To the extent possible, personnel are assigned on a project basis, so that they may become familiar with the individual businessmen involved in a given area and work more closely with them. This personal relationship was evident during field visits to successfully relocated firms; relocation staff members were generally greeted warmly as friends and colleagues by the relocated businessmen.

Cooperation with commercial and industrial brokers. As a matter of policy, PRA encourages commercial and industrial real estate brokers to participate actively in the business relocation process. PRA does not attempt to circumvent sales or leasing brokers. Instead, it tries to work directly with them. Prior to acquisition of a specific area, the boundary maps are made available to members of the Society of Industrial Realtors and cooperating brokers, upon request. These maps contain the number of businesses to be relocated and the estimated date of condemnation.

A list of commercial and industrial space available throughout the city is also compiled from information supplied by cooperating brokers. It is distributed to all business displacees seeking new space. It is also circulated among the Philadelphia Gas Works, Philadelphia Electric Company, PIDC, and 200 brokers and attorneys in the Philadelphia area. It is revised and brought up to date at least every six months. The list identifies the listing broker, and PRA does everything it can to protect the interests of the brokers. In many instances, tenants of buildings to be acquired are encouraged to work through the brokers leasing them their present space. This cooperative work is formalized through the Philadelphia chapter of the Society of Industrial Realtors, and is reinforced through personal contacts between PRA staff and SIR members. In effect, PRA helps to bring brokers and displaced businesses together. In addition, the business and industrial relocation staff has retained a real estate consultant to advise them on particularly knotty relocation problems — especially those involving industrial and manufacturing firms.

Prompt processing of forms and claims. The entire relocation staff is oriented toward "getting the job done" and worrying about satisfying federal auditors later. They operate on the principle that flexibility and adaptability to the demands of particular problems are more important than a rigid adherence to regulations which may result in *avoidable* delays in compensation. Through the organization of the staff and its files, an effective procedure for rapid handling of claims for compensation and reimbursement has been developed. In the great majority of cases, firms eligible for the Small Business Displacement Payment receive payments at the time of vacating. In addition, less than 1 per cent of those apparently eligible for the SBDP are denied it in Philadelphia.

Staging and timing of business relocation. The PRA business and industrial relocation staff consciously seeks to take advantage of the existence of the many renewal projects in Philadelphia, which are in varying stages of development and execution. These several project areas provide relocation resources for both permanent and temporary moves. This effort is illustrated in several of the cases discussed below. A large, multi-project program is not an unmixed blessing, however. Pressures for displacement of businesses from one project area frequently lead to problems when sites and/or buildings in other project areas designed to provide relocation resources are not ready on schedule. As a result, the business relocation personnel are constantly under pressure to pay particular attention to the *timing* of moves. In some instances, moves have been consciously delayed in order to permit the completion of relocation resources in other project areas. This, too, is illustrated in the cases studied.

Encouragement of group action by relocatees. Because Philadelphia is a major commercial and industrial center, many concentrations of businesses in similar lines of activity are found throughout the city. Particularly in wholesaling and distribution activities (although not exclusively in these areas), there are economic and financial advantages in having the businesses located in close proximity to one another. PRA has developed a conscious policy of encouraging and assisting groups of such businessmen to join together (either as developers or tenants) in order to provide themselves with appropriate locations and facilities in project areas. A variety of imaginative financing and legal arrangements has been developed as a result of this policy. Some of these are illustrated in the cases discussed. A major consideration in the evolution of this policy has been to retain income and employment within the corporate limits of Philadelphia.

Cooperation with local agencies. PRA is independent of the formal governmental structure of the city and county of Philadelphia. As a result, it must work closely with both municipal and county agencies in order to carry out its programs, including business relocation. This has been realized through both personal contacts with local officials and formal organizational arrangements. Several of the cases studied bring out this important point.

Perhaps the most important agency with which strong working cooperation has been developed is the Philadelphia Industrial Development Corporation. PIDC was organized as a non-profit partnership of the City of Philadelphia and the Greater Philadelphia Chamber of Commerce in 1958, "to help Philadelphia industries to obtain additional or more modern space and to attract new industry to the city." Its operations are financed jointly by the chamber of commerce and the city. It also receives financial assistance from the Commonwealth of Pennsylvania under the Industrial Development Assistance Act.

PIDC owns land which it makes available to industry, develops industrial parks and sites for industry, and arranges financing for industrial development. PIDC participates in *real estate* loans only. These include land acquisition costs, development costs, and plant construction costs. Normally, private financing is arranged through sources selected by the operating company. PIDC creates a mortgage on behalf of the operating company, and takes title to the property. Because PIDC is a non-profit corporation, obligations on its real estate are tax exempt. As a result, private lenders can and will make loans at lower rates of interest.

The operating company remains as the equitable owner of the property. It cannot sublease the property, although it may sell subject to PIDC approval. Mortgage payments are made by the operating company directly to PIDC, which in turn makes payments to the private lender. In effect, the operating company under a PIDC participation must remain in the tenant in occupancy. The operating company builds up an equity interest in the property over time, and may sell the property or prepay the mortgage subject to the approval of the mortgagee. PIDC is an important and effective resource for industrial relocation in Philadelphia, and works closely with the PRA business and industrial relocation staff.

State Business Dislocation Payments. In Pennsylvania, a Business Dislocation Payment is available to selected businesses under the terms of Section 609 of the 1964 Eminent Domain Code of the Commonwealth of Pennsylvania. This payment is available in addition to the Small Business Displacement Payment. However, it applies only to retail and certain wholesale businesses which are able to demonstrate that they are unable to relocate without a "substantial loss of patronage." Over half of the firms which have received such a payment in Philadelphia have discontinued operations following dislocation. Approximately 45 per cent have relocated, and have been compensated because they have lost a considerable amount of business.

Tenants under long-term leases are usually eligible for an amount equal to the rent they would have paid for the remainder of their lease, up to a limit of 24 months. The maximum payment is $5,000, and the minimum is $250. For purposes of the Business Dislocation Payment program, owner-occupants of affected properties are considered to have a 24-month lease. The actual payment is based upon a judgment about the percentage of patronage that will be lost through relocation. This judgment is made at the time the property is vacated. Tenants under short-term leases or without leases are typically not eligible for such a payment.

During 1965 and 1966, state Business Dislocation Payments were made to approximately 60 firms in Philadelphia. Another 32 applications were rejected. The payments averaged $2,560, ranging from $400 to $5,000. Approximately 40 firms received both a state Business Dislocation Payment and a federal Small Business Displacement Payment. Although it has not been widely used, the BDP offers one additional alternative means of compensating small businesses in retailing and wholesaling for the financial impact of dislocation. It represents one further opportunity for the business relocation staff of PRA to offer assistance to affected firms.

Despite the varied and large relocation work load, very few evictions have been necessary in Philadelphia. This is a reflection of the emphasis on advice and assistance to businesses, the organization of the business relocation staff to process claims expeditiously, and the availability of alternative relocation resources afforded by many projects in the execution stage.

Food Distribution Center (FDC)

Although the FDC was developed entirely outside the framework of the federal urban renewal program, this experience provides a number of important lessons that could readily be transferred to the framework of Title I activities. As a relocation, its primary lesson lies in the coordination of the timing of moves from older locations in another redevelopment project area to the FDC.

In 1954, the Greater Philadelphia Movement proposed the relocation of Philadelphia's wholesale produce and seafood district on Dock Street to a new location on what was then a municipal dump in South Philadelphia. The new location would be immediately adjacent to new interstate highways and the approaches to the Walt Whitman Bridge to New Jersey, affording access in all directions to the distribution area served by the Dock Street wholesalers. The produce and seafood wholesaling district was antiquated, inefficient, unsanitary, and increasingly unprofitable. By 1954, a smaller volume of business was being transacted than had been handled in 1931. In addition, the area was part of the Washington Square East Renewal Area, which included the Society Hill redevelopment adjacent to Independence Mall.

A major objective was to retain the food distribution activities in Philadelphia. The city, working through PRA, condemned and acquired approximately 388 acres of dump and blighted area. A total of $15,000,000 was expended to fill and stabilize the land, and to install site improvements. The area was designated as the Pattison Avenue East Redevelopment Area in April 1955. A non-profit corporation was formed to serve as redeveloper of the project area under contract with PRA. This was the Food Distribution Center Corporation. No federal funds were used.

The site was acquired and prepared from 1956 to 1958. Construction began in June 1958. The first three buildings were the produce and seafood center, containing a total of 95 stalls. The construction cost was $3,803,000.

The Philadelphia Fresh Food Terminal Corporation was organized as an association of produce dealers. This corporation leases the produce market and seafood market stalls from FDC. FDC was financed with $1,000,000 advanced by the city and a $2.8 million bond issue purchased by local life insurance companies and banks. The Philadelphia Fresh Food Terminal Corporation is the prime tenant in the seafood and produce market area. Members of the associations of produce dealers and seafood dealers are the occupants and subtenants. All of the prospective subtenants put in seed money for some of the preliminary financing.

The stalls are standardized at 25-feet wide and 100-feet deep. Of this depth, 25 feet is front loading dock, 60 feet is interior storage and work space, and 15 feet is rear loading dock. Innovative architectural designs provided an open plan with ample parking and docking facilities for the future. The stalls have a ceiling height of 20 feet, which permits offices on the mezzanine level at the rear of each stall. These offices are rented out by FDC. Of the 104 offices available, 80 were rented by mid-1967; 34 were occupied by food brokers. The remainder were rented to jobbers, market news agencies, food association services, and the offices of the Philadelphia Fresh Food Terminal Corporation.

There has been 100 per cent occupancy of the produce and seafood stalls since the terminal facility was opened in June of 1959. All tenants must be members of one of the two associations. All Dock Street merchants had a priority as relocatees, and when the center was opened all of the original tenants were relocatees. The dealers' association has the right to approve subtenants and the terms of leases. In addition to 70 produce wholesalers and 25 seafood wholesalers, there are three restaurants in the facility.

Food Distribution Center.   Limited parking and accessways meant daily congestion in the old Dock Street produce market (above) in Philadelphia. The relocation site (below) of the Philadelphia produce market provides a marked contrast to the inefficiencies evidenced in its former location. (Photos courtesy Philadelphia Redevelopment Authority.)

The rent paid by the Association covers debt service for FDC. When the mortgage is paid off, the facilities will be owned by FDC. If they are ever abandoned, title reverts to the city.

PRA played an important role in several aspects of the development. Its condemnation authority was used for the initial acquisition of the 388-acre site, and PRA (using city funds) prepared the site prior to acquisition by FDC.

Most importantly for this study, PRA held off eviction of the Dock Street wholesalers until the new produce and seafood market facilities were ready. Then a mass move was arranged over one weekend in June 1959. The businesses closed on a Friday evening in Dock Street, were totally relocated on Saturday and Sunday, and opened for business in the new facilities on Monday morning. This required a great deal of planning and careful timing on the part of the PRA business relocation staff.

The wholesale produce and seafood markets occupy only one segment of the total food distribution center. FDC both leases and sells land to food processors and distributors. By mid-1967, all but two acres of the original 388 were either leased or sold. As an integral part of the development, a truck port and service station complex is included within the Center. Sleeping and shower facilities are also provided for truck drivers in this facility.

Although the relocation of the Dock Street wholesalers to the food distribution center was a group effort and a joint decision, as is usual in such cases there was one individual who spearheaded the drive. In addition to organizing the merchants into the Philadelphia Fresh Food Terminal Corporation, he moved his banana warehousing and ripening firm to a three-acre tract in the Center which was purchased from FDC. The 75,000-square-foot M. Levin and Company warehousing and ripening plant was the first purchase of land in the Center, and the first building constructed.

The Philadelphia Fresh Food Terminal Corporation has a 20-year lease from FDC, with six five-year renewal options. Other relocatees have moved into the Center as well. A variety of financing arrangements has been developed, including advances from the revolving Industrial Development Fund of the City of Philadelphia. Moreover, PIDC has participated in the financing of some of the plants and warehouses in the Center.

This experience illustrates the critical importance of imaginative financing arrangements, many of them tailored to meet the needs of specific purchasers or tenants, which expedited the development of the Center. An organization of small merchants (the produce and seafood wholesalers) made it possible to arrange for leasing and financing which would not have been feasible had they been acting individually and independently.

This case further exemplifies what a community can do, within or without the framework of federal urban renewal programs, in reclaiming unused and unproductive land for highly productive purposes. In the process, Philadelphia retained an important industry and the jobs associated with it. Actual city funds required were minimal, because much of the money used was an advance to be repaid over time from rent receipts of FDC. Moreover, the creation of the site for the Food Distribution Center made it possible to proceed with the redevelopment of the Society Hill area.

Style Setter Fashions

Style Setter Fashions is a dress manufacturing firm which was originally located in the Independence Mall Project Area, Unit 3. The firm occupied 10,000 square feet on the fifth, seventh and ninth floors of a loft building. In their former location, they paid $400 per month rent and employed 40 workers.

The actual relocation can be described as "self-relocation," because the new space was found through an SIR by the president of the firm. However, PRA must be regarded as the initiating cause in bringing the broker and business together. Each was attracted to the other through the efforts of PRA. Once it was learned that the firm was dealing with the broker, PRA remained on the sidelines to "protect and respect" the interests of the industrial broker. This sensitivity to the workings of industrial brokerage paid off handsomely in the Style Setter Fashions case.

The move occurred in October 1964. Style Setter Fashions moved to another loft building. They now occupy 14,300 square feet on the eighth floor. Their monthly rental is $900, and employment has risen to 70.

PRA's role in this case was to process compensation for moving expenses as rapidly as possible. The firm now has all of its operations on one floor, better loading facilities, and a larger elevator. The owner of the firm indicates that business has increased considerably. He commented, "Being forced to relocate caused an unprecedented expansion that might otherwise not have occurred. We have much greater efficiency and lower insurance costs, which have offset any costs of moving and rental increase."

Fifth Street Wholesalers' Association

In 1961, approximately 30 businesses located in the 300 block of South Fifth Street formed an association to find new locations, immediately after they learned that their properties would be acquired as part of the redevelopment of the Washington Square East Project, Unit 2. The properties were actually condemned in 1962. Among the 30 original members of the Association, there were approximately 18 wholesalers, mostly in the dry goods field. The area was the wholesale dry goods center of Philadelphia.

At the instigation of PRA, the Association investigated the possibility of becoming redevelopers in another area. They felt strongly that they should remain together in order to retain their identity as a wholesaling center.

The group approached PIDC, but was unable to obtain financing from that source. However, they did receive advice and counsel about arranging financing.

Few members of the Association had much cash. In addition, several businesses were tenants and were not at that time eligible for SBA financing as relocatees. However, PIDC did suggest a condominium arrangement as a reasonable solution to their financing and ownership problem, but few were willing to give up their independence through joint ownership of any new facility.

The Association retained a very imaginative attorney, who initiated lobbying efforts in the Pennsylvania Legislature to have enabling legislation passed that would permit condominium ownership. In addition, the attorney approached SBA and was partially instrumental in obtaining a reversal of SBA's position with respect to financing real estate purchases by displaced tenants.

With these legal barriers out of the way, the Association then worked through PRA to attempt to find an appropriate site. They could not afford the one which they preferred, which was directly across the street from their ultimate location. PRA then suggested the present location at the northwest corner of Fifth and Spring Garden streets. The site was available and could be utilized for the proposed condominium, but it was not properly zoned. PRA instituted a petition to change the zoning of the parcel to permit wholesale use. This petition was approved by the city council.

It was then necessary to obtain funds for a downpayment on the site. At this point, a number of the original participants withdrew. The final organization stabilized at eleven members. Each was required to put up a *pro rata* share of $17,800, which was 10 per cent of the purchase price for the land. Following this, SBA agreed to provide the necessary financing, but some of the businesses were "too well off" to qualify for SBA financing. With the assistance of PIDC and their attorney, the Association sought financing for three of the individual businesses. In two cases, the Association was able to arrange mortgage financing; in the third case, the individual businessman made his own financing arrangements. Eight of the firms received SBA loans.

Eight of the eleven members of the Association were owners and three were tenants in their old locations. Construction began in 1963, and was completed in early December of 1964. During this construction period, PRA was instrumental in convincing the Post Office Department to assign all of the businesses addresses on Spring Garden Street, which is a main thoroughfare. The Post Office Department wanted to give them street numbers on Fifth and Sixth streets, but the group felt that their identity as a mall would be better preserved if they had addresses on the same street. PRA also arranged for digging and new construction in Fifth Street to be delayed until after the relocation.

In terms of the actual move, PRA's most important action was to hold off notices to vacate until after Christmas of 1964. This permitted the firms to take advantage of the Christmas sale season at their old and known locations. The eleven firms all moved to the new location during the week after Christmas. The grand opening was held in January 1965.

The new location is a mall on 2.6 acres of land. The site cost $178,000, and the building cost the Association $422,700. The total square-footage is approximately 47,200 square feet. Each member of the Association owns his own space in the building, together with a *pro rata* share of the pedestrian mall and parking area. Each owner has an obligation for a proportionate share of maintenance of the roof, building exterior, parking lot and mall. The completed structure was a shell which included heat, lighting, walls and unfinished floors. Air conditioning ducts were installed, but the compressors were not. Nine of the owners joined together for a central air conditioning system for their nine stores. Finishing of floors, painting, partitions and shelving were the responsibility of the individual businessmen. The group later combined to purchase a burglar alarm system for the entire mall. The president of the Association indicated that group effort on these items is extremely important because they were able to obtain better service and facilities at lower prices than would have been possible had they operated individually.

Eight of the occupants of the mall are dry goods wholesalers. In addition, there is one furniture and appliance wholesaler, one manufacturer of slip covers and draperies "for the trade," and one vending machine distributor. The latter is a tenant, which is permitted under the by-laws of the Association. The original participant died before the mall could be occupied.

Nearly all of the firms occupy less space than they did in their former locations. However, all of those interviewed agreed that they had better use of their facilities and much more efficient layouts than was previously possible. In addition, they believe that they now have an identity which attracts business to them. The availability of on-site parking has considerably enhanced the volume of their trade. In addition, the site is very close to the Spring Garden Interchange of the Deleware Expressway, which makes it easier for customers to reach the mall from a much wider area than was possible in their former locations. All of the businessmen interviewed indicated that business and profits were considerably higher, after a preliminary decline during the first few months.

The president of the Association emphasized the importance of identifying leadership for any group such as this in the early stages of the development, to carry the project through to completion. He also is most enthusiastic about the idea of such groupings for small businessmen. He voluntarily speaks before other groups of businessmen faced with displacement, urging them to join together in similar arrangements to cope with their relocation problems.

Charles P. Mills and Son

This commercial photography and photo-finishing firm moved to its own new building in May 1966. This site is in the Independence Mall Redevelopment Area, Unit 2. The firm formerly was located in two buildings which it owned. One was in the Washington Square East Urban Renewal Area, Unit 3; the other was in the Washington Square East Renewal Area, Unit 2. The former was condemned in December 1962.

Mills began his planning in 1960, when he first learned that the property in Unit 2 was to be acquired for urban renewal. That was a relatively new building, constructed to provide expansion to a second story at a later date. Location was extremely important to the firm, because much of its business comes from advertising and publishing firms in the immediate vicinity.

PRA personnel toured the entire area with Mills, showing him several alternative locations. They wanted to retain him in the city, and understood his need to be in the same general vicinity as his two former locations. PRA personnel suggested the new location to Mills. The difficulty was that the site was zoned for institutional use. PRA was intrumental in placing an application for a change in zoning before the city council. Originally, the proposal was rejected. PRA went back to the zoning committee and finally succeeded in having the zoning changed.

A further obstacle that was originally encountered was a requirement in the reuse plan that the building should be 45-feet high. Mills was able to obtain an exception to this requirement for the two-story studio section in the rear of the building, but not for the front section. To compensate for this, Mills now has four retail tenants on the ground floor along Seventh Street, a commercial art company as a tenant on the third floor, and an advertising agency tenant on the fourth floor. Three of his tenants are relocatees from other project areas. The PRA business relocation staff was instrumental in bringing these tenants to Mills. This facilitated his move by providing him with further income to support the building, and it simplified the relocations of the tenants as well.

In order to assist Mills further, PRA held up the order to vacate at the Unit 2 building until the new structure was ready. In addition, PRA acquired the Unit 3 property as an early acquisition. This provided Mills with additional funds to finance the construction of his new building.

Mills is extremely happy with the new location, because it allowed him to consolidate his operations. His is a large commercial photography and photo-finishing establishment, with approximately 60 employees. Mills reported that his new production layout is much more efficient, and that the rental income from the building is sufficient to warrant having to comply with architectural and height requirements.

Mills was particularly pleased with the conscientious efforts of the PRA staff to accommodate his needs. These included finding an appropriate location in the first place, initiating efforts to have zoning and height requirements changed, using early acquisition to provide him with necessary funds for construction, deferring notices to vacate until the new structure was ready, and finding tenants for his rental space.

I. Klayman Company

One of only two abattoirs remaining within the city limits of Philadelphia, Klayman Pork Products slaughters and dresses hogs. The company was located in the West Mill Creek Renewal Area. The company had been at this location since 1897. Its property was condemned by PRA in June 1965.

The first contact between PRA and Klayman occurred in 1963. Klayman was put in touch with PIDC in April 1963 to investigate the possibility of financing a new plant.

The major difficulty with this relocation was that abattoirs are permitted only in areas zoned "Least Restricted" in Philadelphia. The scarcity of such sites led Klayman to obtain an option on ten acres of land in New Jersey.

The PRA business relocation staff learned that the Mack Warehousing and Trucking Company owned land near the Tacony-Palmyra Bridge adjacent to the Frankford Arsenal, which met the zoning requirements, and which was for sale. The owner was asking $30,000 per acre for the nine-acre tract. Klayman regarded this as too high a price, and the land was finally purchased for approximately $231,000. An automated plant was constructed on the site for approximately $1,000,000.

PIDC participated in the financing, with an $800,000 loan from a local bank on an installment sale agreement. Although this was privately owned land, PIDC was still willing to participate because it was "in the public interest."

At the time of the relocation, I. Klayman and Company employed 125 persons. Planned employment in the new plant is 300. Klayman was responsible for demolition of the existing buildings on the site and construction of the new plant, subject to approval by PIDC. Business volume has expanded dramatically, as has employment. In addition, the new location is very close to the new Delaware Expressway. By 1970, the Klayman Plant will be approximately 15 minutes away from the food distribution center, in which several important customers of Klayman are located.

In this instance, PRA and PIDC worked closely together in arranging the financing for Klayman. In addition, PRA found the site with the necessary zoning.

Whitman Chocolates — Pincus Manufacturing Company

The Whitman Chocolate Company occupied several buildings on a site immediately to the north of the new United States Mint in the Independence Mall Project Area. This property was acquired as part of the Independence Mall Project in 1959. The structures did not conform to the plan for the project area, and conflicted with the architectural style of the new U. S. Mint.

At the same time, Philadelphia was anxious to retain the Whitman Chocolate Company, because it employed approximately 1,200 persons. PRA agreed to acquire the Whitman property as an early acquisition so that Whitman could move to a new plant in the North Philadelphia industrial park near the North Philadelphia airport. This industrial park was developed by PIDC. Whitman acquired a 36-acre tract from PIDC, with low-interest financing from PIDC on the land. Whitman then proceeded to build a plant of approximately 450,000 square feet during 1959 and 1960. An additional 50,000 square feet of plant area was added later.

Whitman Chocolates – Pincus Manufacturing Co.   These photographs show the imaginative renovation of the Whitman plant. The older section of the plant shown in the foreground was replaced with a new addition to the remaining section. Space was thus provided for Pincus Manufacturing Co. (Photos courtesy Philadelphia Redevelopment Authority.)

Whitman Chocolates. The relocation site provides single-story production space in an industrial park. (Photo courtesy Philadelphia Redevelopment Authority.)

By arranging for early acquisition of the Fourth and Race streets property, and facilitating PIDC financing of Whitman's new site, PRA was able to "save" Whitman Chocolate Company for Philadelphia.

Meanwhile, the older, multistory buildings on the old Whitman site were demolished. The redevelopment plan called for the rehabilitation of one 900,000-square-foot, four-story building which had been constructed in the 1940's. Part of the agreement was that the loading docks and doors which faced the new U. S. Mint had to be moved around the corner. The remaining building was basically a shell, since it contained no heating plant and had one exposed wall.

PRA attracted the Pincus Manufacturing Company (PBM Clothes) to this site. Pincus was formerly located in older, less efficient space, which was not in a redevelopment project area.

The site and remaining building shell were sold to Pincus at the appraised value of the property. It was specified in the transaction that the structure would be rehabilitated, the truck doors and loading platforms moved to the rear of the building away from the Mint, and that off-street parking and loading be provided.

This transaction was possible because PIDC participated in the financing of the acquisition and rehabilitation of the Whitman building by Pincus. This meant that the low-interest financing could be obtained, and made the transaction attractive to Pincus. This is now the only manufacturing establishment remaining in the Independence Mall area.

Pincus acquired the property in 1964 for approximately $350,000. The firm spent an additional $650,000 in rehabilitation and expansion. They employ approximately 600 workers, and have increased their business markedly in the new location.

Region III

The HUD Region III office is located in Atlanta, Georgia, and serves the entire southeastern United States. The regional business relocation officer maintains continuing contact with field representatives throughout the Region. Periodically, seminars and training sessions are held in the Atlanta office to bring field representatives up-to-date on new developments and programs relating to business relocation.

The regional business relocation staff maintains current awareness of the business relocation activities of LPA's throughout Region III. This staff attempts to assume a leadership role in encouraging LPA's to do as effective a job in business relocation as possible. Moreover, a number of experimental or innovative undertakings have been encouraged through the regional office.

Within the limits established by HUD in Washington, there is regional concern for standardization of procedures relating to business relocation. Checklists of land acquisition procedures have been distributed to all LPA's in the Region, indicating the role of appraisals in determining what is realty and what is personalty. This is considered a critical issue in the business relocation process and is a determination which must be made early.

The Region III relocation staff believes strongly that business relocation and acquisition are closely interrelated, and should be planned and carried out together. Acting on the belief that the nature of the move determines what is to be acquired and what is to be moved, they encourage LPA's to bring their business relocation personnel into contact with displacees at the same time that acquisition personnel and appraisers approach them.

The Region III office is attempting to accelerate the processing of relocation plans. Both relocation plans and approvals for payments in excess of $10,000 should be processed in no more than four working days. In the case of self-moves, Region III still requires three bids to be received.

The regional business relocation staff urges the top administration of each LPA to be concerned with business relocation. The staff has distributed information to LPA's with no business relocation experience, citing the types of activities that have worked in other communities. This helps the inexperienced LPA's to avoid making the same mistakes that have been encountered in the past.

Cooperation with SBA. The area office of SBA is located in Atlanta. This is a coordinating office, as opposed to operating regional offices. The HUD Region III office has made an extra effort to involve SBA in urban renewal activities throughout the Region. Region III requires additional information from LPA's on the development of a business relocation plan, emphasizing plans for SBA loan contacts. Each LPA is required to complete a business relocation survey form for transmittal to the Region III office and the SBA Atlanta area office.

The Region III office and the SBA area office have arranged for each LPA to receive a letter from its SBA regional office offering services and advice about loans. This is based on information about the progress of projects provided from the regional office to the SBA area office. The LPA, in turn, is requested to provide them with a list of anticipated displacees. A receipt is required for this list. Each affected business is also requested to sign a form acknowledging that it has received information about SBA loan possibilities.

Each regional SBA office is instructed to make direct contact as soon as the project execution date is set. This is the date on which a loan and grant contract is signed, *not* the date of a letter of consent. By this time, the regional SBA office has a reasonable idea of which firms will actually file for a loan.

The SBA area office will approve SBA loans on property involving early acquisition, provided federal funds are used to acquire the property. SBA provides the Region III office with a monthly report on all DBL's and EDL's pending and closed during the month.

Stimulation of Negro-sponsored developments. The assistant to the regional director for intergroup relations is specifically charged with the task of encouraging the development of commercial projects which are Negro-sponsored. In most cases, these are shopping centers which are also occupied by Negro-operated businesses. A major objective is to mobilize the capital and assets of Negro financial institutions, most of which are concentrated in Region III, to make it more effective in assisting displaced Negro businessmen to find appropriate relocations. At the time of the interview, nearly a dozen such centers were in varying stages of development throughout Region III. In attempting to promote these developments, particular attention has been paid to the SBA Lease Guarantee Program and to franchising for businessmen seeking new lines of activity.

Atlanta, Georgia

Urban renewal in Atlanta (1960 population, 437,000) is handled by the Atlanta Housing Authority. In September 1967, AHA had one completed urban renewal project, nine in execution, and three in the planning stage. The estimated total business relocation work load was approximately 535 businesses, of which some

438 had been relocated by September 1967. Business relocation is under the jurisdiction of the chief of relocation for the urban renewal division, with one staff member devoting full time to business relocation.

Preliminary contacts are made with each affected business during the survey and planning stage. A booklet (*Facts about Business Relocation*) is distributed to each potential displacee. In addition, he is told where to obtain further facts about business relocation, such as advice on timing and his entitlements for compensation and reimbursement.

Because of the large number of extremely small businesses encountered in urban renewal projects in Atlanta, a special effort has been made to utilize technical schools to retrain displaced businessmen and equip them for the job market. In addition, the volume of very small displacees has placed special emphasis on the problems of qualifying a business for an SBDP. Tenant firms in particular have frequently filed no federal income tax returns in the past. Arrangements have been made with the Internal Revenue Service to permit such businessmen to apply to file returns for the previous two years without penalty. In most cases, these businesses have then become eligible for an SBDP, on presentation and certification of copies of their income tax returns, because they could then demonstrate that they were in fact "in business."

Johnson's Supermarket

The Johnsons are a Negro couple who operated a small grocery store in University Center Project R-11. They were tenants, and occupied 750 square feet in a one-story brick building which was seriously deteriorated.

It was necessary to find them a location where there was a suitable market for their services. They received an SBDP, and also obtained the first SBA Displaced Business Loan granted in Atlanta. With the proceeds of this $20,000 DBL, they built a modern market structure containing 2,250 square feet, which was located outside any project area. Their business has increased to the extent that they have expanded the building twice since the move.

The business relocation personnel of AHA found the location for them. It had to meet the requirements of a good site for a neighborhood grocery store; it is in a shopping center area on a heavily traveled road. AHA worked closely with the Johnsons in helping them obtain the DBL. They moved from tenant to ownership status.

Obie L. Cook Company

This printing firm originally owned its property in the Butler Street Project (R-9). It is both a press (commercial printing) and a repairer of printing equipment. The owner would not entrust the moving of his plates, type drawers and other equipment to a commercial mover. He feared substantial loss through damage or breakage. After considerable negotiation, approval was obtained from the Region III office to permit the firm to make a self-move. AHA also agreed to allow several months for the completion of the move. The actual move took place between October 1963 and April 1964 — a period of six months. Moving expenses totaled $16,807.

Obie L. Cook Company moved outside the project area. The firm owns its own property in the new location. This move was "successful" because the firm was permitted to handle the moving itself, and allowed a period of time sufficiently long to enable it to handle valuable and breakable materials and equipment carefully. In addition, minimal interruption of production occurred.

Douglas, Georgia

The town of Douglas, Georgia, with a population of less than 10,000 persons, is the smallest selected in this study. It is located in an economic area characterized by low to moderate income levels and relatively limited growth potential. Yet, with its small population and low income levels, the community has carried on an aggressive urban renewal program and has used a great deal of imagination in aiding displaced businessmen to relocate successfully.

In 1967, two urban renewal projects had been completed in this city and a third was approximately three-fourths finished. The areas encompassed by the projects have included only a few business firms — less than 15 businesses have been displaced in total — and as a consequence, business relocation does not receive central attention in this program. Nonetheless, considering the critical problems that the agency faced in relocating displaced low-income businessmen, its efforts have produced generally successful relocations.

An additional problem that was encountered in Douglas was the relocation of a church. Because of their non-profit status, churches often face special relocation problems in that they are not eligible for many of the benefits accorded business firms.

Gaines Chapel

In the first project undertaken in Douglas, a small Negro congregation of the African Methodist Episcopal denomination was slated for acquisition. This church was the Gaines Chapel, which consisted of three substandard structures located in the project area. One of the structures was a parsonage, the other the church sanctuary itself, and the third was a small recreation building with kitchen facilities to serve social gatherings.

The congregation of this church was clearly not in a position to raise significant sums of money to build a new church. Moreover, the old church and adjacent buildings were of very low value. The church structure was a frame building which had been moved to the project site and encased in brick many

Gaines Chapel before relocation (above). In addition to the hazards of this substandard structure, Sunday services were frequently disrupted by the noise of passing trains. The new site (below). Many of the bricks used to construct this new church were taken from the old structure. (Photos courtesy Douglas Urban Renewal.)

years before. Interior remodeling had occurred in 1953 following a fire, and the frame walls were covered with sheetrock siding at that time. The foundation was weak and the roof supports in dangerous condition; in fact, the entire roof was sunken badly and leaked. The appraised value of the church itself was only $5,600, and the value of the site for all three buildings was only $1,800. When contrasted with the surrounding neighborhood, the parsonage was in relatively good condition.

The project site was slated to be redeveloped for industrial use, and thus all the homes in the area, in addition to Gaines Chapel, were to be razed. The key problem of relocation centered around moving the church to an area that could conveniently serve the same congregation. However, this had to be done at a cost within the means of the members of the church.

Sometime before urban renewal, the congregation of the church anticipated the need to move and purchased a small lot in an area to which they estimated a large portion of their present congregation would eventually move. This foresight proved valuable except for the fact that their site was much too small (about half the size required) for both a church and parsonage.

The congregation explained their problem to the LPA, a one-man operation, and asked for his help. The site they had purchased was also located in an urban renewal project area, the second to be designated in the city, but was not acquired by the LPA with the rest of the properties in the project area. Land adjacent to the church's site was purchased by the LPA and resold to the church so that the congregation would have a total building site at least 150-feet wide and 250-feet deep. The congregation then used the proceeds from the sale of their condemned property both to satisfy a mortgage on this property and to make a down-payment on the construction of the new church.

The parsonage, which was in the best physical condition of the three buildings owned by the congregation, was repurchased from the LPA by the church at a fraction of its acquisition price and moved to the new site. It was then renovated for use again as a parsonage. The old church was also purchased from the LPA so that the bricks and other usable materials from the structure could be used to build the new church. The actual construction work on the new church was done by members of the congregation. With the help of the LPA, the assistance of a retired building contractor was also obtained. The contractor was paid a nominal fee only to coordinate the efforts of willing professional builders and laborers from the local area who participated.

When completed, the congregation had a new modern church and a renovated parish house in a redeveloped and growing area of town. Financially, the church was now in slightly more debt than before (approximately $4,000), but the higher value of the property far exceeds this additional debt.

The cooperative effort among the church congregation, the LPA, and other willing members of the community inspired many of the other small Negro congregations of churches in the city to improve their facilities. In this case, the "demonstration effect" was a highly significant factor.

Gaskin Avenue Shopping Center

Relocation efforts in Douglas have involved businesses with gross revenues of less then $3,000 per year. This is clearly not the typical small business, but it does demonstrate the feasibility of relocating even the smallest business firm.

One of the leaders of the Gaskin Avenue Shopping Center development was the owner of Richardson Grocers. With the help of the LPA, this grocer obtained an exclusion from the urban renewal acquisition plan for his property. In addition, he purchased adjacent property from the LPA for development purposes. He then constructed a new store on the adjacent property, and avoided any business interruption by moving his inventory from the old store to the new during off-business hours.

Richardson's Grocery was the first of many structures built side-by-side which subsequently formed the Gaskin Avenue Shopping Center. The Richardson structure served as the anchor of this project and encouraged others to relocate on this site.

One such example is King's Barber Shop which relocated from another project area to this site long before demolition in the other project actually began. He was able to change from tenant to owner status with this relocation by constructing a small, twenty- by forty-foot structure. Local financing made this possible, and his mortgage payment is less than $50 per month. His business has increased from two to three barber chairs and he additionally furnished space for another relocatee — Jackson Cab — as well as utilizing some of the space in his structure for a fish-market operation.

Clearly, these efforts are modest in scope and size. However, they do illustrate the fact that even very small, marginal businesses serving highly localized markets can be successfully relocated. With the increased economic viability of the area, these businesses should continue to increase in volume and profit.

Greensboro, North Carolina

The medium-sized city of Greensboro (population 135,000) has embarked on an intensive program of redevelopment which has received substantial encouragement from the local community. This LPA had five major urban renewal projects in execution in 1967. A significant portion of their activity was centered in a revitalization program for the downtown area.

The CBD of Greensboro had faced net losses of businesses during the previous fifteen years and had, since 1958, worked actively to reverse this movement. Of particular interest is the organization titled DARE (Downtown Area Renewal Effort) which was created to assist in this effort and to provide coordination among the many public and private groups and agencies working to this common end. This organization's activities have direct implications for business relocation.

Operation DARE was the brainchild of the Redevelopment Commission of Greensboro. It is essentially a coordinating organization for five major citizens'

committees. They serve as advisory groups to the redevelopment commission
and provide liaison between the redevelopment staff and businesses and private
citizens in the community. The committees organized under this DARE program
are:

1. **Public Information Committee.** This committee is composed of the Jaycees,
the chamber of commerce, and other qualified groups and individuals. They
sponsor a newsletter entitled *Your Downtown.* This committee also provides the
stimulus for other publicity about urban renewal efforts.

2. **Business Impact Committee.** Representatives from the merchants' associations, the chamber of commerce, business and professional womens' clubs and
other groups and individuals concerned with the economic future of the
downtown area serve on this committee. They have explored the feasibility of
various schemes to improve downtown shopping. This committee also formed a
downtown development association, whose function it was to attract industry to
the downtown area.

3. **Design Committee.** This committee is composed of professional engineers,
architects, ladies' garden clubs, and other groups and individuals concerned with
the aesthetics of the downtown area. It explores various alternative approaches
to physical design and ways of adding eye-appeal to existing structures. One
project undertaken by this committee was the upgrading of business signs in the
downtown area.

4. **Legal Aspects Committee.** Representatives of the local bar association,
women's auxiliary of the bar association, and counsel from several large
businesses in the area take part in this group. They explore legal problems
associated with carrying out downtown urban renewal and new methods of
accomplishing downtown improvement through legislation or administration.

5.   **Private and Public Investment Committee.** Representatives of local banks,
savings and loan associations, and other types of financial institutions form this
committee. The central concern of this committee is to investigate and
coordinate various ways to obtain financing for downtown redevelopment.

These various committees provide both meaningful coordination of the
overall renewal activities and dissemination of information to the public
concerning these efforts. They also take maximum advantage of local talent and
engage the self-interests of groups and individuals in the overall efforts of the
redevelopment commission. Members of the redevelopment staff feel that this
committee organization under DARE has been quite successful in obtaining
city-wide cooperation and support for urban renewal. Since the projects have
involved downtown businesses, these committees have been helpful in business
relocation activities as well.

The organization of the redevelopment commission provides for a separate
function entitled "Business Relocation Advisors." It separates business relocation from family relocation. At least one full-time staff member is working on
business relocation efforts at all times. In addition, the director of project
operations also aids in business relocation problems when necessary. By 1967,
the staff had handled the relocation of approximately 100 businesses or
non-profit organizations.

In their relocation activities, the staff of the Greensboro LPA has been involved in the relocation of some seven churches. The LPA has provided, in most cases, relocation sites in redevelopment project areas that were ideally suited for the respective churches. Although no special provisions are made for non-profit organizations, and they are not eligible for the SBDP, the redevelopment agency has attempted to acquire the properties and time the acquisitions to provide churches with ample opportunity to select an appropriate site and construct their new churches prior to being displaced. By working closely with the churches and their diocese, and further by encouraging the churches to locate near public housing areas which contain a large portion of their congregations, the LPA has achieved generally successful results in its treatment of churches.

Business relocations have involved a full range of services, including direct help in planning the move, subsequent layout of the new structure, and supervision in the moving process. The relocation staff provides service seven days a week and often during the evening in order to meet the particular problems of businessmen. One enlightening point made by the relocation staff was that businessmen seldom can find time to give full attention to relocation during the day while the business is in operation. The prevalence of this situation was borne out in subsequent interviews with displacees who indicated that on many occasions they had called the relocation staff during the evening and on holidays with perplexing problems.

A final point of interest concerning the general program of business relocation conducted in Greensboro is the publication of a working manual on relocation published recently by this LPA. This *Relocation Manual* is a 56-page compendium of information, forms, and general advice concerning what the displacee must know and do about moving and obtaining appropriate relocation payments. This comprehensive document is an invaluable aid to both the staff and displacees.

Church Relocations

Two churches, the Saint Phillip's A.M.E. Church and the Bethel A.M.E. Church, represent relocations that have been particularly successful. Each improved both its physical structure and its location.

Saint Phillip's Church is a small congregation which was displaced from one urban renewal project area and was provided space in another project area. A considerable amount of public housing was constructed near the new location which housed a significant portion of the congregation. Without careful coordination and planning, relocation might not have been possible. Churches face special problems in finding suitable sites. They not only require the proper approval, but also must locate near their respective congregations. This is particularly true when most of the congregation is in the low-income bracket without means of suitable transportation.

Bethel A.M.E. Church is a case in which the church was displaced from its site in a renewal project area and relocated within the same project area. Here again, the provision of an appropriate site was the key issue. Also, coordinating the demolition and site preparation to provide a continuity of operation for the church was necessary. In both of these cases, the LPA provided every assistance possible within existing regulations.

The relocation of churches presents special problems to the relocation staff. There are only limited areas in which help may be provided and the staff must take fullest advantage of these devices. The areas in which the LPA may be most effective and helpful in church relocations are: (1) a fair and equitable purchase price with particular concern for direct property losses in removable fixtures of the church, (2) help in locating or providing suitable relocation sites for the construction of new church facilities, and (3) allowing the church adequate time to construct new facilities and vacate its present facilities. These three factors are critical because they represent the effective range of assistance that can be provided by the LPA staff.

H & C Catering Company

Of all the relocation efforts in Greensboro, this case has received more publicity than all the others combined. This publicity in itself demonstrates the LPA's effectiveness in publicizing the services it can provide and the successes it has achieved in business relocation.

This firm operated from several small and deteriorating buildings in a location that presented significant problems of traffic congestion. Its storage and expansion potential was extremely limited. As a tenant, the owner of the business saw little future in attempting to upgrade the property significantly. The layout of the building complex was extremely inefficient. More importantly, it had a run-down appearance that could hardly be expected to attract customers wishing to discuss the catering of parties, picnics or other similar affairs.

H & C Catering began operations in 1962. It had been at the location from which it was displaced for only two years. The principal operation was conducted from several small trucks which delivered sandwiches and coffee to factory workers in and around Greensboro. Although the owner had hoped to expand into other types of catering activities, his old location effectively precluded this expansion. While the potential demand for both the delivery lunches and general catering services was great, the proprietor faced limitations at the old location and found difficulties in resolving this problem before urban renewal was initiated.

The owner of this firm was notified by the LPA's relocation staff of the impending project and the implications to his business through a personal visit. The initial contact of the redevelopment staff member was to inform the owner

H & C Catering Co. prior to relocation (above). The physical structure sharply limited the market potential of this catering firm. After relocation (below), the business firm, with the aid of a substantial SBA loan, was able both to enlarge facilities and to upgrade the catering services offered. (Photos courtesy Greensboro Redevelopment Commission.)

that he was there as the firm's "vice president of relocation." That is, the relocation staff was ready to provide the necessary time and services to help the business relocate.

The businessman first informed the relocation staff of his limited background and experience in coping with relocation problems, and his desire to take full advantage of any help they might provide. Since the business had already acquired a site that was suitable for relocation and construction of a new building, one of the first problems was to obtain adequate financing not only to complete the new structure but also to acquire new equipment and provide additional working capital. Although the businessman had established a good credit reputation among lending institutions in the city, his experience in business was limited and he had been unable to obtain financial commitments from any institution he had approached. The relocation staff member made arrangements for a meeting with an SBA loan officer. They also helped the businessman prepare financial statements so that the amount of funds required could be identified. The staff further assisted the proprietor in completing the application for an SBA loan. A staff member accompanied the businessman on periodic visits to Charlotte to negotiate with SBA. After considerable negotiations and planning, a loan for $85,000 was granted.

The SBA loan made it possible to increase the size of the business substantially. By SBA policy regulations, an increase in space occupied was limited to 33 per cent. However, redevelopment staff members were especially ingenious in computing the total area occupied in the old location to justify the significantly larger structure. The staff included the square-footage of the owner's automobile which was used for storage for the business, the basement of a house which was likewise used for storage, and a room in the bookkeeper's home which was also used to maintain the accounting ledgers of the firm. This was an exceptional effort by the LPA staff, but one in which the regional SBA office concurred because of the unusually scattered character of this specific business enterprise.

A significant amount of planning help was provided this businessman in both the construction of the new building and the selection of equipment. The LPA staff suggested that the new building include a small space for a restaurant to serve a growing demand from a nearby housing development designed for the elderly. Also, they advised the owner to build considerably more storage space than he had originally planned so that he could utilize further economies by buying in carload lots. Administrative offices were also included so that the business could move more heavily into the catering business. A specific example of the type of help given this businessman was a comparative cost study performed by a member of the redevelopment staff. The business consumed a large quantity of ice used in the preparation and maintenance of food. A comparative study was conducted on the feasibility of purchasing a large ice machine as opposed to purchasing the ice as was done in the past. On the basis of the recommendations by the relocation staff, the new machine was purchased and has resulted in significant cost savings.

Robert Cole, Inc., old location (above).   Inadequate facilities made it necessary to produce and store large signs on the roof and in other areas exposed to the elements. New location (below). Large sliding doors provide access to an ample work and storage area entirely under cover. (Photos courtesy Greensboro Redevelopment Commission.)

Following relocation, the change in the character of the business as well as the physical structure was dramatic. The physical plant includes over 9,000 square feet of space and incorporates loading docks for the trucks as well as parking spaces for employees and customers. The SBA loan, in conjunction with the SBDP and direct property-loss payments, enabled the businessman to purchase new equipment that greatly enhanced the quality of food prepared as well as the efficiency of production. After only a few months at the new location, business volume had increased by some 20 per cent. The firm also began to attract customers requiring higher quality catering services.

Robert Cole, Inc.

This case involved substantial upgrading of a sign-making firm. In addition to assistance in planning the move and the layout of the new business structure, the LPA staff worked to obtain every possible benefit for the business displacee.

The Cole firm makes various types of advertising signs and promotional devices that range in size from small notices to signboards 35-feet high. When the firm was initially contacted concerning its displacement and subsequent relocation, the relocation staff found that the owner had already purchased a site for relocation. The basic problems revolved around planning for the timing and physical details of the move, financing the new structure and equipment, and obtaining assistance in making claims for moving expense reimbursement and other benefits available under law.

Although the old location had become less desirable from a functional standpoint and the business owner was pleased to have the opportunity to relocate, displacement posed several problems for him. He had to decide what type of structure to build, where to place equipment, how to lay out the processing plant, and how to resolve other technical issues to operate the business at the new site. A relocation staff member aided the businessman in developing a model of the new plant and in designing alternative layouts to explore the most efficient method of operation. This planning aid also helped in identifying equipment needs and in estimating the total amount of financing required for the move. The LPA then assisted the businessman in his initial contacts with SBA and in the subsequent preparation of necessary financial statements and cost estimates. Another critical phase of the financing involved the acquisition of the old business property by the LPA. This was timed so that the business could receive the money as soon as possible to apply the proceeds toward construction of the new building.

A loan for $82,000 was authorized by SBA. The firm has continued its plans for further expansion through the purchase of new equipment. The new plant has a much more efficient layout and considerably larger storage space. This has enabled the firm to smooth out some of the seasonal variations in business that were caused by the necessity of working outside in the elements, because space under cover formerly was not large enough to meet production requirements. In addition, ample parking space is available adjacent to the building. The new location provides easy access to the large regional market served by the firm.

An interesting sidelight of this case which demonstrates the services provided by the relocation staff involves documentation to obtain the SBDP. The firm was a corporation and thus fell under the general criteria relating to maximum salaries of major stockholders. Its financial statements could have precluded payment of the SBDP without significant assistance from the LPA staff in developing the necessary financial documentation to establish its eligibility. The LPA pursued the point that the last year's operations prior to displacement were not representative of earlier years and should be adjusted according to previous earnings. This interpretation was accepted by HUD and the owners of this business firm received the SBDP.

Louisville, Kentucky

This city of over 400,000 population had six major urban renewal projects in progress in 1967, plus several others in the planning stage. The former six projects had resulted in the displacement of over 1,000 businesses. A major portion of the project acreage is located in downtown Louisville, so that business relocation is a major concern to this LPA. To cope with this workload, the Urban Renewal and Community Development Agency of Louisville has four full-time business relocation specialists in addition to the director of relocation to provide assistance and counsel to displaced businesses.

The business relocation staff in Louisville has considerable business experience and skills. This LPA separates family and business relocation activities completely because of fundamental differences in the skills required in the two types of relocation. The consulting staff are all relatively mature and experienced businessmen with a background of not only dealing with the public but dealing with businessmen and their special problems as well.

The Louisville LPA has been faced with the problem of moving several very large and technically complex businesses. As a result the relocation staff has frequently had to obtain and review moving bids for such companies. Because technical considerations are involved in these bids, the LPA has felt the need to call in consultants to provide advice and assistance in the bid evaluation process. Moreover, by using consultants on the initial group of large moves, relocation staff members developed sufficient expertise in the technical aspects of bid review to permit them to screen these bids themselves. In addition, they have made many contacts within the moving industry and have been able to aid businesses in contacting those movers with the appropriate skills to handle the highly technical phases of heavy industrial moves.

However, fixture appraisals still require the services of a highly qualified specialist in this field. The agency considers this to be a key area of concern. The fixture appraisal and the identification of removables is basic to the development of a plan for moving and for subsequent layout at the relocation site. By working with fixture appraisal specialists, the business relocation staff has acquired the experience and background to enable them to offer some counsel to affected businesses.

This relocation staff has also achieved success in the handling of moves in which improvements at the new site are required by local codes. For example, an existing 1½-inch pipe may be substandard under the plumbing code. Upon relocation, the business firm is faced with the added expense of a changeover to 2½-inch pipe, in addition to moving costs and property losses already incurred. Safety standards also require, upon relocation, coverings for certain types of wire and even floor installations of both wire and plumbing in some instances. The relocation staff has assembled a great deal of technical information on these additional costs so that the business may apply for and receive special reimbursement even though such costs represent "improvement."

Louisville has used the "referral system" in dealing with SBA and has developed excellent relations with this agency. SBA financing has been an important ingredient in the effective relocation of businesses in Louisville.

Jefferson Meat Market, Inc.

The displacement of a business firm often results in a significant change in its method and scope of operation. This is particularly well illustrated by the case of Jefferson Meat Market in Louisville. Before urban renewal the business firm combined retail and wholesale meat sales in a retail neighborhood. The site had only on-street parking and offered virtually no opportunity for expansion. The bulk of the business volume came from wholesale sales of processed meats to larger institutions. However, the owner of this business was greatly limited in his efforts to increase this aspect of the business because of space constraints.

In addition, the physical condition of the facility and equipment made it impossible to obtain a United States Department of Agriculture Inspection Certificate so that the firm could engage in the interstate sale of meat products. Various market opportunities were available in other nearby states, but the firm could not take advantage of this potential. Although the business was licensed by the state, some large customers even within the state were concerned about the physical condition and layout of this processing plant. Its largest customer had indicated that unless significant improvements were made in the interior of the plant and in much of the sensitive refrigeration and processing equipment, it could no longer make purchases of meat from Jefferson. Thus, the owner faced not only an inability to sell outside the state but also a significant curtailment of sales within Kentucky.

The business had grown on a piecemeal basis, with small additions to capacity and equipment being made on an irregular basis. The facility contained a wide variety of refrigeration equipment that represented many different vintages. This arrangement entailed a complex and inefficient electrical system that required an

Jefferson Meat Market (above) in its downtown location prior to displacement. Its present location (below) has the advantages of a modern, efficient structure coupled with access to major highways. (Photos courtesy Louisville Urban Renewal and Community development Agency.)

average maintenance cost of over $300 per month over and above the cost of utilities. Although improvements could be made at the old location, the owner hesitated to do so because he was only a lessee. The condition of the building did not seem to merit either such an investment or a longer-term lease. The building was 85 years old. Since most of the necessary improvements would involve irremovable fixtures, the businessman did not deem it feasible to invest additional sums at the same location. Sale was not possible because of the age and condition of the equipment, and because much of the equipment could not be successfully removed without damage. Most of the refrigeration equipment was not movable, and its market value was much lower that its in-place value.

Another element which complicated the overall problem facing this business was its inability to obtain adequate financing. Because of the condition of the building he rented and the dim prospects of obtaining federal licensing, the financing of more modern and improved equipment had not been possible.

With the advent of urban renewal, the relocation director of the LPA and his staff had many contacts with the firm. Its general relocation problems were identified and steps were taken to provide not only a suitable relocation site but adequate financing. The LPA made arrangements for the owner of the business to purchase a site within an urban renewal area that was well situated to serve the larger wholesale segment of the firm's market. The new location had excellent truck access to major routes within and outside the city and offered ample expansion space for the future. The owner was able to obtain over 25,000 square feet of open space for parking and/or future expansion. He constructed a building of 7,000 square feet — nearly 2,000 square feet larger than the building he previously occupied.

Financing was a major issue in this move. Initially the firm and the LPA met resistance from SBA in obtaining funds to construct the new building and purchase necessary equipment. Under policy regulations that existed at the time, tenants displaced by urban renewal had little opportunity to obtain financing from SBA for new construction. The relocation staff spent a great deal of time discussing this problem with the regional office of SBA. Finally, a formal request for waiver was submitted, to enable Jefferson Meat Market to obtain a loan sufficient to purchase a new building and necessary new equipment. The LPA staff, in conjunction with SBA representatives, then advised and counseled the claimant regarding the necessary financial statements and documentation for the loan application. Because of the special complications of this loan, processing took considerable time. The LPA cooperated thoroughly by deferring demolition of the structure in the old location, even though this meant allowing the business to remain well beyond the planned displacement and demolition date.

Once an SBA loan of approximately $245,000 was approved, the relocation staff helped in planning both the move and new construction. Specifically, the staff counselors advised the business owner to install built-in sewer connections during initial construction in anticipation of a new sewer system that was planned in the urban renewal area. By doing this, the business owner will considerably reduce future construction costs and avoid work interruption that would have been necessitated by renovations required to install identical sewer connections later. The owner expressed much gratitude for this advice, as it incorporated significant potential savings.

Moving this business involved a good deal of technical planning. A significant portion of the actual move was accomplished by the business firm itself. For example, state law required that the transfer of the meat in inventory had to be accomplished under very precise temperature controls; the business owner-manager was required to ride in each truck to ensure that the temperature was maintained within legal limits.

Because the firm was not displaced until after construction of the new structure was completed, little business interruption was experienced. Actually, the move was made in phases over several weekends to avoid any significant interruption, and the owner operated out of both locations during this period until the move was completed. This procedure likewise required the full cooperation of the LPA. Significant moving costs were incurred because of the size and complexity of the move, and the owner received just under the maximum $25,000 as reimbursement for his moving expenses.

The new structure is both quite attractive and functionally more efficient than the old structure, which was designed for use as a retail outlet. The new building was designed specifically to meet the requirements of the firm and to meet the licensing stipulations of both the state and federal agencies. New equipment was also installed with the specific purpose of meeting federal licensing requirements. Shortly after occupancy, the business received the federal license. The high maintenance costs of the dated equipment in the old location have been eliminated. Also, the plant now has complete docking facilities as well as off-street parking spaces for customers and employees. The physical handling of inventory has been improved dramatically. Sales are up considerably — the owner estimates between 25 and 30 per cent — and employment has also increased accordingly.

It was the opinion of the relocation staff at Louisville that this enterprise would have had to close had it not been for urban renewal and the associated relocation of the business.

Joe's Palm Room

This case involved the displacement of a small bar owned by a Negro proprietor. The relocation had several effects which relate not only to the type of business conducted, but to the customers the business serves.

Before being displaced, the owner of Joe's Palm Room was a tenant operating a small bar which catered exclusively to Negroes living in the neighborhood. Displacement presented several problems, not the least of which was transferring the liquor license from one neighborhood location to another. Related to this was the need to obtain the acceptance of neighborhood residents in a new location even if the liquor permit transfer were granted. Finally, the

Joe's Palm Room (above) exemplifies the small neighborhood bar, typically difficult to relocate. At its new location (below). Imaginative architecture was instrumental in achieving neighborhood acceptance of this restaurant and cocktail lounge. (Photos courtesy Louisville Urban Renewal and Community Development Agency.)

business was confronted with the problem of obtaining adequate financing in a community that had been, according to the owner, reluctant to lend to Negroes.

The license transfer was achieved through the persistence of both the displaced businessman and the relocation staff members, who met together with the appropriate licensing agency and explained the particular problem raised by urban renewal displacement. In addition, redevelopment staff members met with neighborhood groups, church congregations, and other interested parties who protested the location of a restaurant-bar in their neighborhood. Two factors accounted for their success in overcoming neighborhood resistance: the backing of relocation staff members, and the physical appearance of the planned restaurant-bar. On the latter point, careful consideration was given its design so that the structure would enhance rather than detract from the neighborhood. It presents the general appearance of a professional office building rather than that of a bar or restaurant. This was an important feature in "selling" this relocation to local residents.

In order to obtain adequate financing, the relocation staff advised the businessman to meet with SBA staff members to discuss loan possibilities. With the help and encouragement of the relocation staff as well as SBA loan officers, the businessman was able to obtain a loan of approximately $120,000. This financing made possible expansion into both food service and liquor sales, with approximately twice the square-footage in the new structure as in the old.

As a result of this relocation, a Negro businessman, who was a tenant when displaced, is now the owner of a much larger restaurant-bar facility that adds to the neighborhood in which it is located. The clientele is now integrated and the owner estimates a 30 per cent increase in revenues over his highest volume year at the old location. The new site provides off-street parking space — a critical factor for such an operation — whereas the old location had only on-street parking. Finally, the expanded business establishment employs nearly four times as many persons as at the old location.

Preston Street Shoe Mart

This case is an illustration of the grouping of a small number of independent businesses within a single, common-wall shopping center for purposes of relocation. Specifically, the Preston Street Shoe Mart, composed of four stores, is a condominium in which three of the four stores are owned by displacees who previously operated businesses in the same general area.

Because of the long-standing and widely known tradition of "bargain" shoe offerings in the Preston Street area, many of the small shoe store owners felt it imperative for them to remain in the same general area after redevelopment. With the cooperation and encouragement of the Urban Renewal Agency of Louisville, a site in the urban renewal project area was purchased by three displacees plus a fourth member who was a private developer. The four businesses formed a corporation with which to purchase the land from the LPA. The corporation then sold, in fee simple, four parcels of land to each of the four corporate owners. The corporation still exists to maintain the common areas of the development.

The timing of this project is one of the key areas in which the LPA made a significant contribution. The construction of this condominium was planned so that the first of the four stores could be completed and occupied prior to the completion of the remaining portions of the structure. The LPA recognized the timing considerations of the other businesses and left their building standing until the new stores were constructed. No business interruption resulted in this instance because of planned timing and the fact that the move could be carried out after business hours. Once the first store was completed and the old store located directly adjacent was vacated, the old building was demolished to make way for the completion of the remaining connecting structures.

The new location now provides, in addition to more modern surroundings and efficient layout, off-street parking for approximately forty cars. According to one owner-manager, sales are up 10 per cent over the previous location and he is pleased with the outcome of the move.

Westerfield-Bonte Company

This move involved not only very high costs but highly technical personnel. Much coordination and cooperation were required between the LPA and the business firm.

The firm is a specialty printer for the legal profession. The nature of the operation requires close contact with their customers on a day-to-day basis. It is necessary for copy to be delivered for approval and returned immediately because of the statutory deadlines for the printing of briefs and other legal documents. It was therefore critical that the business remain within easy access to the courthouse and to the many lawyers with offices in the CBD. After an intensive search of the nearby area, a commercial structure was identified that generally met the needs of the business firm, except that it was not within easy walking distance from the courthouse and municipal complex. The owners, while pleased with the larger size (approximately 50 per cent more space), were concerned about the implications of the new location to their business and the additional costs associated with the need for frequent delivery service by truck to coordinate the printing process.

At the same time, several advantages were obtained with the new structure. Loading docks were now available where they had not been in the old location. There is also employee and customer off-street parking to compensate in part for the necessity of some customers to travel to the printing plant by auto. At the time of the interview, the business owners had observed no significant change in their sales volume, but did note a slight (4 per cent) increase in costs because of the increased transportation expenses.

The move involved the transfer of heavy but delicate machinery requiring riggers and other experts in the handling and installation of such machinery. A critical consideration in the move was the fact that no interruption of the business could be tolerated. Legal briefs must be out on a specific date or the client loses the opportunity to appeal; only a short time is given to publish such briefs. The firm is under constant time pressure and is subject to lawsuit if these deadlines are not met. In order to solve this special problem, the firm operated in both locations for some time so that it could adhere to its time commitments. The LPA aided the firm in identifying potential movers and in providing the necessary substantiation for the reimbursement of moving costs. The cost of the move exceeded the $25,000 maximum (the total moving cost for this firm was $30,500) and the LPA was also able to obtain the city's participation in the amount which exceeded this maximum.

Mobile, Alabama

Mobile, Alabama, with a population of 200,000, has a relatively limited urban renewal program. In 1967, the LPA had two projects in execution which had displaced approximately 185 business firms.

One of the major factors influencing the selection of Mobile for inclusion in this study is its effort to apply the SBA lease guarantee program to assist in the relocation of small, minority-group-owned businesses. In addition, the relocation of a funeral home presented special demands which required the imaginative use of both project land and financing techniques to accommodate a "problem" displacee.

Broad-Beauregard Plaza

This case is an exception to the general rule applied in this study that only completed relocation efforts should be included. Because of the potential importance and timeliness of lease guarantee insurance (whether issued by the Small Business Administration or a private insuror), this case is included to illustrate the potential effectiveness of this relatively new tool of relocation. At the time of this writing, the relocation effort was still under way, with every indication of a successful, if delayed, completion.

The lease guarantee program embodies a rather simple concept, even if its application becomes rather complex. It simply provides guarantees for the rental payments of a business over a specified period of time. The instrument is by no means new; large, well-established firms have used this device for many years. The policy itself serves various purposes. It is a means by which a developer or lessor of a shopping center (or any other rental commercial or industrial space) may minimize his risks and also obtain capital for his venture. It does so by covering the mortgagor's debt service, thereby making the loan more attractive to an institutional lender. More importantly, the lease guarantee insurance policy is designed to enable small businesses (including those displaced by urban renewal) to compete for shopping center space or any other location on the same basis as larger firms with more financial resources and better credit ratings. This latter application of lease guarantees has the potential to expand significantly the effective availability of alternative relocation sites to displacees. In addition, the lessee may be able to negotiate for much more favorable lease conditions.

Every effort is made to encourage private insurors to participate in this program. In the Mobile case, an insurance company has entered into a contractual agreement with SBA to the effect that the private company will be the primary insuror and that SBA will reinsure up to 80 per cent of losses over a stipulated amount.

Under the plans established in 1967, approximately seven displacees from urban renewal projects in Mobile will relocate as lease-guaranteed tenants in Broad-Beauregard Plaza, a racially-integrated shopping center. The displacees are all Negro operators of small retail businesses. Prior to this arrangement, these businesses were unable to find suitable relocation sites. The lease guarantee commitments from the private insurance company and SBA will provide the displacees with the necessary leverage through reduced risks to the lessor to obtain the needed and desirable space. The commitments have also enabled the developer to obtain the financing required.

The LPA in Mobile has encouraged this financial arrangement. It has also offered complete cooperation by staging demolition, and providing land in the project area for construction of the plaza. As additional experience is gained with the lease guarantee, it should prove an invaluable asset to LPA's in locating and promoting appropriate sites for small business displacees. Likewise, this device can provide an assist to mortgage financing of developments designed to provide relocation sites.

Hodge Funeral Chapel

The relocation of the Hodge Funeral Chapel is a case in which a Negro entrepreneur faced special problems of relocation because of site restrictions and neighborhood objections to commercial re-zoning. In addition, the owner had the common problem of acquiring sufficient funds to finance the construction and equipping of a new business establishment. As a sidelight, it is interesting to note that the owner-operator of this funeral home is also one of the principal promoters and developers of the Broad-Beauregard Plaza.

The owner of this funeral home met with great difficulty in obtaining a suitable site for relocation. In initial attempts, the owner found several locations that were suitable from a commercial standpoint and acquired options on these sites. However, he was unable to exercise any of these options because he could not obtain the necessary zoning variances. These denials were based on objections from the residential neighbors of the proposed locations. Although the businessman suspected that his race was a deterring influence, he believes that the most serious difficulty stemmed from a general reaction against having a funeral home as a neighbor.

After obtaining and subsequently losing several options in this fashion, the owner was able to acquire a four-acre parcel in the Broad-Beauregard Street Urban Renewal Project from the LPA. This site was well adapted to the construction of a funeral home.

Finding an appropriate location was only part of the relocation problem, however. Another critical issue was obtaining adequate financing. The venture involved a substantial improvement over the structure from which the firm was displaced and called for a considerable investment — over $200,000. Although the owner was able to raise some needed capital by selling two subdivided parcels of his newly acquired land to service station chains, more money was required.

The relocation staff of Mobile referred this funeral home operator to the local SBA office to explore his eligibility for a Displaced Business Loan. The owner was given substantial help in the preparation of the loan application. A loan was approved by SBA for $70,000, to be used for working capital, equipment purchases, and the construction of a new funeral home building. The owner, after further negotiation, was able to obtain a somewhat larger loan from a private insurance company to aid him further in financing this project. Interestingly, the insurance company that helped him finance the new structure maintained a small branch office in the Hodge Funeral Chapel building at its original location. It likewise became a tenant in the new structure.

The combined help of the redevelopment staff both in providing a relocation site and in arranging the SBA and private loans enabled this businessman to upgrade and enlarge his business substantially. A dramatic change has occurred in his revenues. During the first year at the new site, they were nearly double those at the old location. The appearance of the neighborhood has also been enhanced by the construction of this funeral home.

Nashville, Tennessee

In 1967, the city of Nashville, Tennessee had three major urban renewal projects in execution and two in the planning stage. The area under metropolitan government includes a population of nearly 250,000 people. The urban renewal program involved a significant portion of the CBD and surrounding commercial area, and had displaced over 600 businesses. Many very small businesses as well as very large manufacturing firms are included in this total.

The business relocation staff of only two full-time men has had to cope with both of these extremes. Their handling of "mom and pop" stores demonstrates the importance the staff places on the smaller type of relocation effort. The staff also emphasized the use of "temporary relocation sites" in the relocation process, together with dual moving expense reimbursements in conjunction with these temporary relocations.

Acme Cash Market

This business, approaching its twentieth year of operation at the time of the move, is truly representative of the "mom and pop" type store. The owners of this convenience market occupied a small corner building in an area that was rapidly deteriorating. This one-room building, containing 1,000 square feet on a single floor, had no off-street parking. In addition to the decline in physical condition of the neighborhood, the development of several public housing projects elsewhere in the city had resulted in the loss of a large portion of the former local customers of this market. In addition, a grammar school expansion and park development had further displaced a number of the neighborhood families.

When the owners of this business were initially contacted, the relocation staff member found that both husband and wife were in their middle sixties. The husband was already receiving social security payments. This factor, plus the marginal status of the business in terms of gross sales and profits, caused some hesitation over encouraging the owners to relocate. However, the owners were in relatively good health and they felt that some additional income, even the small amount from the grocery operation, was needed. After some searching, a grocery operation in another part of town was found whose current owner wished to sell his business and inventory and transfer the lease. An agreement to purchase was made and a three-year lease with a three-year option was obtained by the displacees at precisely the same rent they paid in their old location.

This business was eligible for a Small Business Displacement Payment. In fact, this payment was required to assemble the necessary capital with which to purchase the new grocery operation. The seller had made it clear that the business could not be turned over until full payment was made — in cash. This was possible only through the efforts of the LPA. In order to bring about this relocation, the housing agency staff had all the necessary documentation prepared in advance and drew a check for the SBDP. A staff member carrying the check met the relocatees at the new grocery location when the moving van arrived. Since regulations prohibit payment of the SBDP until after the business has physically moved, the check passed from hand to hand as the transferred equipment was unloaded. This ensured compliance with regulations and yet facilitated the move. The relocation staff thus performed a simple but critical function.

The owners of the displaced business also received direct property-loss payments exceeding $2,400 plus minor moving costs. Without this total compensation of nearly $5,000, as well as the help and cooperation of the local redevelopment officials, this move could not have been accomplished. In all probability, the business would have discontinued.

Consumer's Drug Co. was displaced to allow street widening. The temporary location was used so that the business could rebuild on its former site. (Photos courtesy Nashville Housing Authority.)

In their new location, the displacees indicate that grocery sales have risen somewhat. They are quite pleased in their new environment. Because they purchased a going concern, no immediate improvements were required and no significant business interruptions were incurred.

Consumer's Drug Company

This case involves the temporary relocation of a drugstore so that the business could return, after redevelopment, to the identical site from which it was displaced. Also, the relocation staff of the Nashville Housing Authority was able to obtain reimbursement for both the move to the temporary location and the move back to the original (now redeveloped) site.

The owner and manager of Consumer's Drug Company was faced with the problem of relocation when an urban renewal project acquired and demolished his small drugstore. The building he occupied was of relatively low value (less than $15,000 for the two-story structure plus land) and had been standing more than 75 years. Its location directly on a corner with little clearance, as well as the physical condition of the building, placed it on the list of structures to be razed during a street-widening and general redevelopment project.

After advising the LPA that he wished to return to the original site if possible, he received considerable help in facilitating this aim. The relocation staff aided the businessman in finding a nearby building in which to relocate his drugstore on a temporary basis. It was a small warehouse-type structure which he rented under a short-term lease, located just one-half block away from his drugstore. Since he had been in business at the same location for nearly 20 years, the proprietor felt strongly that he had to remain in the same vicinity in order to retain the clientele that he had established over his many years in business.

Because of the nearness of the temporary relocation site, the move was made with very little business interruption. Redevelopment of the project area, insofar as it affected the drugstore operation, was completed in less than two years. During this time, the drugstore operation continued with very little effect on the business. Once site preparation was completed, the druggist constructed a building which provided nearly 70 per cent more usable square-footage than in his old store. In addition, the new building offers off-street parking and a much improved general appearance.

A side issue of this move was the fact that a barber who had rented space in the old drugstore structure also moved on a temporary basis and returned as a lessee of the druggist after redevelopment. Thus, both businesses were effectively relocated in this effort.

In his new structure, the owner is enjoying significantly improved sales. He was very pleased with the cooperation and help that he received from the relocation staff of the LPA. In addition, he subsequently completed the upper story of his new pharmacy building to provide rental office space for a doctor.

Economy Type Service

Economy Type Service, a small typesetting firm, was a tenant in an area slated for urban renewal. After being informed that he would be displaced from this project area, the businessman sought to find a new location for his business. After consultation with the relocation staff of Nashville, he purchased land in another area of town so that he might build a small plant specially suited to his needs. Subsequent discussions with the LPA revealed that the newly purchased property would be partially taken because of street widening in the area. After further negotiation, additional width was provided from adjacent city-owned land in exchange for the depth taken from the owner of this business. Without this coordinative effort by the LPA and other city agencies, this relocation could not have materialized or resulted in the much larger and improved plant that was constructed.

At his new location, the owner of this typesetting firm has been able not only to move from tenant to owner status, but also to carry out long-run expansion plans that were impossible at his old location. His revenues have increased by more than 40 per cent at the new location, and he no longer has to contend with the problems of congestion and lack of parking space that he faced at his old site.

Shannon Antiques

This case not only illustrates the successful handling of a very difficult business relocation, but it also shows the extent of service and the type of effort that may be required to accomplish some business relocations. It further identifies a problem that is not uncommon among the very small business concerns — inadequate financial records.

Shannon Antiques was a tenant that had been in the project area only two years prior to its declaration. The proprietor operated a small antique refinishing shop while his wife, in the same building, sold fishing bait. The building that he occupied was over 60 years old and was in substandard physical condition. Although considered totally disabled as the result of injuries incurred in World War II, this businessman found it necessary to supplement his VA pension by operating some form of business enterprise on a limited basis.

When the owner of this small business was initially approached by relocation staff members of Nashville, a basic difficulty was immediately apparent — the owner had no documentary proof that he was in business. He had never maintained any kind of systematic records nor had he even filed income tax statements. Since the VA required an annual statement of income in order to maintain the businessman's pension, redevelopment officials met with VA staff members to utilize their records in developing and substantiating the existence of business records for this firm.

After assembling all of the data available, LPA staff members took the businessman to the local IRS office, explained the situation, and submitted delinquent tax returns for the previous two years so that some official record of his gross sales could be established. By compiling these sales records, average gross sales in excess of the minimum necessary for receipt of the Small Business Displacement Payment were established and application for this payment made.

The SBDP was an essential element in the move; the businessman had little chance of successfully relocating without it. With it, he was able to purchase a property in an area some forty-five miles from Nashville and complete a partially finished building that he acquired on the relocation site. He resumed and in fact expanded his business with these improved facilities. He is now the owner of his business structure rather than a tenant. The bait business which his wife previously operated is much better situated than before and this segment of their business has increased significantly.

As a result of the time-consuming and diligent efforts of the relocation staff, this businessman was able to relocate and continue his modest business with very little interruption. At 68 years of age, he claims to have more refinishing work than he can actually handle. Moreover, he is quite pleased with the independence that his new location has given him. In his words, "relocation provided a new lease on life."

Region IV

Although the Region IV Relocation Branch is concerned with all phases of business relocation, they have focused a great deal of attention on the initial appraisal aspects of commercial property acquisition and relocation. The staff believes strongly that one of the keys to successful commercial relocation is the accurate and comprehensive appraisal of *both* realty and fixtures in planning for a move. With such appraisals, focusing particular attention on irremovable fixtures can eliminate many problems of acquisition and planning.

Because larger business firms have highly technical equipment as well as a wide variety of fixtures that may either be removed and relocated to the new site or acquired as part of the property, it is imperative that a careful and systematic method be established to identify and value these items. This process is critical to help the displaced businessman decide which items he wishes to declare as direct property losses, which items he will remove and relocate to the new site, and which items are to be acquired as a part of the real estate.

Another problem directly related to the initial appraisal of the property is the situation in which the tenant of an acquired property had made extensive improvements. Although the treatment of tenant improvements varies from state to state, it is certainly clear that complete and comprehensive appraisals and identification of the feeholder property and the tenant property (as well as third-party property, should it exist) are necessary for an equitable resolution for either the landlord or the tenant. All too often a tenant learns about the purchase of the property after the appraisal and purchase have been made, without being given the opportunity to identify those improvements upon which he may be able to enforce a claim.

In many instances, the appraiser involved in the initial appraisal is competent to appraise only the realty, and has little knowledge of the specialized fixtures that are incorporated in the structure. In fact, the appraiser may be unaware of the legal definition of a fixture and thus includes (or excludes) fixtures without proper identification and/or valuation.

In an effort to provide more consistent and accurate initial property appraisals, the Region IV office has established suggested formats for acquisition and relocation appraisals. These suggested standard forms are distributed to the various LPA's under its jurisdiction. The staff has also initiated a campaign to make LPA's aware of the provisions pertaining to the movement of fixtures and the moving costs associated with the installation of replacement fixtures.

Another approach employed within this HUD Region and others has been to encourage the use of expert appraisers who specialize in fixture appraisals. Several LPA's have utilized such consultants in business relocation cases, and have often found their fees to be more than offset by the savings realized from their use. These consultants have also been useful in screening competitive moving bids where the movement and installation of equipment is involved. Because of the technical nature of the services performed, this analysis of bids often reveals areas of non-compliance with regulations as well as inconsistencies with respect to standard (normal) costing of such services. Such consultants have also been useful to certain business firms in planning the technical elements of the move because of their basic familiarity with engineering problems.

Chicago, Illinois

Chicago is the nation's second largest city with a population of over 3.5 million; it is also the largest city included in this study. By 1967, the Chicago Department of Urban Renewal had initiated and/or planned nearly 70 urban redevelopment projects, of which 25 were completed. These projects had involved a total of 3,400 acres of land within the city; another 4,000 acres were included in projects in the planning stage.

The staff of the Chicago Department of Urban Renewal is large and involves a complex organizational structure. It is divided into eleven major divisions. Relocation is administered by a separate division which, at the time of this study, was further divided into thirteen separate sections. An organizational change was in process at the time of the visit to Chicago. The relocation division was being structured so that commercial relocations would not only represent a separate section, but would also be divided into a commercial claim review section and an SBA unit.

Functionally, the division was already operating along these organizational lines. Several staff members were specifically responsible for business relocations. The idea of commercial relocation specialists has long been ingrained in the relocation organization. The director of relocation stressed the point that experience had demonstrated that family relocation specialists could generally not handle the special problems of business relocations, especially those that involved the initial organization of business groups and business financing.

There are several distinctive and outstanding features of Chicago's business relocation efforts. For example, most of the nearly 3,000 business displacees have been very small businesses that, based upon the experience in other cities, present some of the most difficult relocation problems. Because of the limited managerial talent which many small business operators possess, the relocation division has taken special steps to emphasize both the training and consulting aspects of relocation, in addition to providing assistance with reimbursement claims. In addition, the relocation division has placed particular emphasis on obtaining SBA financing. The staff has given displacees special help in seeking Displaced Business Loans, other SBA financing, and private loans. Among the many types of assistance offered in Chicago, the following represent the most distinctive and imaginative efforts to assist business displacees.

Small Business Opportunities Corporation. The Chicago Small Business Opportunities Corporation is a not-for-profit corporation that is partially funded through Title IV of the Economic Opportunity Act of 1964. SBOC initiated a relatively new program to aid disadvantaged businessmen in Chicago. It represents a potentially powerful tool for relocation. In addition, SBOC has undertaken a cooperative program to aid businessmen displaced by urban renewal. Although the goals and scope of the program conducted by the SBOC were not specifically designed to aid business displacees, it was the feeling of both the LPA relocation director and the executive director of SBOC that needed business training and consulting could be provided, in part, by an agency such as the SBOC. Of particular significance was the fact that SBOC had been able to combine various talents drawn from the School of Business Administration, University of Chicago, and from several research and consulting organizations, such as the Real Estate Research Corporation, to supply aid, advice and training to disadvantaged businessmen.

Procedurally, SBOC is furnished with a list of displacees from each project by the relocation staff. A letter is then sent to each business firm informing its owner of the various services available to those who wish aid in reestablishing their business firms. If displacees choose to avail themselves of the services, they are then assigned a consultant who is generally a staff member of SBOC. Alternatively, a "volunteer" counselor might be assigned to aid the business on a one-to-one basis. Volunteer counselors are drawn from the business community and generally represent the junior executive ranks of some twenty firms which have agreed to cooperate in this program.

The School of Business Administration, University of Chicago, has provided help in two major ways. First of all, they have furnished graduate students as counselors to supplement the SBOC staff in helping businessmen solve specific problems. Also, through their Industrial Relations Center, they have conducted training courses for cooperating businessmen and the SBOC staff members.

At the time of the interviews, the SBOC program had helped only a few displacees from urban renewal projects; the direction of the SBOC is toward disadvantaged businessmen generally and not simply displacees. On the other hand, the type of training and counseling service offered by SBOC is very often needed by displacees and is probably best provided by a specialized organization.

Group relocations of small businessmen. One of the most significant and innovative contributions Chicago has made in aiding business displacees is the counsel and encouragement it has provided in consolidating the relocation efforts of groups of small businesses. Specifically, one staff member of the Chicago Department of Urban Renewal has been largely responsible for the formation of business groups to acquire and develop relocation sites jointly. The "group" move has an important place in business relocation. It is particularly significant in Chicago since the creation of small business shopping centers was a key element in the overall redevelopment plan. More importantly, these group efforts provided a means that might not otherwise have been available for the displacees to find new locations for their businesses and to obtain the advantages of close association with similar or complementary types of businesses.

Liaison with Small Business Administration. Perhaps the most notable element in the Chicago business relocation program is the success that has been achieved in obtaining both DBL's and regular SBA loans for displaced businessmen. The relocation staff identified financing as a key issue in business relocation early in their program. Since the 1961 Housing Act which authorized Displaced Business Loans, the staff has actively sought ways to familiarize displaced businessmen with their opportunities under the Act, aid the businessman in the preparation of the necessary application forms, and counsel them concerning the necessary capital and other requirements of the DBL. Having become thoroughly familiar with SBA regulations concerning DBL's, the relocation staff has been in a position to brief the loan applicant fully before meeting with SBA loan officers. In this way, the prospective borrower has been prepared to provide complete financial data and pro forma statements on his business operation and its financial requirements, as well as its forecasted ability to generate sufficient cash to repay the loan.

Because of the complexity of the SBA loan program with its specific and continually changing provisions, the help provided by the relocation staff has proved an invaluable aid to businessmen in qualifying for loans. The wide range of clients which have sought and obtained DBL's through the help of the relocation staff in Chicago is best illustrated by the fact that Chicago has obtained one of the largest SBA loans on record — $1,500,000 for the relocation of a privately-owned and operated psychiatric hospital. In contrast, loans as small as $5,000 have also been obtained for displacees.

Bell's Shell Service Station

Mr. Bell, operator of a successful Shell service station located in the Hyde Park-Kenwood Renewal Project, was one of the early recipients of a DBL in Chicago. He was one of the first displacees in Chicago to receive an SBA loan for the purchase of real estate when he had been a tenant at the time he was displaced.

In this case, Mr. Bell was not only given considerable help in obtaining financing, but he was also provided aid in finding and purchasing a new site approximately five blocks from his original location. Mr. Bell was a local civic leader and had been in business for many years. The location from which he was displaced was an excellent one, and the LPA made every effort to provide him with an equally desirable location in the same approximate area. He was given

Bell's Shell Service Station (above) at its old location. The new location (below) offers greater ease of access and an expanded, modern facility. (Photos courtesy Chicago Department of Urban Renewal.)

first priority for a location within a redevelopment area which was next to the Harper Court development, a retail center composed of business displacees.

The relocation staff provided considerable help in arranging the SBA loan. Not only did the DBL involve the purchase of real estate for a displacee who was previously a tenant, but this loan also included the participation of a local bank. Because of the equity requirements established by SBA for this loan, a commitment from a local bank was necessary so that the businessman could obtain the $145,000 he had requested. With his excellent business record and status in the community, Mr. Bell obtained a 20-year commitment from the bank and a 15-year commitment from SBA. This staggered term arrangement provided for a more advantageous cash flow for the business and made the total desired loan possible. In this case, the bank holds a prior lien on the property over SBA.

Although the new station had been in operation only three months at the time of the field survey, the volume of business at the new location was up considerably over that at the former site. Mr. Bell was quite enthusiastic about the treatment he had received from the LPA. He felt that the combination of assistance in obtaining the new site and help in acquiring necessary financing were crucial to the successful relocation of his firm.

Dr. John Givens

The case of Dr. Givens indicates the critical role that financing can play in helping the displacee acquire a suitable relocation structure and site when factors other than individual and/or business credit and collateral are involved.

Dr. Givens is a Negro physician who had a large and growing practice in the Near West Side Project Area. Dr. Givens owned the building he occupied, and rented a portion of this building to other business and professional men. When notified of the impending purchase of his building, Dr. Givens set out to find financing for a new professional building. Although Dr. Givens had established credit with more than one financial institution in Chicago, he was unable to borrow sufficient funds from a private institution because of their aversion to the "West Side." Dr. Givens felt it imperative that he maintain his practice near the residences of the people he served. He remained steadfast in his conviction that a new well-designed professional building would by an asset to the neighborhood in spite of the reluctance of financial institutions to finance such a venture.

When Dr. Givens turned to the relocation staff for help in securing a loan, he was first given information concerning regulatory requirements and basic financial criteria for DBL's. Next he was provided considerable aid and assistance in contacting SBA, in processing the application for a loan, and in developing the various financial data required by SBA. When this physician received the $90,000 SBA loan he had requested, he was in a position to purchase the land and construct a building with combined value of nearly $110,000. This building now serves as an example to the surrounding community of the combined efforts of the LPA and SBA, as well as adding one of the most advanced architectural designs in the area.

Since moving to his new location, Dr. Givens has nothing but praise for the help he received from the LPA. His practice has grown even more rapidly than at the previous location and he is able to serve the same neighborhood in his medical practice.

Jeffro Plaza

The Jeffro Plaza relocation is a case in which the relocation staff was not successful in obtaining SBA financing for a group of business displacees, but then turned to private sources for funds and aided the businessmen throughout the negotiations for these funds. In addition, the relocation staff was instrumental in the formation of the businessmen's group which eventually comprised the Jeffro Development Corporation. Also, the site for the new plaza as well as a temporary relocation site were provided by the Chicago Department of Urban Renewal.

Because of the redevelopment project conducted in conjunction with the University of Illinois campus expansion, many very small wholesale and retail merchants were displaced from locations scattered throughout the West Side area. Most of the affected merchants had not consciously considered either the inherent advantages of being located close to one another or the relationship of their own operations to those of their neighbors. It was apparent to the relocation staff, however, that many advantages could be gained by the formation of a group of merchants to find and build a center in which to relocate.

Several of the wholesale-retail merchants in the area were encouraged to form such a group, but they lacked effective leadership and the motivation to pool some of their resources. As one merchant described it, he had been located next to or near several of the others for many years but felt nothing in common with them. They often spoke, but seldom shared common problems, and almost never considered the possibility of joining in a common venture. Thus, the initial task of the relocation staff was to "sell" the idea of pooling capital in order to provide the best and most potentially successful relocation site. Also, the relocation staff felt that the identification of a leader among the businessmen interested in forming a group was critical.

Many meetings were held with various businessmen located in a three-block area around the University of Illinois campus to inform them of the provisions under which they would be relocated and assisted, and to make preliminary attempts to draw several of the businesses into a corporate group. This effort required many meetings over several months and involved literally hundreds of man-hours of work for the relocation staff. Finally, the decision was made to form the Jeffro Development Corporation with a nucleus of fourteen displaced business firms.

Most of the business firms included in this corporation were family businesses that had been in existence in this same area for half a century. Based upon their history of performances and their longevity, it appeared that the firms would have little problem in attracting the necessary capital to purchase a new site and construct the planned center. However, they found loan funds extremely difficult to obtain because of their relatively small size. They therefore sought help from the relocation staff in obtaining an SBA loan. After lengthy discussions with SBA officials, it was determined that because the new corporation included some members whose buildings had not been purchased by the municipal department of urban renewal, it was not eligible to qualify for SBA financing.

The relocation staff then turned to private lenders in an attempt to obtain funds. After considerable searching and negotiation, a loan of $1.1 million was obtained through a mortgage company and a life insurance company. With these borrowed funds plus the equity investment of the various corporate members, the Jeffro Development Corporation was able to purchase a five and one-half acre site in the Roosevelt-Clinton Industrial Project from the Chicago Department of Urban Renewal. The group paid over $550,000 for this site.

Once financing for the purchase of the land and construction of the buildings in the new center had been arranged, another pressing problem emerged. A temporary relocation was required for the business firms between the time they had to vacate their old premises and the completion of construction of their new building. The relocation staff was instrumental once again in negotiating a lease for the group with the owners of the Central National Bank Building located within the project area. This temporary relocation was significant for at least two reasons. First, it provided the displacees with the necessary space to carry on their business operations during the interim period of nearly a year. Second, and possibly more important in the long run, is the fact that the businessmen had to work together under less than perfect conditions. The temporary relocation site was clearly not designed for retail trade. Its crowded conditions, while uncomfortable and less than entirely efficient, did prompt a spirit of camaraderie that had not existed before. In spite of the temporary and makeshift nature of their bank location, the merchants found that their sales increased from 25 to 50 per cent during their year of waiting.

Once the new center was completed, the fourteen business firms moved in. All have subsequently enjoyed a considerable increase in sales and operating efficiency over their original locations. Although the corporation was unable to obtain SBA financing for its joint facility, eight of the individual businesses were subsequently assisted by the LPA in obtaining SBA loan commitments to purchase new fixtures and equipment, make leasehold improvements, purchase additional inventory, and pay certain non-reimburseable moving expenses.

According to one of the original leaders of the group, nearly every one of the members of the Jeffro Corporation had first tried to relocate individually from their old Maxwell Street area locations. None was able to find a desirable site. It was only after many frustrations that each agreed to consider the possibility of combining efforts for his own self-preservation. Even after the formation of the fourteen-firm group (there are eleven limited partners and three general partners), many individual members were skeptical about the success of the venture in the new location. As a result, several contracted for a conservative amount of space and made a minimum investment in the corporation. In light of the success that nearly all have achieved after the opening of the new center, this conservatism was an unwarranted planning error; many now require additional space.

This relocation produced increased sales and profits for the member firms, as well as an efficient facility which has ample off-street parking and is a definite asset to the neighborhood. It offers many lessons that can be applied in other similar situations. The concept of a "group" move was accepted because of the efforts of the relocation staff. The persistence and imagination of the staff in pursuing private funds after failing to obtain SBA loan commitments to purchase the land and buildings serve as an example of the aid that can be provided businesses in this critical area. In addition, the temporary relocation site required a good deal of imagination in utilizing a facility that would have otherwise remained vacant. Finally, the follow-through provided by the staff in helping to arrange SBA financing for some of the firms after they had relocated illustrates the period of responsibility assumed by the relocation staff.

53rd-Kimbark Plaza

The shopping center at 53rd and Kimbark streets in the Hyde Park-Kenwood Project is an example of a successful relocation of small local business firms displaced from sites within the same project area. In a very real sense, this was a "ground-breaking" venture in that it represented one of the first of such efforts in Chicago as well as in the nation.

In this case, a group of sixteen local retailers and professional men already operating businesses or offices in the project area formed a corporation for the purpose of developing a new shopping center as a relocation site. Here, as in the case of Jeffro Plaza, it was necessary for the relocation staff to provide much of the stimulus to form the organization. At the time of incorporation, condominiums were not legal in Illinois. The group established a merchants' association to manage the center. Each merchant has one vote in the corporation regardless of his representative stock ownership. The corporation is basically a real estate holding company in which each occupant-owner participates on the basis of his occupied square-footage as a percentage of the total square-footage in the center.

The new center occupies a site of approximately two and one-half acres which was purchased from the Chicago Department of Urban Renewal. There is off-street parking in the center for approximately one hundred cars. When the structure was completed, each occupant was provided with space that included central heating, an incinerator, and air conditioning. The owner-"tenants" then installed their own internal improvements, which in some instances were quite extensive.

One of the major contributions and innovations of this effort at the time was the priority given the displaced businesses in obtaining a suitable site for the construction of the new center. This was one of the first instances in which the urban renewal plan contained a specific provision designating an area to be used for the construction of a facility by business displacees. One of the advantages of the occupancy priority in this case was the fact that the actual relocation involved a move of only a short distance. The merchants therefore remained in the same general neighborhood and tended to retain their old customers in the new center.

Because of the small size of the businesses involved, the newly formed corporation faced some difficulty in obtaining mortgage funds. In this instance, as in the case of Jeffro Plaza, a life insurance company provided the financing with a mortgage commitment of approximately $600,000. In addition to providing aid in obtaining financing, the relocation staff also helped the corporation in having plans and specifications drawn up for the construction of the new buildings in the center.

Several of the business firms were successful, with the aid of the relocation staff, in arranging SBA loans. One of these cases involved an elderly couple (approaching retirement age) that was able to obtain a 20-year loan from SBA. Although unusual, this instance of a long-term SBA loan to an elderly couple does demonstrate both the economic soundness of the center development and the effectiveness of the relocation staff in supporting displacee applications for financing.

Another business firm in the 53rd and Kimbark development — a supermarket — received two SBA loans: a DBL and a regular SBA loan. The DBL was made to the supermarket owners to enable them to invest in the new center up to the allowable one-third expansion limit. Because of the need for more square-footage of display and storage space to support a larger volume of sales, the owners felt that they had outgrown SBA. However, with the aid of the relocation staff, they were able to obtain a supplementary SBA loan to finance the remainder of the venture. As a result, they effectively doubled their square-footage after relocation, and their sales volume nearly tripled. Unfortunately, as in the case of some Jeffro Plaza establishments, they could use even more additional space today.

The 53rd and Kimbark Plaza is almost a landmark in Chicago in that it produced many "firsts" for the LPA. According to the staff, many of the lessons learned at 53rd and Kimbark were then applied to Jeffro Plaza and subsequent efforts.

Detroit, Michigan

Urban renewal in Detroit, one of America's larger cities, is administered by the Detroit Housing Commission. In 1967, this administrative arm of the municipal government was involved in 28 redevelopment and 13 neighborhood conservation projects which covered more than 10 per cent of the entire land area of the city.

Business relocation is a separate function under the organizational structure in Detroit and is administered by two full-time "business claims specialists." These two staff members had displaced and attempted to relocate more than 1,300 businesses by 1967. Clearly, the ratio of businesses displaced to available relocation staff provides little opportunity for personal contact and a wide range of personal services in most cases.

The relocation staff has focused most of its attention on processing relocation claims for displaced businesses. Considering the size of this task alone compared with available staff, it is not surprising that this particular service monopolizes their time. To help alleviate the problem of meeting the needs of many businesses with only two staff members, two organizations have been established to aid in the process of business relocation.

Mayor's Committee for Industrial and Commercial Development. This committee was established to help reverse the decline in the CBD and to provide general assistance to businesses in the Detroit area. This committee has no direct powers. Public relations is one of its major functions. In this respect it can be of help to displaced businesses. Although the committee has no direct responsibility for displaced businesses, its members will provide aid if requested by displacees or other business firms. Their help consists of contacting and coordinating the efforts of city agencies such as the zoning board, the public works department, and other agencies that affect the business environment.

Mayor's Committee for Total Action Against Poverty (TAP). The TAP program in Detroit and the related Small Business Development Center are organized to supplement the role of the relocation division of the Detroit Housing Commission by offering financial and technical aid to small businesses affected (but not necessarily displaced) by urban renewal, redevelopment, or conservation projects. This organization offers counsel to individual businesses concerning SBA loans. In addition, the SBDC staff initiated local workshops on "How to Relocate Your Business," and business seminars and group counseling sessions that are appropriate to meet the immediate needs of small businesses.

Both of these programs were still in their infancy in 1967, and it was difficult to judge their effectiveness based upon current results. However, the potential of this type of supplementary help is significant, particularly in larger cities with relocation staffs burdened by heavy work loads.

Delta Iron Works, Inc.

Delta Iron Works is a small machine tool shop which works exclusively on job or custom orders. This firm operated from a location that had two serious drawbacks — poor access and inadequate space. The owner had contemplated a move, but because of a long-term lease could not seriously consider this alternative. Upon being informed of the impending displacement, the owner, working with the relocation staff, located a new site a few blocks from the area from which he was being displaced. He then proceeded to plan for the move.

Two critical factors then emerged. First, a comprehensive appraisal was made by a private consultant who identified and valued the fixtures owned by the firm. Because the owner was a tenant, this initial appraisal was a central factor in his reimbursement for the move. This consulting engineer also helped plan the move, which subsequently cost over $16,000. The second major element of help was provided by the LPA in effecting a zoning variance. The relocation structure purchased by the businessman was not appropriately zoned for its intended light-industrial use. With help from the LPA, however, he received the necessary approval.

The move brought about several improvements in the business operation. Materials handling is considerably more efficient. The business can now accept contracts for much larger job orders because of improved access and fenced-yard storage. The owner considered the two factors of the zoning variance and the extensive help provided in planning the move to be major elements in the success of his relocation.

Lauri Brothers Market

This business is an independent supermarket that successfully relocated in the near-downtown area of Detroit. As a result, the owners greatly expanded and improved the business operation. The critical factor in the success of the move was the aid given the business in its making the relocation reimbursement claim, particularly since this claim involved extensive fixture appraisals.

The market had been located since 1930 at the site from which it was displaced. At that location, it was faced with a lack of space with which to expand as well as a lack of off-street parking. In addition, because of recent urban renewal activities in the vicinity, the predominantly Negro market which they served had been reduced considerably and dispersed to other areas. When notified of the impending dislocation, they sought a relocation site which could accommodate the market they had previously served. A vacant auto dealership structure was purchased and refurbished by demolishing approximately one-third of the structure to make it usable as a supermarket. The site is a corner location that provides access from two main arteries of the CBD.

Although operating costs rose considerably at the new location, the store increased its business volume by more than two and one-half times. The cost of the actual physical move was over $22,000, much of which was attributable to a large amount of fixture removal and reinstallations. In one specific instance, the installation of refrigeration lines through a trench beneath floor-level involved significant expenditure. This installation expense could be approved only after numerous on-site photographs of the equipment were taken by the LPA and forwarded to the HUD regional office to substantiate the claim. Without this extra effort on the part of the LPA, payment of much of this large moving claim would probably have been denied — or at least significantly delayed.

Smith-Nager Glass Corporation

This relocation resulted in considerable upgrading of the business with associated improvements in both sales and profit. It also involved financing by SBA as well as a change in tenure status from tenant to owner.

This company places emblems on glassware. It was operating from rented basement quarters at the time it was displaced by urban renewal. Because of both its location and the condition of the structure housing the business, this firm faced the problem of attracting customers into the main showroom to view samples of its fashioned glassware.

The operation requires space for not only the display and sale of glassware, but also the manufacturing equipment used to decorate the glass. Although no glass is actually manufactured in the firm, various pieces of heavy equipment are required to print and bake designs on the glassware. Thus, the locational requirements included both showroom and production space for the business.

The business owner was able to purchase a small, light-industrial plant that had served as security for a defaulted SBA loan. Because the owner was eligible for a DBL, a 20-year SBA loan was granted for the purchase of this commercial structure. With this loan of $21,000, plus the SBDP, the owner was able to make substantial improvements in the appearance and general layout of the firm, and purchase additional equipment. These improvements have had their effect on the business. According to the owner, revenues increased some 25 per cent during the first five months at the new location. Expansion plans are under way and the businessman speaks highly of the help and cooperation he received from the LPA.

Fargo, North Dakota

Fargo, although the largest city in North Dakota, is relatively small with a population of approximately 50,000. Redevelopment efforts have been scaled to this population size; the city had initiated two projects by 1967. Although the first project involved relatively few businesses, the second displaced approximately eighty business firms.

Redevelopment and the related business relocation function are conducted by an essentially "one-man" operation. This is partly the result of the scale of urban renewal efforts in Fargo, and partly because of Fargo's general philosophy that the urban renewal agency is not permanent. That is, the urban renewal agency was established to accomplish one purpose — that of completing two central-city projects. Once this task is finished, there is little guarantee that urban renewal will be extended to other areas.

The second urban renewal project undertaken in Fargo posed a problem for the LPA because of the size of the case load of displaced businesses relative to the size of the staff. Complicating this problem was the fact that little peripheral retail-commercial development exists around Fargo. Thus relocation resources are distinctly limited. The downtown area, generally around Broadway, represents the hub of retail-commercial activity for the entire Fargo region. It was established policy that the retail businesses displaced by this project should be relocated, if possible, within the downtown area. Otherwise, they faced the high probability of being lost as businesses anywhere. Further, it was felt that those businesses displaced, particularly those which presented special problems of relocation because of the nature of their business and the attitude of the businessmen involved, could be best assisted by "business advisors" who were colleagues in business rather than public officials. The rationale of this policy stemmed from the general attitude of the community and the desire by a few businessmen to stimulate the downtown area.

The executive director of the LPA and the mayor met with interested businessmen and organized a business relocation committee to help displaced businesses relocate successfully. Local businessmen who were appointed to the committee represented a cross-section of local business and industry, but particularly included representatives of local financial institutions. Each businessman was assigned one or a group of businesses requiring relocation assistance. He was to provide his advisee(s) counsel on matters relating to the acquisition of a new site, sources of available financing, and other related problems. In addition, it was hoped that the committee member could provide encouragement and establish rapport to obtain displacee cooperation beyond that which would be possible through an urban renewal agency staff member.

The involvement of the business relocation committee members varied significantly, from providing relatively little help to establishing an effective and productive relationship which resulted in a successful relocation for the displacee. The business relocation committee, once organized, held meetings one day each week to discuss as a group the specific problems each member had encountered with his business assignee. These meetings also served to determine the appropriate distribution of business relocation cases. Generally, the assignment was made on the basis of the committee member's background and experience, and also any knowledge about or personal acquaintance with the displacee. Each of the four banks and four savings and loan associations located in the downtown area of Fargo provided committee members. As an example of the assignment criteria, business displacees were often assigned to the representative of the financial institution where the displacee had a commercial or personal account. In some cases, two or more committee members were assigned to a specific business firm because of the complementarity of their background and/or relationship with the displacee.

Carlson-Robbins Furniture Company

This case involves a move from one site in the Downtown Urban Renewal Project Area to another site in the same project. In the process, the owners of this retail furniture store acquired a considerable increase in square-footage and greater efficiency in the use of space. In addition, the firm obtained an SBA loan for improvements to the new structure.

Furniture stores often present a dilemma in relocation. While they have an affinity for downtown locations, they also have large and bulky inventories that require considerable amounts of storage space. This means that they need and seek relatively low square-footage costs; however, downtown or near-CBD locations are usually the most costly. Because of these somewhat conflicting relocation goals, displaced furniture stores can pose special problems for the relocation staff.

In this instance, the business firm, with the help of the LPA, acquired a structure that could be converted to provide ideal space for a furniture store. The building in question was owned by a railroad company on land designated as right-of-way. Because of the peculiarities associated with the ownership of this land by the railroad, only the building could be sold to the business firm (formerly a tenant at its old location). The land was leased on a long-term basis. Although a significant amount of refurbishing was necessary to adapt the building for their purposes, the business owners made excellent use of this space which had previously been occupied by an auto dealership.

After being informed of the SBA provisions pertaining to displaced businesses, the owners contacted SBA concerning a loan. This loan was granted, and with additional capital from the business, over $30,000 was spent in remodeling the relocation structure. The member of the business relocation committee assigned to this case was chairman of the board of directors of a major downtown bank in Fargo, and contacted the firm early in the relocation process to offer help. In this case, the business required little direct assistance but the displacees expressed appreciation for the offer and the encouragement from this committeeman.

At the new facility, the furniture store has noted a significant increase in business volume over that at the old location. Although the new site offers no off-street parking as the old location did, the business firm does not consider this a detriment.

Dakota Food Equipment, Incorporated

This business is a supplier of restaurant equipment. It was located in two separate buildings, one owned and one rented, prior to displacement. The layout and storage facilities of these two structures were not well suited to the needs of this business. The owner was therefore not terribly dismayed at the prospect of displacement. However, he faced two basic problems in the move: (1) finding a suitable relocation site, and (2) obtaining adequate financing.

In both of these elements of the move, the business firm was provided assistance by a member of the business relocation committee. The committee member was a business consultant who owned his own firm in Fargo. He initially contacted the owner of Dakota Food and aided him in his search for a new business location. In addition, the owner was given help and encouragement in his search for funds. The firm eventually received an SBA loan for over $50,000, in order to purchase a relocation property and construct a building.

As a result of this relocation, the business firm was able to consolidate its two-building operation under one roof, and provide much more efficient storage space on a single level. The firm has also increased its off-street parking capacity and has employed two more persons. Revenues were up nearly 30 per cent during the first year at the new location.

Morrie's Tavern

This case exemplifies the role of the business relocation committee in Fargo in helping a displacee upgrade his business. Morrie's Tavern was located in a deteriorating area of Fargo, which had been planned for urban renewal for some time. In addition to the owner, three other persons were employed at this small bar which offered only on-the-premises drinks.

This tavern owner was assigned two committee members — a representative from a local savings and loan and a real estate broker   to help in his relocation. While the broker provided some help in locating a new site, particular aid was provided by the savings and loan executive in securing an SBA loan for the purchase of a new business structure.

The business was changed to a cocktail lounge and package store. The name has been changed to "Chub's Pub and Package Place." The business owner now employs nine persons on a full-time basis. Sales increased approximately 50 per cent over the old location; much of this increase was attributable to the addition of a package store operation. The business was not licensed for retail liquor sales at the previous location, but was able to obtain the additional license authority when it transferred to the new location.

Grand Rapids, Michigan

Urban renewal in Grand Rapids is conducted under the Municipal Department of Community Improvement and Inspection Service. Four projects were completed or in execution and an additional five were in various stages of planning in 1967. The LPA is a city department, and must meet the same fiscal requirements as any other city department. This type of organization can have a distinct effect on the general staffing and organization of the urban renewal program, and more specifically on the program of business relocation. In Grand Rapids, one person has the total responsibility of family and business relocations, and has thus far carried out these duties without assistance. During the execution of four major projects by 1967, over 100 businesses and 350 families were relocated as a result of urban renewal in this city of approximately 200,000.

The second and third projects carried out have involved very few families because of their orientation toward the downtown area. They have, however, included a significant portion of large and well-established manufacturing firms which were relocated from the central core to outlying suburbs and industrial parks developed by the city. Because manufacturing has played a central role in downtown development, many of the larger businesses that were displaced were staunch supporters of urban renewal. Their operations were "locked in" the CBD, and they found relocation difficult without some form of support. The structures that housed the businesses were designed for manufacturing purposes — a currently inappropriate use in the evolution of the CBD — and were essentially unsaleable in their present condition. Because several firms faced this dilemma, the urban renewal projects which eventually displaced them provided a vehicle for a move that many sought but could not finance.

One of the key issues involved in moving larger manufacturing firms is the acquisition of the property and the associated appraisal of realty and fixtures. Many of the firms needed little guidance in selecting a site, financing the structure to be constructed on this site, or executing the move. For this reason, the basic relocation problem for such firms revolved around the planning and implementation of the project itself, and the associated acquisition of their properties. Consultants were utilized in many instances to submit initial appraisals on the realty and fixtures and to aid in the general acquisition process.

In essence, the downtown projects in Grand Rapids had as one of their central goals the relocation of inappropriately and inefficiently located industries to areas that were more appropriate from the viewpoint of both the businesses and the city. The mutual benefits that could be gained from many industrial moves helped account for the success achieved in these business relocation efforts.

Leitelt Iron Works

As indicated above, one of the principal reasons for conducting the two major CBD urban renewal projects was to relocate large manufacturing concerns operating in the downtown area. The Leitelt Iron Works exemplifies such a firm. Its relocation illustrates the importance of an appraisal consultant in aiding both the business and the LPA.

The president of the firm indicated that without urban renewal, he would have been out of business by 1970. This establishment was engaged primarily in large machine job order work; that is, custom work for other large manufacturers in the area. Because Leitelt used very large machine tools in its activities, and because large machinery must be delivered to the plant for repair and machining, access and efficient handling were fundamental to a successful operation. Throughout its early growth years, the firm had acquired three different structures (one four-story structure and two one-story structures) located on three different but adjacent lots. As a consequence of this configuration, materials handling costs and other associated costs were extremely high.

The main building was nearly 85 years old and was in need of complete renovation. Because the oil heating system and electrical wiring were obsolete, maintenance and utility costs were extremely high. A full-time heating engineer was needed simply to maintain the old furnaces. The physical appearance also left much to be desired. The president indicated that one large customer had terminated dealings simply because of the general appearance of the physical plant.

Another critical shortcoming of the old plant was access. The main building was located adjacent to a river and had only one door as an entrance and exit. Since the major portion of the large machine-tool operation was conducted in this building, it necessitated transporting machinery from one building to the other to complete the total service process. Aside from delivery complications, even visiting the firm was a problem because of narrow streets and a scarcity of parking area. There was only limited off-street parking for employees and on-street parking was difficult to find for both employees and potential customers.

All of these disadvantages led to a move to liquidate the firm in 1954. Pressure to liquidate continued among the stockholders until the property was acquired by the city.

A move from the old location had been anticipated for some time by Leitelt Iron Works. Long before urban renewal entered the picture a suitable site for relocation was selected and purchased. However, before the firm could move, it had to raise the necessary capital to finance the new structure. For all practical purposes it could do this only by selling its existing property and using the proceeds to invest in a new plant. Urban renewal made this possible and provided a portion of the planning help to make this move a reality.

Today, the firm is housed in a single, one-story structure that is nearly 20,000 square feet larger than the combined square-footage in all three buildings at the old location. In addition, the firm has nearly three-fourths of an acre of space for parking and yard storage of heavy machinery.

Since this was the first large industrial move in Grand Rapids, the services of an engineering consultant were used. The appraisal of irremovables by this consultant greatly facilitated acquisition and relocation. The firm was able to apply the proceeds from these irremovables toward the purchase of new equipment. In the actual move, the consultants also reviewed bids and counseled the firm regarding the most economical and efficient methods of moving without interruption to business.

Leitelt Iron Works. Three views of the old location in downtown Grand Rapids. Production was inefficiently dispersed in several buildings and off-street parking was extremely limited. (Photos courtesy Grand Rapids Urban Renewal Agency.)

Leitelt Iron Works is now located in an outlying industrial area. This modern plant offers both greater efficiency of operation and improved appearance. (Photo courtesy Grand Rapids Urban Renewal Agency.)

The actual move was quite complicated and involved heavy-machinery moving equipment, riggers, electrical work, and a partial self-move. The LPA made arrangements for a 90 per cent partial payment of the total relocation claim in order to provide funds as soon after the move as possible.

The new location has proved very beneficial to this business firm. Not only did maintenance costs and certain overhead charges decline considerably, but sales also rose nearly 50 per cent. There has been a marked change in the attitude of stockholders with this turnabout in fortunes, and prospects are quite high for continued operation of this business.

Wurzburg's Department Store Warehouse

Wurzburg's Department Store is one of the largest and best-known stores in the downtown area of Grand Rapids. It was also one of the first businesses to be affected by the urban renewal program. The relocation of its warehouse thus had a significant "demonstration effect" on other local displacees. It involved a very large move, high moving costs, and the use of specialized consultants on the appraisal of irremovables.

The firm owned a warehouse located in a declining section of the CBD. The president of Wurzburg's stated that they were quite anxious to get out of this structure since it was not designed to be a warehouse. The multistory building was originally a retail store, but with the economic decline in the area, it was converted to warehouse space. The layout of the building was very poor for storage, and inventory handling was difficult. The firm was forced to use passenger elevators in handling their merchandise. For this reason, they could not make effective use of the upper floors. Also, floor-loads were limited so that only certain types of lighter materials could be stored on the upper floors. Finally, the building was old and constructed in such a way that it required very high maintenance costs.

Once displaced, the firm quickly found vacant warehouse space in a convenient location, since the area in the CBD was in a declining state and many vacant commercial buildings could be found. In leasing their new warehouse facility, they were able to obtain a loading dock with covered parking for trucks as well as off-street parking for all employees. The new structure is much less expensive to maintain and is rented on a long-term lease with an option to purchase. The new structure is ideally suited for storage, having high ceilings and freight elevators. In this facility, the firm can handle inventory not only for its downtown store but also for its two new branch operations without the requirements of additional employees or space.

The acquisition of the structure at the old location involved the appraisal of irremovables and obtaining consulting advice on the moving costs. A central reason for the good relations between the firm and the LPA was the treatment of irremovables in the acquisition. In addition, because no moving-cost reimbursement limitations existed at the time, the full moving expenses of approximately $48,000 were paid.

St. Paul, Minnesota

This city, with a population of approximately 320,000, had four urban renewal projects in various stages of completion in 1967. Over 500 business displacements were involved. The vast majority of business displacees were in the downtown project of St. Paul, which covered 12 blocks of central core area. Nearly 400 businesses were displaced from this project alone.

The LPA of St. Paul is organized so that both property management and business relocation are carried out by the same division. The LPA feels that this organizational structure has many advantages because the property management function is well coordinated with the relocation function. Property management staff members are well aware of their tenants' needs and can also coordinate the timing of the move with relocation staff members, who are closely involved with obtaining relocation sites for displacees. There are currently four full-time staff members working in these two functional areas.

Two useful and innovative elements of the St. Paul relocation program have centered on a business relocation advisory committee established by the chamber of commerce, and an inventory of available commercial property maintained by the relocation staff.

Business Relocation Advisory Committee. The chamber of commerce, in cooperation with the LPA, organized a business relocation committee for the purpose of assisting displaced businesses with particularly difficult problems of relocation. Another critical function of this committee was to establish good public relations between the business community and the LPA.

Inventory of commercial structures. Perhaps one of the most interesting facets of the St. Paul program is the degree of cooperation that has been obtained from local real estate brokers, and particularly the local real estate board. The relocation staff has assembled and maintains a master list of available commercial space throughout the entire city. This provides an accurate day-to-day inventory of potential locations for displacees.

Initially, the inventory was developed with the cooperation of local real estate brokers. At a mass meeting, brokers were given a large stock of forms on which to list individually all of their commercial property listings. A master list of these properties was then developed according to the following categories: retail, office, manufacturing, and building site. Within each category, the structures were arranged by geographical zones. The relocation staff attempts to match the needs of business displacees with the available properties, and refers the displacee to the broker(s) handling those properties which appear to be suitable relocation sites. In all cases, the normal commission is charged by the broker. The relocation staff serves simply as a clearinghouse and referral agency.

The list is updated regularly with data from cooperating brokers and by posting advertised properties from the daily newspapers each day. The staff claims a high degree of success with this relocation technique.

Gerber Jewelers

The owner of this retail jewelry store, who also owned the business structure he occupied prior to displacement, purchased an existing building approximately one and one-half blocks from his old location. This newly purchased building was completely remodeled. This substantial renovation effort required a considerable investment. The displacee was encouraged by the LPA to contact SBA in order to obtain the necessary loan. After a long series of negotiations that involved not only the businessman, but also his lawyer, a loan was granted.

Because of the revitalization that has occurred in the St. Paul CBD, as well as the more strategic location of his new structure, Gerber's has nearly doubled its sales at the new location. In addition, two employees have been added.

Of special interest in this case is the imaginative renovation effort made by the businessman and financed by SBA. This approach, in addition to the economies gained through renovation as opposed to new construction, provided prime downtown space near the previous location of the firm.

Vitamin Council. Another example of a manufacturing firm (above) inappropriately located in the CBD. In its new plant (below). This firm renovated an existing structure and adapted it to its specific needs. (Photos courtesy St. Paul Housing and Redevelopment Authority.)

Vitamin Council

This firm manufactures patent medicine and non-prescription lotions. It was renting its space at the time of displacement and faced the prospects of a move even without urban renewal. Because of a high growth rate, significant expansion would have been necessary in the near future. Responding to these circumstances and requirements for a new location, the relocation staff provided both assistance and cooperation that resulted in a highly successful relocation.

After the initial contact with the business owner, the relocation staff proposed as a relocation site a sound structure that was not to be demolished, located in an industrial redevelopment project area in the city. The owner-occupant of this building, a soap products manufacturer, was approached by both Vitamin Council and the LPA. The agency staff provided help in the negotiations for the purchase of this building. Vitamin Council thus became an owner rather than a tenant.

In addition to the help provided this firm in acquiring the relocation structure, the LPA also made available additional land adjacent to the newly acquired site for purposes of expansion. This was a critical issue in this relocation effort since the firm would have found the relocation structure unacceptable without further room for expansion.

The LPA also referred this business to SBA as a possible source of financing for the new structure. After some negotiation, a loan which had the participation of a local commercial bank was granted for an amount over $200,000. The loan was staged, first to cover acquisition and then new construction.

This relocation effort provided the opportunity for a business with high growth potential to relocate at a strategic time in its development. The move has enabled this company to expand into new fields of production and to increase substantially the efficiency of its existing production. These advantages may not have been possible without the cooperation and assistance of the relocation staff of St. Paul.

Region V

The Region V office in Fort Worth, Texas was the only one not personally visted during the field interviews. Through correspondence, however, it became apparent that the business relocation personnel in the Region V office were well aware of the character and quality of business relocation efforts of LPA's operating in the Region.

The Region V office appears especially well organized for prompt and rapid handling of any problems or claims for compensation in excess of $10,000, which must be cleared for approval through the regional office. For example, prompt consideration and approval were given to the third-party contract between the Oklahoma City Urban Redevelopment Agency and the University of Oklahoma City, which is discussed in detail in the section on Oklahoma City. Quick and favorable consideration was given to the temporary, on-site relocations of Capitol Typewriter Company and Johnnie's Shoe Repair in Little Rock, as indicated by the correspondence in the files of the Little Rock Housing Authority. Moreover, there is at least one case in which a payment in excess of $10,000 was approved in writing within two days in order to expedite the relocation of a substantial business in Little Rock.

Little Rock, Arkansas

Urban renewal programs in Little Rock are operated by the Division of Urban Renewal of the Little Rock Housing Authority (LRHA). As of September 1967, LRHA had five projects in execution, with four completed. All relocation cases included in this study come from the Central Little Rock Project (Ark. R-12), which was still in execution. This 508-acre project contains the entire central business district of Little Rock. As of December 1966, over 200 business relocations had been completed from this project alone, with over 400 business relocations completed from all projects.

Organization and procedures. The business relocation staff consists of a director and two business relocation counselors, who are the field representatives. The relocation section has prepared and distributed throughout the agency a manual entitled *Policy and Procedure for Non-Residential Relocation,* which indicates the steps, procedures, policies, forms and HUD references pertinent to business relocation activities.

This manual is one indication of the highly effective internal organizational structure for business relocation in LRHA. As a result, processing of claims is prompt and efficient. Moreover, a highly systematic filing program has been established which permits rapid and easy access to information on any individual relocation case. There is extremely good coordination of activities among the several sections of the LRHA Division of Urban Renewal. This is quite important, since property acquisition and disposition are handled in two different departments which are separate from the business relocation section.

The Division of Urban Renewal has established a PERT/CPM program for each project. The scheduled timing for each phase of the project program is noted on large wall charts. These are kept current, with an indication of the excess or deficiency in activities at the end of each month. If necessary, field personnel are transferred from one project to another to keep the program as nearly up to date as possible.

The business relocation section is also responsible for the management of all property acquired and owned by LRHA in its urban renewal activities. After clearance, they are often rented on a temporary basis for parking purposes. The section also collects rents on LRHA-owned properties from business occupants. The formula for monthly rentals is normally 0.6 per cent of the acquisition price of the property, which is prorated on a square-foot basis for a partial occupancy of a structure.

Initial contacts are made with displacees prior to acquisition. An affected business is required to give 30-days' written notice of its intention to move. This allows the business relocation staff time to inspect the property, make an inventory, advise on moving as opposed to sale of equipment, and advise on the specifics of the move. Once the inventory is prepared, inspected and approved, three bids are normally required. The business must have bids in hand 15 days before the actual move occurs.

Staff members advise and assist in preparing and filling out claims for compensation. They help in assembling the documentation for SBDP's. This cuts down the amount of time required in filing and approving a claim in most instances. The business relocation staff has developed a checklist which is used in each case. Local forms have been designed so that the relocatee's burden of documentation is eased.

Informational brochures have been prepared by LRHA and are given to each relocatee who is to be affected by the program. The relocatee is asked to sign one copy of the brochure. This copy is retained in the case file to indicate that he has been shown the form and has had its meaning explained to him.

As a result of this procedure, particularly fast action has been possible through the regional office in clearing claims in excess of $10,000, as well as in obtaining approval for special circumstances (e.g., temporary relocation for Capitol Typewriter Company). In one case, approval of a claim in excess of $10,000 was obtained within two days.

Normally, LRHA reimburses the business directly for its actual and necessary moving expenses, rather than paying the mover. If this policy creates a special problem for the business, however, direct payment is made to the mover. LRHA usually advises the affected business to remain in the old location until the property is acquired, so that it may qualify for an SBDP.

LRHA works closely with the local real estate board and encourages its members to make direct contact with relocatees. Information is continuously exchanged between the board and LRHA.

The LRHA business relocation staff conducts a follow-up interview through a questionnaire in each case, approximately one year after the relocation. In this way, they try to improve their policies and procedures. Of more than 50 such interviews read during the study, all displacees reported increased business in their new locations. The vast majority also expressed satisfaction with the manner in which they were treated by LRHA. In many instances, displacees who are concerned about the relocation program are referred to others who have already moved, so that they can confirm for themselves the kinds of treatment they may expect to receive.

Public Relations and Information. LRHA has a highly developed public relations program for businesses about to be displaced by urban renewal. A detailed projector-slide talk has been prepared, which is shown to groups of relocatees. An attempt is made to show this to every businessman who will be affected by relocation or rehabilitation. Normally, meetings of approximately 30 affected businessmen are arranged under the sponsorship of the local chamber of commerce. These meetings are attended by the director of business relocation, either the executive director or the assistant executive director of LRHA, the chief of the division of urban renewal, and either the regional director or the chief loan officer of SBA. These meetings acquaint the affected businessmen with the relocation program, and especially with the people with whom they will be dealing. An effort is made to meet each businessman personally at the end of the meeting. Representatives of the local real estate board are also invited to be present at these meetings, to explain the process of looking for and obtaining new space. The basic theme is that LRHA wants to cut red tape in the entire process as much as possible. Each individual businessman is invited to visit the project office to discuss his particular move and his special problems, as well as to learn the rules of reimbursement in detail.

Cooperation with SBA. LRHA has a good working relationship with the regional office of SBA, which is located in Little Rock. There is good personal rapport between LRHA and SBA personnel concerned with business relocatees. Through September 1967, a total of 16 DBL's had been obtained through SBA. LRHA keeps the SBA staff informed well in advance about the characteristics of the firms most likely to be seeking SBA financing. In turn, SBA cooperates in keeping LRHA informed about the progress of loan applications.

The SBA staff reported that as of September 1967. no DBL's in Little Rock were delinquent. SBA claims that every DBL and EDL in Little Rock had been approved within 21 working days. SBA Loans have been obtained for working capital purposes, land acquisition and construction, new construction, and leasehold improvements. SBA generally encourages an affected business to apply for a DBL rather than an EDL, because the permissible term is longer and the maximum number of dollars allowable is greater.

Cooperation with Little Rock Industrial Development Company (IDC). The IDC is a private, profit-seeking land development corporation sponsored by the Little Rock Chamber of Commerce. It assembles land for industrial purposes, and has developed the West Side Industrial Park, to which several firms from the Central Little Rock Project have moved. IDC was organized with $200,000 from private businesses in Little Rock. It will sell or lease land, and build and sell or lease buildings. There is a repurchase clause on land sales to discourage speculation. Of seventy occupants in the West Side Industrial Park as of September 1967, seven were relocatees from the Central Little Rock Project. IDC prefers to sell rather than to lease, in order to generate more turnover of its money. To achieve this, it will sell on a land contract or installment sale basis. There is good cooperation between LRHA and IDC, although IDC's developments are not designed exclusively as a relocation resource.

Treadway Electric Company, Inc.

This wholesale distribution firm handling electric supplies and lighting fixtures was located in the Central Little Rock Project. It had occupied 40,000 square feet on three floors of rented space since 1923. Treadway moved to its new location in the West Side Industrial Park in April 1966. Moving expenses totaled $21,500.

The former location was in the wholesale district, and had very serious parking problems. Treadway did a great deal of walk-in business in the old location, which has virtually disappeared in the new outlying location. This is not considered a serious loss by the firm.

This case illustrates the effectiveness of good cooperation between the business relocation staff and the relocatee throughout the entire relocation process. The firm approached LRHA in January of 1965 with a request for assistance and advice. The planning process started at that time. Treadway asked LRHA to honor the lease under which they (Treadway) were operating, when LRHA acquired the property. LRHA agreed to this arrangement.

Treadway built its own new plant in the West Side Industrial Park on five acres of land. This allows room for expansion of the present 40,000 square-foot building. The new building is on one floor and much more efficient. Tailgate-height loading bays are now available on site, which expedites shipments considerably.

The business relocation staff gave advice from the outset about the necessary documentation for compensation of moving expenses. Treadway was helped in developing their bids, the bonding requirements, and insurance coverage. They were further helped in making and documenting the inventory of their supplies. As a result, the entire move was accomplished in four days.

Because of the cooperative work on documentation, the moving expense payment was approved in *four* days by the Region V office. The letter of approval contained a notation of commendation to the LRHA staff for "the excellent manner in which this move was processed and documented."

Anticipating rather high moving expenses, LRHA closely assisted in the handling of moving bids. Careful planning of the move made it possible to keep expenses below $25,000. Treadway agreed that LRHA was extremely helpful in this regard.

Timing the move was also an important consideration. Although the new facility was not fully completed, Treadway had all incoming shipments sent directly to the new location approximately three weeks before the move. This meant that they had some inventory at the new location to handle their customers' needs almost immediately, and it also reduced moving expenses.

Because of the effective handling of this move, Treadway changed from a vociferous opponent of urban renewal to a confirmed supporter. The president of the firm said that he thanked the LRHA business relocation staff at the time of the move, and he was still thankful for their help.

Johnnie's Shoe Repair

This establishment claims to be the largest shoe repair and shoeshine establishment in Arkansas. It was a tenant in 1,325 square feet of ground-floor area at 413 Louisiana Street in the Central Little Rock Project Area. The building was acquired by LRHA on April 30, 1964. The owner-operator opposed urban renewal and relocation as vigorously as possible. He wrote directly to and visited U. S. Senators and Congressmen seeking help and relief. At first, he refused delivery of registered mail notifying him to move, and subsequently denied having received any such notice.

Because his was a long-time and established business at the 413 Louisiana Street location, the owner believed that any move outside of this area would do him serious damage. On March 31, 1965, Johnnie's Shoe Repair was voluntarily moved to a temporary relocation site at 208 West Capitol Avenue. The claim for property loss and moving expenses was delayed because this was a temporary relocation. It was necessary to obtain approval from Region V of HUD to authorize the temporary relocation. This was in a block marked for total clearance. Finally, through the persistent intercession of LRHA, Johnnie's Shoe Repair received $3,000 property loss compensation in November 1965.

Although he knew that this would be a temporary relocation, the owner invested approximately $12,000 in property improvements in the temporary location. In 1966, he acquired a site at 115 Main Street. He applied for and received a DBL from SBA to finance property acquisition and construction. While construction of the new building was progressing, the area of the first

Johnnic's Shoe Repair (above) in its original location. Its final location (below) shows a dramatic upgrading in appearance and customer access. (Photos courtesy Little Rock Housing Authority.)

temporary relocation was vacated, with the exception of three businesses. Notices to vacate as of November 30, 1966 were given to these three businesses. Johnnie's refused to acknowledge these at first, and LRHA was afraid they might have to resort to a business eviction for the first time. Finally, a second temporary location was voluntarily selected at 208 Main Street. This move occurred on December 3, 1966. Subsequent to this, LRHA was able to arrange for an SBDP for the firm, even though it had not yet moved to its permanent location site. This concession was later acknowledged by the owner to be extremely helpful, and an indicator of the good faith of LRHA.

Finally, on July 3, 1967, Johnnie's Shoe Repair opened at its new location. The proprietor also owns the building, and occupies the ground floor with his business. The second floor is rented to a restaurant, and the third floor contains a private club. Through the assistance of LRHA, an agreement was obtained from the owner of the adjacent building to construct on its north wall, saving Johnnie's a great deal of construction expense.

The proprietor is now one of the most enthusiastic supporters of urban renewal as one could imagine. He is particularly complimentary about the treatment and assistance he received from the business relocation staff of LRHA. His business has increased significantly at the new location, and he is particularly pleased to be a property owner. The location, which he originally regarded as unsuitable, has turned out to be a very substantial generator of traffic and business.

Capitol Typewriter Company

This firm was originally located at 216 West Capitol Avenue. They had signed a 30-year lease for their new location at 307 Main Street, but could not obtain occupancy until December 1966 when the current lease expired. The firm tried to buy up the remainder of the existing lease from the present tenant, but was refused. Both locations were in the Central Little Rock Project Area.

Both the firm and LRHA wanted Capitol Typewriter to remain in downtown Little Rock. The bulk of its business comes from firms and shoppers in the CBD, and it is an important resource in the CBD. Capitol Typewriter had been looking for a new location for three years prior to the move, because they knew that a move was inevitable.

Because it was necessary to have Capitol Typewriter vacate the Capitol Avenue premises to permit clearance and new construction in that block to proceed, LRHA obtained approval from the Region V office to reimburse Capitol Typewriter for a move to a temporary relocation. This on-site location was an old bank building which most recently had been used as a recruiting station for the Army, Air Force and Navy. It was owned by the U. S. General Services Administration (GSA) and scheduled for acquisition and demolition by LRHA. This property was acquired in November 1966 from GSA, which assisted LRHA in having the boiler repaired to allow occupancy by Capitol Typewriter.

Capitol Typewriter Co.   These three photographs show the relocation sequence from the original location, to the temporary relocation, and finally to the present site. (Photos courtesy Little Rock Housing Authority.)

The firm moved into the new location on November 21, 1966, and was compensated for $4,700 in moving expenses. Prior to this move, a total of $6,700 was expended by Capitol Typewriter Company in remodeling the structure. This expense was reimbursed by LRHA, and was permitted by the Region V office to be included in project costs.

LRHA also assisted Capitol Typewriter in obtaining a DBL from SBA in the amount of $85,000 for leasehold improvements. The president of the firm gives full credit to the LRHA business relocation staff in providing assistance and advice in documenting the loan application, as well as in expediting the processing of the loan.

Capitol Typewriter moved to its final location at 307 Main Street on April 15, 1967. The president of the firm is most enthusiastic about the treatment and handling he received from both LRHA and SBA. He reported significantly increased business at the temporary location, and good business at the final location. He attributes much of this to the ease of moving which was made possible by the assistance provided by LRHA.

This case emphasizes the importance of adaptability on the part of the LPA, particularly in seeking exceptions from HUD regulations and guidelines when it is in the interest of the community and the project to do so. Special permission was necessary to include as project costs the moving expenses of Capitol Typewriter to the temporary location. The same was true of the remodeling expenses at the temporary relocation, which were paid by LRHA as a project expenditure. Moving expenses to the final location constituted a federal grant. Advertising expenses of Capitol Typewriter for its temporary relocation were not reimbursable. Timing was affected by the fact that LRHA had to own the temporary relocation before the move could be effected.

National Investors Life Insurance Company

This case involved a complex land exchange and the relocation of a small but growing local insurance company that was retained in the Little Rock CBD. In addition, a very substantial building in the project area was rehabilitated in accordance with the renewal plan.

National Investors Life occupied a 75-year-old, two-story former bank building on a downtown corner of Main Street. The building, in the Central Little Rock Project Area, was in good condition. The total building area was 7,000 square feet. At the time of the move, National Investors Life had 72 employees.

LRHA agreed to early acquisition of the National Investors Life property. This was necessary because the property to be acquired by National Investors Life, known as the 555 Building, was owned by two separate parties. National Investors Life purchased one-half ownership, and arranged for an exchange of its Main Street property plus cash for the other half. LRHA agreed to stipulate the acquisition price it would pay for the Main Street property so that a firm agreement could be worked out for the exchange. The owner of the half-interest in the 555 Building insisted on this arrangement so that he might take advantage of the tax treatment of property owners under public takings. He wanted to avoid a substantial capital gains tax.

The location to which National Investors Life moved is at Second and Broadway. The building was constructed to house a service station, garage, and roof-garden dance pavilion, and was advertised as the largest service station in world. It is a five-story concrete and steel structure built in 1923.

Transfer of title between National Investors Life and the part-owner of the 555 Building to the Main Street property occurred in August 1962. LRHA acquired the property on July 15, 1963. The offer and acceptance contract in the first sale stipulated that National Investors Life could occupy the building for 11 months rent-free. LRHA honored the remainder of this period at the time of its purchase nine months later. After September 1963, rent was $750 per month, based on a monthly rental formula of 0.6 per cent of the agreed acquisition price.

The 555 Garage Building was rehabilitated extensively by National Investors Life. The rehabilitation was subject to LRHA approval of specifications. There was no problem in this regard, and indeed the rehabilitated building won several architectural awards.

The total area of the National Investors Building is 84,000 square feet, of which National Investors Life uses 52,000 square feet. The company has expanded its operations and employment dramatically since the move. The actual move occurred between April 3 and April 10, 1964. Most of the move was effected over one weekend, so that business was not interrupted. This was regarded as critical by National Investors Life, because they had to maintain service for their policy-holders at all times. LRHA was given full credit for effective cooperation in making the rapid move possible.

As a sidelight to this case, space on the first floor of the new location and the entire second floor are leased to a number of retail and office tenants. The creation of this rehabilitated space has provided an important relcoation facility in downtown Little Rock. A restaurant, barbershop and two attorneys who are now tenants in the National Investors Life Building were relocatees from other parts of the Central Little Rock Project.

Oklahoma City

The Oklahoma City Urban Renewal Authority (OCURA), organized in early 1964, is the LPA for Oklahoma City. As of September 1967, there were three projects in excecution: University Medical Center Project (R-20); John F. Kennedy Project (R-35); and Central Business District Project, Section 1-A. All cases generated in this study are from the Medical Center and John F. Kennedy project areas, which are contiguous to each other. The total business relocation work load in these latter two projects is approximately 925 businesses. As of September 1967, approximately 150 had been relocated.

National Investors Life Insurance Co.   These two views show the dramatic and imaginative changes in the relocation structure resulting from major renovation by the displaced firm. Other displaced businesses are tenants on the ground floor of the rehabilitated building. (Photos courtesy Little Rock Housing Authority.)

Estimates by the director of the Business Research Center at Oklahoma City University (which will be discussed in more detail below) indicate that probably 800 of the businesses will actually relocate. Of these, some 600 are extremely small (one- and two-man firms), and as many as 300 may be classified as marginal. There is a large proportion of one-man businesses operated in homes. These are predominantly personal service establishments: beauty shops, barber shops, shoe repair shops, etc.

Although Negroes constitute approximately 12 per cent of the total population of Oklahoma City, nearly 80 per cent of the population of the Medical Center and John F. Kennedy project areas is Negro. The bulk of the Negro population of Oklahoma City, as well as the vast majority of Negro-owned and operated businesses, are concentrated in these two project areas.

Organization and procedures for business relocation. The OCURA business relocation staff consists of three white males. All are long-time residents of Oklahoma City, and one has substantial real estate background. During the fall of 1966 and early spring of 1967, OCURA was totally reorganized. This resulted from the fall 1966 elections, when a new mayor, a new city council, and a new city manager were installed. From October 1966 through January 1967, Mr. Wheeler Frisbie, Director of the Business Research Center at Oklahoma City University, was on leave from OCU and served as Deputy Executive Director of

OCURA. During that period, he effected a thoroughgoing reorganization of the structure and functions of OCURA, and prepared the operating manual for the agency.

Although much of the professional and operating staff of OCURA had been on the job less than one year at the time of the interviews, a high degree of intra-agency cooperation and dedication to the job was evident. In dealings with small business operators in particular, the business relocation staff shows a high degree of empathy with their problems. Essentially, small businessmen in particular are treated as people, rather than as items on the case load. In large part, this reflects the approach of Mr. Frisbie, who regards business relocation as an important opportunity to renew *people* as whole individuals. This means attempting to make relocatees better businessmen — or simply to make them businessmen. One formally stated goal of the business relocation program in Oklahoma City, for example, is to bring every relocated business to the point at which it can add *one* employee. In their business relocation activities, the OCURA staff works closely with the Business Research Center at OCU. Every effort is made for the initial contact with each affected businessman to be a personal one. This occurs in the preliminary planning stage, usually through a representative of OCU. The details of this procedure are discussed below.

The business relocation function is extremely well-organized, and particularly impressive files are maintained on each affected business. This makes for prompt and effective handling of problems that arise during the course of the business day. As a matter of policy, OCURA tries to avoid temporary on-site relocation to areas which are scheduled for subsequent clearance. This policy is one more reflection of the essentially personal attention which is given to each business relocatee. The hallmark of business relocation in Oklahoma City is personal concern for each affected businessman. A further evidence of this concern is the fact that a business relocation consultant was hired in 1965 to study in detail the problems of businesses in the Central Business District Project, and to recommend approaches that would result in minimum disruption of business operations and activities in Oklahoma City. The format utilized by this consultant was applied by the Business Research Center staff at OCU for the Medical Center and John F. Kennedy projects.

Contract with Oklahoma City University. In August 1966, OCURA entered into a one-year contract with the Business Research Center at OCU to develop a program and procedure for business relocation activity in Oklahoma City, and to carry out many of the component parts of that program. OCU does most of the background and planning work for business relocation, as well as contacting and advising each individual businessman affected by renewal. This leaves the business relocation staff of OCURA free to concentrate on the actual moving process and on expediting the processing of claims for compensation and reimbursement. The administrative staff of OCURA is highly enthusiastic about the results of the contract with OCU, which was renewed for a second year in August 1967.

The OCU staff consists of thirteen full-time and nine half-time professionals.

Their contract with OCURA is an operating contract, not a demonstration contract. During the preliminary planning phase of each project, a representative of OCU makes a personal call to each business displacee who has been identified in the preliminary business relocation survey of the project area. In the Medical Center and John F. Kennedy project areas, this preliminary survey was also carried out by the OCU staff. In the preliminary interview, information about the specific requirements and needs of the business is obtained, as well as an indication of the capabilities of the business to pay rent or acquire space in another location.

Through the preliminary interview, it is usually possible to identify the kinds of problems confronting the business. For example, it is explained to the businessman what sort of records are required in order for him to qualify for an SBDP. The basic thrust of the OCU program is to relocate as many businesses as possible, to keep them in business, and to make better businessmen out of the operators. In many instances this involves making them consciously functioning businessmen for the first time in their careers.

Prior to direct contacts with individual businessmen, the OCU staff conducts market surveys of areas in near proximity to the project areas. Data on residents, their incomes, expenditure patterns and shopping habits are developed and analyzed. As a result, the "needs" for businesses in every area of Oklahoma City have been identified and mapped. This permits the OCU staff to give advice on *where* it makes sense for different kinds of businesses to relocate.

In addition, OCU conducts periodic surveys of vacancies, rents and prices in areas to which dislocated businesses might appropriately move. These are classified by size, rent level, type of operation and the like. This information is available to potential relocatees for their use in planning the move.

Once a firm has been placed on the work load of OCU, two kinds of advice and assistance are available. First, individual counseling and consulting on their particular business problems are provided. They are advised about the basic requirements of record keeping and documentation for relocation, and the appropriate procedures for selecting a proper site for the relocation. This advice and analysis include consideration of timing the move, in terms of how long the surrounding area will support the business in its present location. By working with the individual businessman, OCU attempts to speed up reimbursements and other payments through OCURA and HUD.

One of the major problems confronting OCU is to assist extremely small businesses in proving that they are in fact in business, and constructing income statements to qualify them for the SBDP. In many instances, these firms have not filed income tax forms in the past. Efforts are made to obtain forgiveness for this from IRS. Although no policy commitment has been made by IRS, the requests are being decided on an individual basis "on their merits."

In addition, specific advice is given to individual businessmen with respect to their future business activities. For example, two Negro upholsterers were advised to expand their areas of activity, and now have both Negroes and whites in their clientele. Several businessmen have been encouraged to obtain franchises. Franchising firms offer good training for this work, and the businessmen have been able to offer new services to the same market area they previously served. Others are encouraged to enter new lines of activity. In a few instances, when it is quite apparent that the individual is not well suited or equipped to be an independent businessman, he is advised to discontinue operations. Under such circumstances, OCU makes every effort to obtain job training for the individual. In addition, job references are provided. More than twelve such discontinued businessmen have been placed thus far.

Once the individuals have been given basic information and their particular problems analyzed, they are encouraged to attend one of several seminars offered at OCU. A modest course fee of $5 is charged. The original concept of providing training for broad management has been revised, in favor of more emphasis on record keeping, bookkeeping and preparation of income tax returns. The basic idea is to prepare the businessman for relocation, and for more effective business operations in the new location. A long-run objective of the OCU relocation program is to attempt to convince each business to hire one more person after settling in the new location.

As of September 1967, a total of 275 individual businesses had gone through the OCU program. In this process, OCU maintains close and continuing liaison with OCURA. In addition, once the move is completed, OCU continues to consult with the individual businesses on such matters as layout, signs, advertising and financing.

In the actual moving process itself, the OCU staff helps the individual businessman to evaluate and identify his specific locational requirements and capabilities. Then the businessman is referred to one or more brokers who are cooperating in the program, to find potential new locations. OCU helps the businessman evaluate the alternatives that are before him, and advises on actual site selection.

The OCU program involves a great deal of time and effort for individual firms. For example, Mack's Tire Shop (one of the cases discussed below) required over 100 professional hours of advice and consultation. Nearly 60 hours were consumed in working on the SBA EDL for Mack's. In another case (a shoe repair business), OCU taught the owner's wife to keep books. She is now studying cost and profit structures for appropriate pricing. As a result of OCU advice, this shoe repair firm, owned and operated by a Negro couple, took on a line of shoes for retail sale. This was based on market research conducted by OCU. After six months of work with OCU, the couple reported making more money than they ever had before.

The critical point about the OCU program is that it involves highly personalized advice and training, designed to meet the specific needs of each individual businessman or group. For example, seminars for beauty shop operators were scheduled on Monday afternoons because beauty shops are closed on Mondays in Oklahoma City. Much of the success of the program to date has stemmed from the fact that professionals have been brought into the relocation process during the early planning stages of a project. Moreover, as "third parties" the OCU staff has been able to talk pointedly and directly to the affected businessmen. This represents an area of activity which is applicable for many LPA's operating in communities in which there is also a local college or university.

Edmonson's Fish Market

Luther and Fannie Edmonson operated Edmonson's Fish Market in the Medical Center Project. In addition to selling fish, they also sold sandwiches and soft drinks. This business was conducted in a large ramshackle frame and concrete building containing over 4,000 square feet, which was owned by the Edmonsons. The Edmonsons are Negro, and their clientele is almost exclusively Negro. The property was acquired by OCURA in August 1966. The proceeds netted little to the Edmonsons, because they had a very large mortgage on the property and other outstanding debts. The business moved to a new location outside the project area in February 1967. Moving costs were $350. The claim was filed on May 15, and a check was issued on May 19.

A sidelight to this case is the fact that they were moved by Fairgrounds Transfer Company, a moving establishment also located in the Medical Center Project Area. This was another relocatee firm. OCURA encouraged businesses moving from the area to use local moving firms to the extent possible. The Edmonsons remained as tenants in their former property for three months. They received an SBDP, less three months's rent, on June 8. They are tenants in the new location, and pay $100 per month.

The most important point about this case is that the new location is a former gasoline service station which has on-site parking. It is on a corner which affords considerably greater ease of access than was the case in the former location. The new location was found for the Edmonsons by the OCURA business relocation staff after considerable searching of the area. The Edmonsons were not inclined to accept the new location at first, but were convinced by OCURA that it would be a better location for them. The area is much smaller, but the operation is considerably more efficient because of better layout and improved parking facilities. In addition, the new location is on the edge of a Negro neighborhood whose residents are substantially more affluent than those of the former location. The 1965 gross in the old location was $8,045; net was $135. In 1967, gross sales were expected to exceed $12,000, with a net of approximately $3,000.

In qualifying for the SBDP, Mr. Edmonson had a great deal of difficulty putting together an income tax statement, especially since he had never filed before. Both OCU and OCURA staff helped him assemble records and a tax statement. They were able to convince IRS not to press for back tax forms, since it was evident that no taxes would be owed.

Mack's Tire Shop

The owner-operator of Mack's Tire Shop employed his son and one other employee at his old location in the Medical Center Project area. The firm moved in January 1967 to an outlying site on U. S. Route 77, the main highway to Norman, Oklahoma. It is a heavily traveled route. The site is near the city of Moore, which has no tire outlet at all. The potential market is extremely good, and was selected on the advice of the OCU staff.

Mack's occupied 1,440 square feet at the old location, at a rental of $80 per month. The firm now rents 1,265 square feet of building area for $100 per month. However, there is more land area in the rear for storage and more room for on-site parking than was available in the old location.

As a result of liquidation of inventory prior to the move, Mack's lost money in 1967. The owner has worked closely with the OCU staff, however, and has obtained a franchise for a new line of tires as soon as he can obtain the funds to finance the new inventory.

The proprietor received moving expenses and an SBDP. He also applied for an SBA Economic Development Loan in the amount of $7,000. The staff at OCU expended 60 professional hours in accumulating the necessary documentation for the EDL application, and in meetings with SBA staff. The loan was approved in September 1967.

The OCU staff also worked with the owner in market research, selection of a location, and advising him on the erection and location of a new sign. Although his interim proceeds declined markedly after relocation, he is enthusiastic about the effort and advice expended on his behalf by both OCU and OCURA. He is convinced that in an operation of his size it would have been impossible to take the time away from his business to find an appropriate new location and to prepare the documentation necessary for the EDL.

Oklahoma Machine Works, Inc.

This firm was located in the John F. Kennedy Project. Its operations were characterized by disarray and inefficient layout at this location. It moved to an industrial zone between May 22 and May 25, 1967. Moving expenses and property loss were compensated in the full legal amount. The payment voucher was filed and approved on June 8, and the payment check was issued on the same day.

Although the president of the firm found the location himself, he had several leads from OCURA. He expressed considerable satisfaction with his handling by OCURA, especially the expeditious processing of his relocation payment.

The new plant is more modern, more efficient, and in a substantially better location to serve its customers than was the case in the old plant. The owner indicated that it was probably the best thing that had ever happened to the company, because they really needed to move from their other cramped quarters. However, they were doing well enough so that they did not take advantage of the possibility of moving until forced to do so by urban renewal.

The timing of the move, including acquisition of the property, was arranged to be most convenient for the firm. In addition, the prompt handling of their claim for reimbursement made it unnecessary to go outside for additional working capital funds at a time when they needed all of their money for new equipment and installations in the new location.

Ophelia's Beauty Parlor

The owner and operator of this beauty parlor is a Negro woman who operated the business from the front room of her home in the John F. Kennedy Project. She had built a small wing on the house for her aged mother. Her property was taken for clearance. She was offered a property to be rehabilitated in the same area, but the combined cost was too much for her. The OCURA business relocation staff searched the area and discovered a duplex residence just outside the project area. It is in the near vicinity of the State Capitol, the University Hospital, and the VA Hospital. The property has a two-car garage with a garage apartment upstairs. It is rented for $65 per month to a Negro couple, both of whom work at the VA Hospital. The owner's mother occupies the ground floor of the residence (she is 85 years old), and the owner lives on the second floor.

The proceeds of the sale of the former property enabled the owner to pay $2,500 down on the new property. She assumed the seller's mortgage at 5.75 per cent, and the seller took back a purchase-money mortgage for the remainder of the sale price at 6 per cent. This was somewhat below the then-current market rates for conventional mortgages in Oklahoma City. Total monthly payments on the new property (including insurance) are now $113. With the $65 per month rental from the garage apartment, the owner is paying less than the $60 per month necessary to carry her former property. The details of this transaction were worked out by the OCURA business relocation staff. It indicates the extent to which imaginative financing can create a favorable situation for a relocated business.

The owner also received a $2,500 SBDP. The bulk of this was used to convert the two-car garage into a beauty parlor. The owner developed such faith in the OCURA business relocation staff that she would not approve the conversion contract or even consult a lawyer without prior approval from them. This illustrates the kind of personal rapport that is frequently developed in Oklahoma City as a result of the individual attention given to business relocatees. It is particularly noteworthy in this case, since the owner was originally quite hostile to the idea of urban renewal and the necessity to move to a new location.

Grayson's Nursing Home

This business was located in the Medical Center Project. The proprietor owned the property, and remained as a tenant at $100 per month after OCURA acquired the property in May 1966. The former location was a large, somewhat dilapidated two-story frame building. It contained 13 rooms, but only two baths, and was 55 years old.

The move was completed between November 23 and November 30, 1966. The new location is in a residential area near a park on the outskirts of town. The new building contains 5,490 square feet on a 100' x 150' lot. There is an additional 50' x 150' lot in the rear for expansion. The new building contains thirteen double bedrooms, five staff and common rooms, and five baths.

Grayson's received moving expenses, property-loss compensation, and an SBDP. It also filed for ambulance costs in transferring ten bed-ridden patients. This was put out to bid in accordance with HUD regulations, but payment was denied because payment for moving "persons" could not exceed $5 per individual.

With the assistance of OCURA, the proprietor arranged a regular SBA loan for construction of the new facility. In the old location, Grayson's was licensed for 22 beds. The owner originally filed for 24 beds in the new location, on the assumption that he would also receive an EDL from SBA. The actual financing acquired through the regular SBA loan enabled him to build 22 beds. However, with the combined assistance of OCURA and OCU, he was able to show through his records that he could support more. As a result, a supplemental SBA Economic Development Loan was obtained in the amount of $9,500 so that he could expand the new building to 26 beds.

The proprietor has attended management seminars at OCU, and has received advisory work in management and bookkeeping. His wife is now the bookkeeper of the firm, as a result of taking work through OCU. These courses and advice were provided free of charge. OCU also helped in the preparation of income tax forms to document the claim for the SBDP, and to document the application for the supplemental Economic Development Loan from SBA.

One result of the move and the construction of the new facilities is that Grayson's Nursing Home had its rating with the state licensing authority raised from 1-B to 1-A. This means that he now receives $265 per month for welfare cases, as opposed to $235 per month at the old location. Also, he could not expand at the old location because he did not have a fireproof building.

Grayson's Nursing Home (above), an old wood-frame building. Prior to relocation, the business had a low rating because of the fire hazards present. Below, a one story, fire-resistant facility at its new location. The character of the new building has led to a higher rating and an increase in the number of beds licensed. (Photos courtesy Oklahoma City Urban Renewal Authority.)

Region VI

The Relocation Branch of the Region VI office of HUD is located in San Francisco. Because several LPA's within this Region have shown particular imagination in developing and applying innovative techniques and approaches to business relocation problems, the regional office has made a special effort to circulate the results of these efforts to other LPA's throughout the Region. One of the ingredients lacking in many areas is a continuing flow of information on workable ideas that may be used in approaching similar problems elsewhere. The Region VI office has attempted, on a modest scale, to accomplish this objective — which is also the theme of the present study.

Fresno, California

Fresno is a city of 150,000 whose LPA has contributed to the economic revival of the CBD through creation of the Fulton Mall as its major redevelopment project. The imaginative and successful business relocation cases considered here are nearly all related to the construction and relocation activities associated with the mall. Indeed, many of the innovative techniques demonstrated in Fresno evolved from the basic design concept and philosophy which underlay the creation of the downtown mall. The mall, while attracting national attention because of its "people orientation," was nonetheless also designed for business. That is, the plan for the mall considered the business interests that existed and which could also be drawn to the downtown area. The Fresno CBD was not truly deteriorating or decaying, nor was it hopelessly blighted. The volume of retail sales was relatively high, but by comparison with earlier periods and with other areas surrounding Fresno, it was faltering. Each year more commercial space was appearing vacant in the CBD, and periods between occupancy became longer. The city administration, sensitive to this situation, identified three alternative courses of action that could be taken to revitalize the downtown area and to reverse the downward trend of retail sales and assessed valuations.

One course of action, which was quickly rejected, was simply to do nothing. A second alternative would have been that taken by many cities — a complete facelifting through wholesale demolition and redevelopment. The third alternative identified by the administration was a program aimed at intensive yet selective reshaping of sections of the city to improve, yet not drastically change, the continuity of city growth. The third approach was the one selected by the city.

An imaginative first step was taken by interested groups throughout the city. An organization of CBD merchants known as the Downtown Association, in conjunction with the redevelopment agency, executed simultaneous but separate contracts with a planning consultant to develop plans for revitalization of the central Fresno area — an area of approximately two thousand acres. Of particular concern to the Downtown Association was a high-sales-volume retail district of approximately sixty to eighty acres.

The idea of the mall, which encompasses approximately eighteen city blocks, was to produce a "center of activity and social interaction." It was to be a pedestrian haven, where business could be conducted in a quiet and friendly atmosphere without direct confrontation with automobiles, trucks, and other sources of congestion and noise.

With this design concept also came the idea of selective improvements with a minimum of actual demolition and removal. Businesses were encouraged to participate, when appropriate, by improving store fronts to complement the general mall design. As necessary, buildings that were impossible to remodel were to be demolished. So, too, were those buildings on the periphery of the mall that were removed to make way for parking structures. In all, approximately thirty-six acres were scheduled for clearance and an additional fifty acres were identified for conservation or rehabilitation. Within the area designated for clearance or rehabilitation, approximately one hundred and eighty businesses were scheduled for displacement. The businesses ranged from very small retail-service establishments to large service-manufacturing firms; however, the majority of the firms were small, single proprietorships. In addition, 95 per cent of the firms displaced were tenants at their old locations.

Because of the basic project design and the environment of the CBD, as well as the imaginative and comprehensive services provided by the relocation staff of the LPA, a large percentage (nearly three-fourths) of the relocated businesses reestablished their operations within the central core area. Another 15 per cent remained within Fresno, while approximately 8 per cent relocated outside the city. Approximately 30 per cent of the displacees discontinued operations. The majority of discontinuances involved businesses operated by elderly people, firms with special licensing problems such as bars and taverns, and firms that can exist only in substandard areas with very low rental rates.

In addition to the basic design approach to business relocation problems exemplified by the mall, several other interesting and imaginative innovations were introduced in business relocation efforts in Fresno:

Temporary relocations. Because of the increased attractiveness of the CBD provided by the mall plan, many displaced businesses indicated a strong desire to remain in the general area or relocate in the mall. Temporary relocations were often used to accomplish this end when suitable quarters were not immediately available, or when site preparation required a waiting period before either moving to the new site or returning to the site from which the business was displaced. In many instances the relocation staff encouraged temporary relocation, and aided the businessman both in finding the appropriate interim location and in obtaining moving expense reimbursements for temporary moves.

Temporary locations. One of the rather unique features of Fresno's business relocation program is the temporary location (*not re*location) of small businesses into vacancies created by displaced businesses within and around the mall. In order to make the most efficient use of structures to be razed, the LPA rented structures on a strictly temporary basis if they were vacated some months before demolition was actually scheduled. Businesses to be displaced are notified that the building they occupy (generally as a tenant) is slated for demolition after property acquisition by the city. This notice is generally given well in advance of the time that demolition is actually to begin so that the businesses may work with the LPA in relocating. In many instances, a new site is found several months before demolition is scheduled. The business then moves, leaving a vacancy. This has two effects: (1) It produces obvious vacancies when one of the primary purposes of the renewal program is to revitalize the CBD, and (2) it leaves a structure vacant and unused when some small businesses have need for such space. Businesses wishing to occupy such space temporarily were given month-to-month leases to emphasize the fact that their tenure was definitely limited, as well as the fact that they were not eligible for relocation payments. However, the attraction of the Fulton Mall was such that businesses wished to locate there even for a short time so that they might "get their foot in the door." This practice indicates both the initiative of the LPA and the attractiveness of the mall, as well as its effect on the surrounding market area.

Preparation of move packages. Several procedures have been established in Fresno which greatly facilitate business moves. One such procedure is called the "moving tour." This involves common bidding by the various movers in the city and a tour of the business to be moved, conducted by the agency staff. A "move package" has been developed by the LPA, which contains pertinent forms and check-lists relating to the move. An inventory of items to be moved as well as peculiarities and specifications of the move are also included in this move package. In addition, the regulations concerning moving claims are detailed here for the business as well as the mover.

Once the business has identified the approximate date of the move, the agency contacts local movers and informs them of the opportunity to bid. Interested movers may then obtain the bid package which provides complete details. They may also accompany a relocation staff member at a designated time for a tour of the business firm, during which the staff and owner of the firm indicate the specific items and special problems associated with the move. Since all movers are conducted on a single tour, they may all benefit from the questions asked and answers given. In addition, the tour arrangement has stimulated interest in urban renewal relocation moves where interest was waning before. It is clear to the movers that the bid is truly made on a competitive basis.

This bidding procedure was initiated by calling all local movers to a group meeting and explaining the job that urban renewal was attempting to accomplish, outlining the difficulties of timing and red tape that were involved, and provided an outline of federal regulations on bid requirements and cost substantiation. The relocation staff stressed the fact that cooperation was needed among movers in order to facilitate the city's aims in bringing about a revitalized downtown. They further pointed out that a great deal of business could be generated that should be conducted in a sound and businesslike manner.

Promotional schemes. In addition to the Fulton Mall, which has received nationwide attention, the relocation staff has worked hard to obtain the full cooperation and emphthy of the local community, particularly businesses affected by urban renewal. The LPA has adopted one interesting general promotional technique which has produced surprising results. This practice evolved when the LPA started receiving unfavorable publicity from advertisements in the paper and on storefronts proclaiming that a sale was being conducted by the business because it was being "pushed out" by urban renewal. The collective effect of these ads and posters did not help the redevelopment agency's image. The relocation staff set out to show the businessmen that such tactics did not help their businesses either.

Their general approach was to point out to each displacee that "nobody likes a loser" and such ads simply conveyed the impression that the business was losing. In contrast, the staff suggested a positive approach in which the business emphasized its role in contributing to the progressive action of the city as well as its move to an improved location to serve the community better. This spirit of cooperation with the efforts of the city in upgrading the downtown area proved to be a much more effective approach for both the businessmen and the LPA.

In addition to suggesting this positive approach, the relocation staff aided the displaced businessman in his general promotional campaign by providing sample layouts for ads as well as promotional signs. This seemed like a small and insignificant effort at first, but the general impact on both attitude and on promotional effectiveness was significant.

Coordination of acquisition and relocation. The Fresno LPA, like many others, is organized so that the acquisition branch is separate from the business relocation branch. Nonetheless, the LPA staff has recognized the pressing need to coordinate acquisition and relocation activities closely. They have taken steps to ensure early contact of the business by the relocation branch when the acquisition branch has identified the business for displacement.

Business relocation report. The Fresno LPA has adopted the policy of publishing a periodic business relocation report. All affected businesses are listed by name and address, and divided between those that have relocated and those that have discontinued operations. In both cases, complete details are given regarding the amount of relocation payments received by each business, with a breakdown for each business by type of payments. For businesses that have discontinued operations, the reports give details on why the business decided to liquidate, and indicate the owner's attitude toward this decision.

This report has served at least two primary functions. First, it permitted everyone to see the exact relocation payments made, to offset rumors concerning excessively large or small claims. Second, the report demonstrated the interest that the LPA had in such businesses and indicated the efforts made to follow up every case.

The success of Fresno's business relocation program stemmed from the application of these techniques to the Fulton Mall Project. The basic design of the renewal program has played a significant role in providing new relocation sites as well as minimize business interruption and displacement. Unlike many similar renewal efforts involving a CBD, the actual construction of the Fresno Mall took less than six months. It was planned so that walkways to stores were provided at all times to allow access to remaining businesses. Because of the nature of the work being performed, retail business in the mall area actually increased during the construction phase.

Asher Brothers Shoes

This firm is a "discount" type shoe store that operates on the basis of high volume. Thus, location was critical to the firm in finding relocation facilities. Asher Brothers had operated in the same location for many years and enjoyed a relatively prosperous business with an established clientele. This firm was subjected to further pressures by the urban renewal planning process. Its displacement from the structure it rented was prompted by a plan to build a city-owned parking structure on the site. The firm was immediately contacted by the relocation staff and offered the use of a vacant agency-owned store nearby as a temporary site until a permanent location could be acquired. This arrangement waas quite satisfactory to the shoe store and a closing sale was initiated. In the meantime, the plan to demolish the structure housing the shoe store was changed and there was no longer a necessity to move immediately.

Although this "reprieve" allowed Asher Brothers additional time to secure a new and permanent location, it placed the business owners in an uncomfortable position. After advertising and conducting a sale based entirely upon impending relocation, they were forced to return to normal day-to-day retailing at their same location.

The problem of moving coupled with the "false alarm" that the business experienced placed a considerable strain on relations between the business and the LPA. However, because of the excellent rapport created by the relocation staff members, the business was aided in obtaining a very satisfactory permanent location. The building in which the firm obtained relocation space was constructed by another displaced businessman. Through negotiations encouraged by the relocation staff, the plans of the commercial structure that was constructed on the redevelopment site were coordinated with the needs of Asher Brothers so that the storage, loading, and sales space could be custom-made for the business. In addition, the firm was given every consideration in timing the move so that business interruption could be minimized.

The business now has an excellent location, near its old location, but with many new advantages. In addition to the more efficient layout, Asher Brothers is now the prime tenant in a new structure and occupies the largest retail space on a busy downtown corner. Business volume has increased significantly, as has that of most businesses in this area. The owner expressed personal appreciation for the efforts of the relocation staff in dealing with a particularly sensitive and difficult situation.

Coney Island Lunch

The Coney Island Lunch is a cafe specializing in hot dogs. It had operated in the same location for over thirty-five years when approached by the redevelopment agency about displacement. Because of the long tenure at this location, as well as optimism concerning the business prospects of the CBD, the owners of this business felt that it was critical to find a relocation site nearby. After several contacts with the relocation staff, a temporary relocation in a vacant agency-owned building just across the street was offered the business until a permanent location meeting their specifications could be found.

Although the location of the temporary site was ideal, the structure was in need of repairs. The firm invested more than $6,000 in repairs, remodeling, and the costs of the temporary move. All of these costs were borne by the owner, but he considered this outlay "insurance" on his gamble that a suitable permanent location in the same vicinity could be found.

This was a wise expenditure, as this firm was later able to obtain rental space in a structure developed by another displacee in the mall area. Remaining in the same general area, plus the overall renewal efforts in the mall, has proved a boon to business. Although its rental was up considerably over the old location, this firm also enjoyed a much higher volume of business as it neared its fortieth year of operation.

Club Brazil

This case involves a small bar in the downtown area that catered basically to a workingman clientele. Although the bar had a profitable business prior to acquisition, the general character of the area in which it was located had been steadily deteriorating. At the time of acquisition, the neighborhood was described as "honky-tonk" and contained over twenty bars in a three-block area.

During the intial interview with the relocation staff of Fresno, the bar owner indicated his desire to upgrade his operation in order to complement rather than detract from the redevelopment project. The redevelopment staff encouraged this businessman in his efforts and contact was made with the displacee-developer who had also provided space for both Asher Brothers Shoes and Coney Island Lunch. Space was obtained at the rear of Asher Brothers Shoes and the business was transformed into an elegant cocktail lounge. It is interesting to note that this business is now the sole survivor among the many bars that were located in this area at the time of acquisition.

Dr. Stuart Snider, Optometrist

Dr. Snider purchased an optometric practice and in the process acquired a considerable amount of dated equipment and a lease in one of Fresno's oldest buildings. Not long after this purchase, Dr. Snider was contacted by the redevelopment agency and informed that he was to be displaced. He was very much distressed at the prospect of moving. He had not been aware of the urban renewal plans nor the possibility that the structure which housed his practice would be demolished. His particular concern was the loss he anticipated from his recent investment.

A central factor in the relocation of this office was the optometrist's desire to remain in the same vicinity. A major reason for purchasing the practice was its established location and professional office. Dr. Snider did not want to lose this advantage. With the combined efforts of the relocation staff and another displacee friend of the optometrist, a temporary relocation site was found in a nearby commercial structure. There Dr. Snider could maintain his practice while awaiting completion of the building that would eventually serve as his permanent relocation site. He personally paid for the move to the temporary location so that he might later claim moving expenses and direct property loss at the time of his permanent move.

The temporary location was quite acceptable to the optometrist's needs, and he was able to retain most of his patients during this period. After a few months, construction on his permanent location was ready and he completed his move.

United Jewelry and Loan

The owner and operator of United Jewelry and Loan, a small pawnshop in downtown Fresno, had been a tenant in this area for many years. The structure occupied by this business was required for an off-street parking site. The relocation staff took immediate steps to find a suitable temporary location for the business. An acceptable temporary location was found in the same block and the businessman moved there at his own expense.

During the initial contacts with the relocation staff, the businessman indicated his desire to become a developer-owner in the same urban renewal project that had displaced his business. His initial intention was to purchase project land and construct a new building to provide a permanent location for his own business. However, in subsequent discussions with the relocation staff and with other displacees in the neighborhood who required relocation space, he became convinced that his pawnshop operation would be inappropriate in the redeveloped environment. Nonetheless, he retained his desire to invest in the new mall project and was successful in negotiating leases with four displacee businesses (Asher Brothers Shoes, Coney Island Lunch, Club Brazil, and Dr. Stuart Snider) in the project area. His decision to develop a commercial structure for rental income purposes was also a decision to liquidate his pawnshop business and convert his operation into an investment property management venture.

The business owner continued to operate his pawnshop at the temporary location until a suitable purchaser of the business was found. When this was accomplished, the proceeds from the sale were reinvested in the project development, and four displacees were provided commercial space for relocation.

Walston and Co.

The relocation of this stock brokerage office illustrates both the coordination and cooperation required to avoid business interruption, and the remarkable results that can be achieved with imaginative rehabilitation. This brokerage company occupied space in a deteriorating building in the CBD that was over sixty years old. It was among the first business firms to be relocated within Fresno. The firm had contemplated a move even before urban renewal, but because of the restrictions of a long-term lease, they were deferring such action. The urban renewal project and the subsequent notice of impending displacement prompted Walston to search for a nearby suitable site. The structure eventually selected reflects a great deal of imagination in that it represents the rehabilitation of an old building into an outstanding commercial structure.

The owner of the new location had purchased an aging five-story hotel structure and transformed it into a single-story, modern commercial structure. This was accomplished by demolishing the upper floors, constructing a brick facade, and completely remodeling the interior portions of the structure.

The physical move of this business firm presented a significant problem in that little business interruption could be tolerated. In order to maintain appropriate service for brokerage customers, the move had to be accomplished during one weekend. The new site was located only two blocks away on the same side of the street, but many problems existed in the installation of needed equipment. The relocation staff devoted a considerable amount of time coordinating this move and obtaining prior approval from HUD to install a new electronic stock-price board at the relocation site in advance of the move. The firm was thus able to move during a weekend and resume operation on the following Monday. This plan was accomplished without incident. The resident manager indicated that business increased substantially after the move. He likewise expressed appreciation to the relocation staff for the opportunities afforded the firm in relocating and for the help provided during the actual move.

Western Union Telegraph Company

The move of a Western Union Telegraph branch office presented a unique experience to the Fresno relocation staff, as well as a number of problems. The primary problem was the fact that the nature of the business permitted no cessation of telegraph service — that is, no down-time could be tolerated during a move. In order to achieve this uninterrupted flow of communications it was necessary for the Western Union Telegraph Company to construct a duplicate business facility at a new location prior to its move.

With the help of the relocation staff, a new site was secured and a new building constructed to Western Union specifications just three blocks away from the old site. While Western Union continued its operation at the old location, the installation of new facilities and underground cables in the new building was completed. When all plans and arrangements were finished, the move was instantaneous insofar as the communications systems were concerned.

This relocation effort involved well in excess of the $25,000 maximum payment allowable under urban renewal regulations. Because of the specialized and technical nature of the equipment involved, the company carried out a self-move. All claims were promptly processed by the redevelopment agency. As this was one of the first moves of this type in Region VI, it provided a guide to other LPA's confronted subsequently with similar problems.

Sacramento, California

The city of Sacramento, the capital of California, has a population of over 200,000. In 1967, it had carried out two major downtown urban renewal projects. The first project displaced some 350 business concerns, while the second project involved nearly 450 businesses and non-profit organizations. In both projects, approximately one-half of the displaced businesses discontinued operations. This seemingly high rate of discontinuance may be explained by the relatively large number of dilapidated residence hotels and rooming houses in both project areas as well as many "greasy spoons" and "grog shops." Sacramento had, for some time, faced a significant problem in coping with the skid-row sections of its CBD. Urban renewal efforts were undertaken in large part to rid the town of these blighted areas. Thus, it is not surprising that many businesses in these areas discontinued operations when urban renewal was initiated. A significant problem still remains, however, because of the high percentage of migratory workers who spend a large part of the year in this city, or who simply retire here. Such individuals have very low incomes and are prone to frequent the skid-row flop houses and other business establishments.

In the face of these very special and difficult problems, the relocation staff prides itself on the degree of personal service that is offered and provided each business displacee. Some of the specific elements of the business relocation program in Sacramento include:

Early and continued assistance. The relocation staff seeks to provide early service to the displacee, and has attempted in nearly every instance to contact him well in advance of the impending move. From this early contact, assistance is provided throughout the move process to the final follow-up to determine the status of the business after relocation.

Business relocation as a specialized function. The redevelopment agency in Sacramento is organized so that business relocation specialists deal exclusively with business firms. That is, business and family relocation are separated in terms of both staff and general function. Three staff members are normally involved in each business relocation — the agency representative, the relocation supervisor, and the chief of relocation and community services.

Relocation manual. A relocation manual detailing the entire relocation process has been developed by the Sacramento LPA. It contains a complete and comprehensive narrative of instruction concerning both family and business relocation. This manual both explains and illustrates the steps in the relocation process for staff members.

Move assistance. A considerable amount of help with the actual physical move is provided those businesses desiring it. The agency provides consultation on this matter as well as handling all bids, awarding the move contract, and generally making arrangements for the move. They consult with the businessmen concerning the layout of the new business and attempt to be on hand to ensure a quick and smooth move. This has meant, in many cases, a minimum of business interruption.

Relocation profile. The LPA of Sacramento publishes a "relocation profile" on each completed project, so that the nature and results of their family and business relocation efforts are evident. Although this publication does not contain comprehensive detail on each displacee, it does provide a useful overview. This has been most helpful to the agency in publicizing its desire and willingness to aid displacees, and in gaining displacee acceptance to make the task of relocation somewhat easier.

A-1 Upholstery and Manufacturing Company

This small manufacturing firm was successfully relocated from a "skid-row" area. Actually, this move involved two businesses. The second firm, Lucas Manufacturing Company, was located in the same structure and was displaced at the same time as A-1 Upholstery. Although conducting separate operations, the firms were complementary to each other. A-1 manufactured new furniture to custom order and reupholstered older furniture, while Lucas Manufacturing operated as an interior decorating firm. When these two business owners met with relocation staff members, they were encouraged not only to relocate together, but also to merge their businesses so that Lucas in effect became a subcontractor of A-1 Upholstery. Relocation staff members aided the firms in their search for a new location. A recently vacated but relatively new structure was found that could adequately house both. With the acquisition of the new space, these former "skid-row" tenants merged.

Although the two firms originally obtained only a two-year lease with an option for an additional two years at the new location, they also have an option to buy and fully anticipate exercising this option. Although the structure from which the businesses were displaced had been leased at a lower rate, it had encountered higher operating costs. For example, insurance on the businesses was prohibitively high and impossible to purchase during the last few months of tenure at the old location. Fires were frequent in this "skid-row" area and it was difficult to protect businesses from vandalism.

The new location offers many advantages over the old in terms of access to major arteries and a general improvement in environment. The new building is equipped with a complete sprinkler system and affords much better efficiency of handling because of large doors in both ends of the structure. In addition, the new site provides a considerable amount of off-street parking whereas the old site offered none.

The move of A-1 Upholstery was somewhat complicated by the necessity of installing 220-volt wiring for some of the machinery, and compressed air lines for the pneumatic staplers at the new location. On these and other moving matters the relocation staff provided full cooperation and assistance. The relocation claim was processed so that payment was received within a month of the move.

Adjustment Bureau of Sacramento

This business firm presented a special problem to the relocation staff of Sacramento because of timing requirements in its physical move. The nature of this business was such that it could well have been ruined if it had been forced to discontinue operations for even a few days. Continuity of operation is essential. Through the coordination and assistance provided by the redevelopment agency, the entire move was conducted during one weekend; the doors were open on the following Monday morning for business as usual.

The essentials of success in this case were, first of all, ample notice of displacement so that appropriate steps could be taken to plan the move. The business owners were able to find a site which met their special locational requirements (close proximity to the telephone company, the post office, and other central-city establishments) and negotiated a rental which was not substantially higher than they were paying in the old location.

The relocation staff worked closely with the business managers both in planning for and in making specific arrangements for the move. All telephone equipment was installed and painting completed prior to the move. Once the move was completed the relocation staff made prompt reimbursement, within one month, for moving expenses incurred and for loss of property.

One interesting sidelight of this case involved the installation of telephone systems. Since this was not a reimbursable expense, the firm could not make a claim for one of the largest expenses it incurred — over $1,000.

A-1 Upholstery and Manufacturing Co. in its "skid-row" location (above) at the time of displacement below, in its new environment. (Photos courtesy Sacramento Redevelopment Agency.)

Henry Taketa, Attorney

In this instance a displacee not only became the owner of his own office building structure at the relocation site, but also supplied office space for many other displacees from the project area. Although the relocation staff of Sacramento did not play a significant role in this relocation, it does illustrate the type of effort that has been encouraged by this LPA.

This attorney occupied office space in a building that was over seventy years old. He owned a one-third fee interest in the structure. From the proceeds of the acquisition price he purchased a site from the redevelopment agency within the same project area. The provision of space by the LPA was a critical factor in this instance, as was their cooperation in the construction of the new structure on this site.

At the encouragment of the LPA, the new building developed by the attorney was designed to accommodate several other tenants displaced from the project area. Today, this new office building not only furnishes space for the relocated attorney, but also houses a physician, an optometrist, an insurance firm, a small newspaper, and a barber shop.

Sacramento Composition Company

This case particularly illustrates the services provided by the relocation staff in planning and executing the physical move of a business if such services are needed by the firm. In addition, this firm was provided extensive help in identifying a relocation site.

This medium-sized printing plant was located in the loft of a dilapidated building nearly 70 years old. Access to the firm was available only by a steep and narrow stairway with two jogs. Because of the poor layout and inappropriate design of the structure for this type of business, machinery and other equipment were difficult to operate and often inaccessible during busy printing periods.

The customers of this printing firm depended upon (and in fact demanded) quick delivery of job lots. One of the critical issues that arose when the business owner was notified of his impending displacement was the desire to avoid business interruption. After initial contact and an identification of the key elements of the move, the relocation staff of Sacramento immediately set out to help the businessman find a relocation site. Many commercial structures were found by the LPA staff. After much deliberation the business owner decided to relocate in a newly constructed unit near the central business district.

The actual move of this printing plant was, with the owner's consent and encouragement, planned and implemented by the relocation staff. Two methods were available to move the large but delicate machinery: It could be dismantled, moved in pieces, and reassembled in the new structure; or a hole could be cut in the roof of the old building and the machinery lifted through the hole by a truck crane and transported to the new location on flat-bed trailers. Because of the necessity of keeping business interruption to a minimum, the latter technique was used. The "hole-in-the-roof" method proved to be both expedient and much more economical for both the owner and the LPA.

In addition to the technical requirements in moving the machinery, there was also the involved job of realigning, readjusting, and resetting the printing machinery at the new site. This task was performed by experts retained by the relocation staff. The layout of the machinery in the new structure followed schematic drawings provided by the business owner.

With careful coordination and imaginative techniques, the relocation staff was able to accomplish the business move during one weekend. This caused the business to lose only two working days during the move.

Walsh's Bar

This "skid-row" bar was successfully relocated to a hotel within the same general area. It was given the opportunity to upgrade its business considerably in the process.

The owner of this small bar was a tenant in his original location and was notified, with substantial advance notice, of the demolition plans for the area. With the help of the LPA staff, he was able to acquire a bar located nearby. He bought the business (the license, the fixtures, stock, and other business equipment) for purposes of relocation.

The owner of this bar abandoned the majority of the equipment and other property in his old location and received the maximum direct property-loss settlement. With this payment, he was able to purchase new fixtures and equipment for the relocation site.

San Francisco, California

San Francisco is a city of over 750,000 population. The staff of the San Francisco Redevelopment Agency (SFRA) had handled nearly 1,000 business relocations by 1967. The vast majority of these business relocations involved small businesses in residential-commercial areas. Its major single accomplishment, however, was the San Francisco Produce Market relocation. At the time of this study, three major project areas were in advanced stages of execution, with three additional projects in early development and planning.

San Francisco Produce Market

This mass relocation involved a $75,000,000-a-year produce market center composed of approximately 38 independent wholesalers. The relocation took six years to complete, and eventually involved the concerted efforts of various levels of government, the redevelopment agency, and many interested and affected local businessmen. During the course of this massive relocation SFRA was able to provide the leadership necessary to bring such a complex move to a successful conclusion.

The old produce center was overcrowded, disorganized, and inefficient. Chief Ahern of the San Francisco Police Department described the traffic in the market area as "complete chaos" during morning business hours. Large numbers of merchants, many customers, and the necessary use of delivery trucks in connection with the produce business all contributed to the congestion in an area of narrow streets with totally inadequate parking and loading facilities. Streets and sidewalks in the area lost nearly all utility except to serve as extensions of the market. In a report submitted to the mayor by Ahern, it was noted that most merchants were breaking the law by storing and displaying produce on the sidewalks. However, the report concluded that the lack of adequate floor space within the business structures, coupled with the inability to expand their facilities, compelled the owners to persist in this violation. Should they be needed, fire vehicles could move through the area only with considerable delay and confusion. It was obvious to all, the retail and wholesale merchants included, that a change in location and expanded facilities offered the only reasonable solution.

According to one produce merchant who was interviewed, the produce dealers had been unsuccessfully seeking a new site since 1921. Though most of the merchants agreed that they should stay together in order to retain the desired market environment, they lacked organization and effective leadership. This, coupled with the anticipated problems of selling their properties in the event of a mass move, deterred any serious relocation actions on the part of the merchants.

San Francisco Produce Market in its old, congested downtown location. (Photo courtesy San Francisco Redevelopment Agency.)

By 1955, conditions at the markets had deteriorated to the point that the area was declared blighted by the San Francisco Board of Supervisors. In 1958, it was designated as the Embarcadero-Lower Market Redevelopment Project Area E-1. The declaration of the project and the threat of condemnation provided further impetus for the search for a new produce site. Ideally this site would be in San Francisco. It would also be large enough both to accommodate the businesses involved in the relocation and provide additional space for the necessary expansion of many of these firms.

At this same time, the U. S. Marine Corps Depot at Islais Creek was being phased out of service and the land was to be sold as surplus. Representatives of the produce merchants were approached by the redevelopment agency and asked to consider the purchase of this land as a site for their new market. However, the merchants were also considering a less costly site in South San Francisco. This alternative site would have meant the loss of a $75,000,000-a-year business from the tax base of San Francisco. Thus the city government of San Francisco also became involved in the search for a new site. Their principal criterion was to find a suitable site within the city limits. Islais Creek met the physical and locational requirements of both the merchants and the city.

Negotiating the purchase of the 24.5-acre site from the federal government involved considerable time and effort by the local government. If the merchants had attempted to negotiate the purchase of the land in their own name as a private profit-making organization, they would have been compelled to bid, on a competitive basis, against other potential users of this site. This situation, in the view of the merchants, was unsatisfactory. They felt they could not meet the competitive price which would have resulted from public auction. The alternative was to encourage the purchase of this site by a government agency, in which case the purchase price would be negotiated. The city attorney's office was asked to outline the necessary steps for the formation of a non-profit corporation consisting of San Francisco citizens, with a board of directors appointed by the mayor. This approach was possible under California redevelopment law and eventually led to the formation of the City of San Francisco Market Corporation.

Under this rather unique organizational arrangement, the non-profit corporation was legally empowered to issue revenue bonds and use the proceeds for the purchase of the produce center site. Actually, the corporation gave the City of San Francisco the money to purchase the site. After the purchase was accomplished, the corporation leased the produce terminal site, exclusive of public streets, for a term of 50 years. With considerable time and effort, the city made the appropriate arrangements with the U. S. General Services Administration to receive first option on the Islais Creek site. A delegation of produce merchants indicated that they were most interested in seeing this transaction materialize.

During the negotiation and transaction period, many problems arose, not the least of which was the price of the site. The price asked by the General Services Administration exceeded by $1,000,000 that amount which the corporation (under the cloak of the city) was willing to pay. After months of meetings, a price of $2,160,000 for the 24.5-acre Islais Creek site was agreed upon; the transaction took place in October 1961.

Because the negotiations between the city and the federal government were prolonged, many of the produce merchants grew anxious and began schemes to relocate on their own. One group found and purchased a site in the city of South San Francisco. In the process, they took over 60 per cent of the produce trade with them. This split among the original group of produce merchants was never reconciled, and today the San Francisco area is served by two major produce markets rather than by one. The San Francisco Produce Market is generally regarded as being by far the more successful.

The San Francisco Market Corporation financed the construction of the new produce market with the remainder of the proceeds from the bond issue shortly after acquisition of the Islais Creek site. The completed structures provided 84 stalls (with dimensions of 25 feet by 100 feet) for displaced produce merchants wishing to relocate, as well as space for some new businesses. The new constructed stalls have both a front and rear covered platform and loading dock, and provide many advantages over the original produce market site other than simply additional space.

The individual stalls are incorporated in four large buildings that face one another so as to provide a very large center area for convenient parking. In addition to the produce stalls, there are three restaurants, a bank, a super-service station, and an office building. Railroad sidings serve the produce stalls and the site provides unobstructed access for ingress and egress.

The individual stalls were designed and constructed to take advantage of the generally cool San Francisco climate. High ceilings and large ceiling fans provide excellent ventilation. Each stall is partitioned at the top with screening so that air flows freely throughout each building. Roll-up steel screen doors are employed for security and protection, and at the same time allow for additional ventilation. These features reduce significantly the need for expensive refrigeration equipment in this produce market.

The ownership and tenancy arrangements for the market are particularly innovative and noteworthy. The corporation which governs the market is a municipal non-profit corporation which is, for all practical purposes, operated by the businessmen in the center. The stock of the corporation may be issued only to the city, which therefore owns the market. In order to qualify as a municipal non-profit organization, the City of San Francisco Market Corporation was required to show that its formation was in the best interests of the city's population. Precedents for such an organization had been established both by the Candlestick Park Corporation and by the many public parking garages in San Francisco that were financed in a similar manner. The overriding consideration in this case was that it was in the best interests of the residents of San Francisco to keep the large produce center in San Francisco, providing employment, income and property tax revenues. The stated intent of the corporation, organized in January 1961, was:

San Francisco Produce Market at its new industrial site. (Photo courtesy San Francisco Redevelopment Agency.)

... solely to render financial and other assistance to the City and County of San Francisco by financing the purchase of the site for a produce and related food processing market from the General Services Administration by financing, constructing, establishing and maintaining on behalf of the city a market for produce and related food processing establishment.

The total cost of both the site and the new buildings on this site was 6.5 million dollars; this sum was financed entirely by revenue bonds issued by the corporation and guaranteed by the city. The contract between the city and corporation stipulated that the revenues derived from the rents of the market would be used, first of all, to pay the maintenance and operating costs of the market. Proceeds over and above these costs would then be used to retire the outstanding debt. Once the bonds are completely retired by the revenues of this corporation, the corporation is by law automatically dissolved and the property holdings of the corporation revert to the city. The bonds were issued for a term of 25 years. A major life insurance company purchased most of the prior lien revenue bonds ($4,100,000) on which a rate of 5 per cent per annum was paid. Subordinate revenue bonds in the aggregate amount not exceeding $500,000 were issued in part for cash and in part as payment for services. These bonds also bear a 5 per cent per annum interest rate.

Each of the displaced businesses that wished to relocate in the market as a tenant was required to pay one year's rent in advance. Each business pays $275 per month for each stall on a long-term lease agreement. After the bonds are completely retired, the tenants then have a rent-free perpetual interest in the San Francisco Produce Terminal, with the exception of maintenance and operational expenses.

The new San Francisco Produce Terminal has been in operation since 1963. In 1967, business for the 34 firms located here had risen considerably. Collectively, the displaced merchants reported an increase of 15 to 20 million dollars in yearly sales over those at the old location. In addition, a significant increase in effective storage space was achieved by the relocation; the displaced firms gained nearly 50,000 square feet of additional space over the old location. Although rentals were increased in some cases, the increases were more than offset by the savings from labor-saving devices. These devices, made possible because of dock height, facilitate the daily receipt and delivery of merchandise.

In summary, the combined efforts of public and private individuals and agencies, under the leadership of the San Francisco Redevelopment Agency, resulted in a truly successful and imaginative business relocation effort. Many of the legal and economic elements are transferable to other communities facing the problem of a declining produce market area. In addition, the organizational and legal framework is applicable to other groups of businesses that significantly affect public interests.

Santa Clara, California

Santa Clara's urban renewal program involved one project which incorporated the entire "downtown" or central business district. In this city of 80,000 population, the downtown is an eight-block area, of which a two-block area had been improved by a new complex of four common-wall structures in 1967. The remaining six blocks of the downtown area had been cleared and made ready for redevelopment.

The size of the central business district is considerably smaller than is usual for a city of this population. This stems from the fact that Santa Clara County is criss-crossed by major shopping "strips" which extend along many miles of major streets and are thus accessible to the residents of all adjacent communities.

Because of the amount of CBD clearance by redevelopment in Santa Clara, as well as the marginal character and small size of many of the businesses that existed in the downtown area at the time of urban renewal, a majority of displacees either discontinued operations or relocated outside the city.

The truly outstanding feature of this relocation program was the number and volume of Small Business Administration loans that were arranged. Less than 150 businesses were displaced in this project. Yet the full time of two staff members of the LPA was devoted to providing personalized service for business relocatees, especially arranging for SBA loans.

Arranging for SBA Displaced Business Loans. A large part of one staff member's time was devoted expressly to the processing of SBA loans for displacees. The result of this individual service has been a volume of SBA loans exceeding

$750,000. Most of the displacees relocating within the CBD have received Displaced Business Loans from SBA. This high degree of successful DBL applications can be explained only by the resolution and vigor of the relocation staff in initiating follow-up actions with both the Small Business Assistance office and the displacee.

When the urban renewal program was initiated, the relocation staff discovered that the majority of businessmen who had indicated a desire to relocate in the Downtown Project Area would require both administrative assistance and financial help. In reviewing the prospects of obtaining loans for these displacees, the staff identified two critical problems: (1) The LPA was inexperienced in identification of eligibility criteria and in the general processing procedures for such loans; and (2) the regional office of SBA was located some distance away in San Francisco.

The staff was convinced that frequent contact with SBA officials would be necessary to obtain favorable consideration for DBL loans. Also, timing associated with loss of business by the displacee and progress of project activities posed an additional processing problem. Consequently, the first step in their program of obtaining adequate financing for the displacees was to clear lines of communication with the SBA regional office. Next, members of the relocation staff familiarized themselves as completely as possible with SBA loan requirements so that they could provide initial screening and judgments as to eligibility. Finally, the relocation staff, in their first loan application, sat through all sessions with the businessman and essentially "walked the loan through." In this manner, they gained important experience in the application of SBA requirements.

As a result of laying this initial groundwork on the processing of DBL loans, the LPA staff then took it upon itself to screen applicants, counsel them concerning requirements and specifications, and finally aid the applicant in developing the statements and estimates of financing required. Procedurally, the following steps are taken within this LPA to aid the businessman in obtaining a DBL:

1. All initial paperwork concerning the loan is completed at the LPA office. The businessman is thoroughly briefed prior to his meeting with SBA. He is informed of the type of materials that will be necessary, and advised on the type of planning estimates that SBA will require before considering the loan. Complete financial records are developed with the help of the relocation staff and/or a professional accountant. The relocation staff of the LPA analyzes the problems of the specific business and helps the businessman produce statements based on both expected costs at the new location and the projected working capital requirements of the business. Only after all of the basic data are developed and assembled is SBA approached.

2. After the loan application is initiated, the relocation staff member responsible to this businessman maintains almost daily contact with SBA either in answering additional questions or in making inquiries concerning disposition of the loan. The average time for approval of an SBA loan under these

circumstances has been approximately twenty days — remarkable time in terms of the experiences of other LPA's studied.

The logic of this approach is persuasive when the question of handling the special problems of business displacees is considered. The redevelopment agency faces on a day-to-day basis the pressing problems of relocating businessmen and of meeting specific time schedules with respect to the project. Its acknowledged responsibility to the displacee has led this LPA to "carry the ball" in pursuing adequate financing for displaced businesses. The success of this effort may be gauged in at least two ways: (1) the number and amount of loans received for displacees that have been relocated in the CBD, and (2) the rapport that has been established by this LPA with the regional SBA office in San Francisco. The confidence that the SBA office has in the Santa Clara LPA is shown in the fact that this office frequently requests the relocation ,staff to look in on relocated businesses receiving DBL's to determine the status of the loan. This close working relationship is an obvious ingredient in the overall success of the DBL loan program carried out in Santa Clara.

The Bike Shop

The special problem confronting the relocation staff in this instance was the fact that when the businessman was displaced from his rental quarters, he was not officially open for business. At the time the redevelopment agency was acquiring properties, the business owner was contacting wholesalers and making general arrangements to open his business, but was not actually conducting the retail segment of his operation at the time of displacement. The task of the LPA staff here was to gather necessary evidence in order to establish the eligibility of this business for both loan and relocation claim purposes.

During conferences with the relocation staff, the businessman indicated that he was negotiating with certain wholesale and retail establishments throughout the state in order to establish sources of supply and open his business in the near future. This activity was enough to qualify his business as a going concern, and the businessman as a legitimate SBA loan applicant. In order to provide the necessary substantiation for purposes of qualification, the relocation staff contacted the dealers with whom this businessman negotiated, and obtained affidavits certifying that he was the operating owner of a business prior to the time of the declaration of the renewal project. This follow-through on the part of the relocation staff took considerable time and effort. However, once the affidavits and other supporting materials were assembled and submitted, the loan application was ruled as eligible and the business was granted a DBL.

With this loan the business owner was able to construct a commercial structure in the project area. He is currently renting space in this building to two other tenants. In 1967 he was even considering moving to a lower rent location himself because it appeared that the space he occupied could bring a greater return if rented than if he continued to use it for his bike shop.

The steps taken by the relocation staff in pursuing to the end the SBA loan for this business illustrates the kind of personal service provided in Santa Clara. The result of this relocation is more space for the business, as well as a change in status from renter to owner.

Common-Wall Group Relocation

One of the most interesting business relocation efforts in Santa Clara involves the development of a common-wall commercial structure which houses three businesses. In this structure are a barber, an optometrist, an insurance agency and an additional investor who was not a displacee but simply a fourth party in ownership of the building. The three business displacees were all relocated from the downtown project and were all tenants prior to displacement. They became fee owners in a prime commercial structure and, with the exception of the outside investor, all have space to serve their own businesses plus additional rental space.

One owner of the common-wall structure is a barber — a lifetime resident and businessman in downtown Santa Clara. When contacted about the pending displacement, he indicated a willingness to buy or build, but had a critical need for financing. The relocation staff set about to obtain an SBA loan for this business.

Since the businessman desired additional space which could be rented, and since this objective was consistent with the overall development plan, a one-third increase in floor space was approved. The original barbershop had occupied more space than it had actually required, so that the one-third upgrade resulted in a considerable excess over current business needs.

The move to the new structure also allowed this barber to make substantial improvements in equipment since the old barber chairs and associated equipment were sold as a direct property loss in the move. The business also received a Small Business Displacement Payment. With the combined proceeds of the direct property-loss payment and SBDP, the barber was able to furnish his new shop with completely new equipment.

Although only 25 per cent of the project was redeveloped by 1967, business had improved substantially in the new location. The barber was quite optimistic about the prospects of his investment. He was also pleased with the advantage of owning as opposed to renting the property.

The second businessman involved in this common-wall relocation effort is an insurance agent. This businessman's situation was much like that of the barber. He was a tenant in the downtown area and had rented an established location in the CBD for some years. He was convinced that his critical problem in relocation was to remain in the downtown area.

The redevelopment staff, in their early contacts with this insurance agent, suggested that he become a developer in the project area as an investor in a condominium structure. The reaction of this businessman to the condominium idea was much like that of several others in this area — he objected to becoming an owner of an undivided part of interest in a business structure. He definitely wanted a building that he could call his own. As an alternative, a structure with separate fee ownerships of common-wall divisions was suggested. This "party-wall agreement" provided individual ownership to each of the businesses within a single structure which met the overall requirements of the redevelopment plan. This approach was well received by this insurance agent, as well as others. This technique proved the key to successful relocation of the business.

The party-wall agreement provided for a sharing of initial costs of the walls common to both buildings which were set on the boundary lines of the divided property. The cost of all exterior walls, slab and roof was also shared by the three parties. The agreement extended to maintenance and repairs to common walls used by two parties, and provided that the costs of such repair should be borne by both parties proportionately. This agreement helped provide small individual ownership without sacrificing the advantages of larger scale developments.

The third displacee member of this common-wall relocation effort is an optometrist. Like his partners in this venture, he was a tenant in the downtown area at the time urban renewal was initiated. As in the other two cases, the optometrist felt it was critical for him to remain in the downtown area. He was also favorably inclined toward the fee ownership possibilities that the common-wall interests provided. In addition, he was very interested in the prospect of becoming not only an owner in fee but also a landlord. This latter status could help significantly towards meeting mortgage amortization payments and improving his general financial position.

In this situation, the displacees not only acquired adequate relocation space, but were also able to change their tenancy status from renter to owner. This was accomplished in each case with an SBA loan which provided expansion room, and indeed space in excess of the displacees' actual current needs. The relocation structure in this instance is divided into individual fee ownerships for each business concern. This approach to relocation provided not only the type of ownership desired by the businesses, but the scale of development dictated by the redevelopment plan. Also, the rental space that each of these businesses offers provided opportunities to house other business displacees.

Region VII

The HUD Region VII office located in San Juan, Puerto Rico serves Puerto Rico and the Virgin Islands. The business relocation staff consists of two relocation specialists, both of whom are natives of San Juan. This is extremely important, because Spanish is much more widely used in Puerto Rico than is English. For a large number of business displacees, the only language is Spanish. The Region VII office has translated HUD regulations and the regulations for SBA.Displaced Business Loans into Spanish.

The Region VII staff maintains extremely close working ties with the Puerto Rico Urban Renewal and Housing Corporation, which is the LPA for the entire Commonwealth of Puerto Rico. These working ties facilitate prompt action when it is necessary. A major problem confronting the Region VII business relocation staff is the fact that so very many displaced businesses in Puerto Rico are too small to receive effective aid through the programs of SBA. Moreover, the high degree of mobility among businesses in Puerto Rico has led the business relocation staff to the conclusion that SBA disbursements should be possible before a formal execution date is set, and a Loan and Grant contract is signed.

San Juan, Puerto Rico

Both housing and urban renewal activities in Puerto Rico are carried out by the Puerto Rico Urban Renewal and Housing Corporation (CRUV). This is a commonwealth agency which operates in all municipalities throughout the island. There is extremely close coordination between housing and urban renewal activities. This is especially important in Puerto Rico, because new public housing facilities also offer relocation resources for many affected small businesses.

Technically, only one of the projects studied is actually located within the political boundaries of San Juan (1960 population: 432,000). However, the San Juan metropolitan area is so densely populated and the localities developed on such an integrated basis that the relocation cases studied in Puerto Rico are treated as if they occurred in one large metropolitan community. This approach is reinforced by the fact that one LPA handles renewal and relocation activities for the entire commonwealth.

As of April 1967, CRUV had completed eight redevelopment projects, and had forty more in execution. CRUV works as an LPA in seventy-six municipalities throughout the island. Staging and phasing of renewal activities are coordinated with the Puerto Rico Planning Board.

In all housing and urban renewal activities in Puerto Rico, much more emphasis is placed on the use of public funds to finance development than is the case on the mainland. While some private financing is encountered, the bulk of development funds have come from the Development Bank (BGF) and from the state-financed Commercial Development Corporation of Puerto Rico (CDC). Moreover, local municipal bond issues are also widely employed.

Several local characteristics distinguish public housing and urban renewal efforts in Puerto Rico. In San Juan, it is estimated that approximately 70 per cent of the population is eligible for public housing. However, some 30 per cent of this eligible population cannot afford public housing. At the same time, land in the San Juan metropolitan area has become extremely expensive. This means that very substantial writedowns are necessary to bring both housing and commercial facilities to rental levels that displacees can afford. It further means that a very high percentage of business displacees are "lost" in the relocation process.

Beyond this, a number of significant features characterize the businesses affected by urban renewal in most project areas in the San Juan area. No matter how small their businesses, most displaced businessmen were owners of their (usually extremely low-value) properties in the former locations. Most of the businesses involved are too small to qualify for SBA financing. Typically, they cannot meet the repayment requirements. Therefore, they most commonly move from owner to tenant status. Moreover, the great majority of displaced businessmen cannot qualify for an SBDP because they have filed no previous income tax forms, and they have no records or books on which to hypothecate these forms even if IRS would allow back filing with no penalty. They cannot prove they were "in business."

A very large proportion of businesses affected by urban renewal have been located in the residences of the owners. Another substantial segment may be regarded as "portable" businesses, being operated out of pushcarts, converted trucks, or cycle-driven carts. Beyond this, the bulk of affected businesses have had very localized market areas, providing personal services, foodstuffs or food and drink (cantinas) to immediate neighborhood residents.

As a result of this pattern of characteristics, CRUV's business relocation personnel have been forced to recognize the reality that a substantial proportion of displaced businesses are so small that they will be lost before they can be helped. Effective help in relocation can therefore be offered to only a relatively few.

Problems of identification and record-keeping on individual business displacee "cases" presented for CRUV represent techniques and ideas, rather than specific relocations of particular firms. One example of this is a concentrated effort by

LPA staff to convince individual municipalities to amend their zoning regulations to permit household activities and businesses in residential areas. This effort is designed to retain the essential life style of the families and businesses relocated. It illustrates the adaptability to local circumstances that is necessary if effective business relocation is to be carried out.

Public Housing Projects

CRUV has established a policy of providing commercial space in public housing developments and in privately financed housing for displacees from urban renewal project areas (e.g., 221-d-3 projects). Business displacees have priority for occupancy in these commercial facilities. A variety of tenure arrangements has been developed. For example, two commercial areas provide rental space for retail stores in one 221-d-3 project acquired by CRUV. Twelve spaces have been rented to displaced businesses in another public housing development in Guayama.

Condominium developments are popular in Puerto Rico, including publicly supported projects. Seven spaces have been sold to displaced businesses in the Luna Condominium. There are also business relocatees in the Quintana High-Rise Condominium. As of April 1967, twelve displaced businessmen had been able to finance acquisition of condominium space through below-market loans from SBA.

San Juan. Relocated small businesses in centers built into public housing projects. (Photos courtesy CREUES.)

CRUV has also reserved sites in public housing project areas which are sold to commercial enterprises for construction of their own facilities. Displaced businesses have priority claims on these locations as well. Arrangements have been made to finance self-help construction for small establishments.

This multi-faceted effort to provide relocation resources in public housing developments recognizes the life style of many families and businessmen in Puerto Rico. It further recognizes that the marginal character of many displaced businesses can provide only enough income to their operators to enable them to live in subsidized housing.

Commercial Development of Puerto Rico (CDC)

CDC is a public development corporation organized in June of 1962 with $1,100,000 from the Commonwealth Legislature and a $1,000,000 line of credit from the Bank for Development (BGF). It is an agency of the Commonwealth Department of Commerce "to promote the creation of commercial centers throughout the island, to establish a loan program for small business concerns unable to obtain financing from other sources, and to assist these concerns in their management problems." CDC therefore engages as a prime developer of commercial facilities, and occasionally advances funds for private commercial development. It has been a redeveloper in several CRUV project areas.

In addition to providing relocation resources for which displaced firms have a priority claim (provided they can otherwise meet eligibility requirements), CDC has become directly involved in the business relocation process in cooperation with CRUV. Its staff assists displaced businesses in their record-keeping and the assembly of documentation to qualify for SBDP's and SBA loans. CDC has also provided facilities in direct response to the needs of displaced businesses in many instances. The resources of CDC are limited, however. Building on a base of approximately $3,000,000 in commonwealth funds, it has generated total assets of approximately $6,500,000. As of April 1967, CDC had 11 projects in execution or planning, containing approximately 450 business establishments to be displaced.

Shopping Centers (Centro Commercial)

With CDC construction financing, commercial centers have been established in Arecibo, Humacao, and Rio Piedras. Each of these is in a renewal project area, and each gave priority to displacees. Nearly all of the relocated firms are extremely small businesses occupying modest square footage. In Arecibo, ten of the twenty businesses were locatees. In Humacao, six of twenty-seven were relocatees. Eleven of eighteen in Rio Piedras were relocatees. In a great majority of cases, the area occupied is less than 1,000 square feet. Rentals range between $2.50 and $3.00 per square foot per year.

Additional shopping centers were planned for development by CDC in project areas in Aquadilla, Cayey, and Quintana.

While these centers provide relocation opportunities for only the relatively more affluent businesses, they represent an important area of cooperation between CRUV and CDC in its role as public developer. This activity does accommodate the needs of a significant, if small, segment of business displacees.

Public Markets (Plaza de Mercado)

One of the basic features of commerce in Puerto Rico is the public market. In centrally located, publicly-owned structures, food merchants rent stalls on a daily, weekly or monthly basis. These stalls are normally quite small (approximately 8' X 8'), and offer minimal facilities. Most of the merchants either grow their own produce or collect it from farmers in the rural areas and bring the food to market daily. Because this is a long-standing tradition on the island, most established public markets are severely dilapidated and deteriorated.

In two instances, CDC has built new public markets in near proximity to the old locations, and the dilapidated structures have been removed as part of urban renewal.

In Arecibo, 152 booths were constructed and occupied exclusively by displacees from the old market. The old market was occupied until the new facility was available. Then a mass move occurred in 1966. Retail establishments occupied 138 booths; there were also six wholesale establishments and eight tobacco stands. Rentals range from approximately $4.00 per week to a maximum of $20 per week.

In El Hoyo project in Cayey, 15 grocery, vegetable and poultry dealers were moved in 1960 to a temporary relocation (which is discussed below), and all were permanently relocated in a new facility on June 30, 1965. The size of the stalls varies from 95 square feet to 365 square feet. Monthly rentals in the old location ranged from $6 to $39. In the new location, the range is between $6 and $16 per month. Most establishments have gross annual sales of less than $4,000 per year.

The Plaza de Mercado in Rio Piedras represents a slightly different arrangement. A large mall-type structure was constructed within two blocks of the old site. All market occupants from the old, congested and dilapidated Plaza de Mercado relocated to it. In addition, a number of retail establishments moved into the new structure. In all, 55 small food merchants located in the new Central Comercial.

This facility has underground parking and loading and all stalls on the ground floor face toward an interior mall, rather than to the street, as is typically the case in a public market. CDC handled all relocations. In addition to the food merchants, twelve retail establishments banded together to form a discount department store on a franchise basis.

San Juan.   New public market facility for displaced food and produce merchants in Rio Piedras. (Photo courtesy CREUES.)

El Hoyo Public Market (Temporary Relocation)

Because they served a highly localized market, a number of businesses have been temporarily relocated while their new commercial facilities were being constructed. In the case of the public market in the El Hoyo project in Cayey, 15 extremely small firms were involved. All were grocery, vegetable or poultry merchants (one did sell sacks of coal as well).

Because it was deemed both necessary and desirable to keep these firms together in a single market facility, as well as to keep the market as close to the original location as possible, it was decided to construct the new market on the site of the old market. Adjacent land was acquired by CRUV and the buildings on it were razed. This site was destined to become the parking lot for the new market. A temporary aluminum building was constructed by CRUV on this site. Between November 1959 and August 1960, all 15 of the businesses moved into the temporary building. They occupied it for four and one-half years, while the old market structure was demolished and a new market building constructed. During this time, they paid rent to CRUV. On June 30, 1965, all the firms were moved from the temporary building into the new market structure. The temporary building was then removed and the area was surfaced for parking.

As a result of this action, an important market facility was preserved for the residents of the community. In the process, none of the businesses discontinued operations, despite the fact that each is extremely small, with annual gross sales ranging from $1,000 to $3,600.

Puerto Nuevo

CDC has developed a warehouse and wholesaling complex in Puerto Nuevo. This is also a port facility, served by four gantry cranes for loading and unloading containers for sea-train and sea-truck shipment. In 1967, there were four warehouse buildings containing a total of 626,000 square feet. These facilities are owned and operated by CDC, which also maintains its offices in Puerto Nuevo. The development is designed exclusively for warehousing and whole-saling operations. Six of the tenants were dislocatees from La Puntilla project in San Juan.

This development is a conscious effort to relocate warehousing activities to the new port facility, and away from the congested and dilapidated warehouse district of Old San Juan. It provides relocation facilities specifically for food warehousing and wholesaling operations. Once again, CDC has worked closely with CRUV in timing and planning this development, and in providing space for displaced businesses.

Rent Insurance

The Commonwealth Department of Commerce has established a rent insurance program separate from the SBA lease guarantee program. It is designed to pay rent to a private landlord in the event that a tenant fails to meet his rental obligations. It also provides insurance against vacancy. The tenant pays an annual premium of 1.5 per cent to 3.0 per cent of the annual rent. A reserve fund of $100,000 was established to initiate the program. The purpose of this effort is to enhance the credit rating of small retailers, to make them attractive and acceptable to shopping center developers and owners. In turn, this improved credit rating of tenants may make it possible for the shopping center developer to obtain financing from private sources more readily.

The program was initiated in Puerto Rico because the U. S. Department of Commerce determined that the development and construction of shopping centers financed entirely with public funds should be reduced to a minimum. Rent insurance represents an effort, therefore, to encourage more private development of commercial facilities. At the same time, private developers are encouraged to make space in their centers available to small businesses displaced by urban renewal. Rent insurance also affords an opportunity to attract private developers to create commercial facilities to reuse areas of urban renewal projects.

Selected References

Anderson, Martin. *The Federal Bulldozer: A Critical Analysis of Urban Renewal, 1949—1962.* Cambridge, Mass.: M. I. T. Press, 1964.

Baltimore Urban Renewal and Housing Agency. *The Displacement of Small Business from a Slum Clearance Area: The Experience in Mount Royal Plaza, Baltimore, Maryland.* Baltimore: by the author, 1959.

Berry, Brian J. L., Sandra J. Parsons, and Rutherford H.Platt. *The Impact of Urban Renewal on Small Business.* Chicago: Center for Urban Studies, University of Chicago, 1969.

Berry, Brian J. L. *Comparative Mortality Experience of Small Businesses in Four Chicago Communities.* Background Paper No. 4, Small Business Relocation Study. Chicago: Center for Urban Studies, University of Chicago, November 1966.

Boston College, Bureau of Public Affairs. *An Effective Program for the Relocation of Business from Urban Renewal Areas.* Boston: Massachusetts Department of Commerce, 1963.

Commercial Loan Insurance Corporation. *Lease Guarantee Insurance.* Milwaukee: by the author, 1968.

Detroit City Plan Commission. *Commercial Renewal Study: A Measurement of Tendency Toward Commercial Blight.* Master Plan Technical Report No. 9, 2nd Series. Detroit: by the author, 1958.

Doctors, Samuel I. *The Private Firm As Manager of an Urban Renewal Project.* Storrs, Connecticut: New England Research Applications Center, University of Connecticut, July 1967.

Greater Boston Economic Study Committee. *Business Relocation Caused by the Boston Central Artery.* Economic Report No. 6. Boston: by the author, 1960.

Groberg, Robert P. *Centralized Relocation: A New Municipal Service.* Washington: National Association of Housing and Redevelopment Officials, 1969.

Harris, Stephen M. "Collision Course: Downtown Improvement and Business Relocation," unpublished manuscript, 1966.

Harris, Stephen M. "When Urban Renewal Forces You to Move Your Business — Some ABC's of Commercial Relocation," *Appraisal and Valuation Manual,* Vol. 8. New York: American Society of Appraisers, June 1965.

"How Business Spurs a City's Revival," *San Francisco Business Week,* September 9, 1961, pp. 87—92.

Joyce, David, and Mary K. Nenno. *The Social Functioning of the Dislodged Elderly: A Study of Post-Relocation Assistance.* Philadelphia: Institute for Environmental Studies, University of Pennsylvania, December 1966.

Kinnard, William N., Jr. "Business Relocation Problems of the Elderly Caused by Forced Dislocation under Public Improvement Programs," in *Essays on the Problems Faced in the Relocation of Elderly Persons,* edited by Chester Rapkin. 2nd Edition. Philadelphia: University of Pennsylvania, 1964.

Kinnard, William N., Jr. *Current Issues in Business Dislocation from Public Improvement Project Areas.* Connecticut Urban Research Reports No. 3. Storrs, Connecticut: Institute of Urban Research, University of Connecticut, March 1964.

Kinnard, William N., Jr., and Zenon S. Malinowski. *The Impact of Dislocation from Urban Renewal Areas on Small Business.* Prepared for the U. S. Small Business Administration. Storrs, Connecticut: School of Business Administration, University of Connecticut, July 1960.

Malinowski, Zenon S., and William N. Kinnard, Jr. *Personal Factors Influencing Small Manufacturing Plant Locations.* Storrs, Connecticut: Small Business Management Research Reports, University of Connecticut, 1961.

Meltzer, Jack, *et al. Selected Aspects of Urban Renewal in Chicago: An Annotated Summary.* Prepared for the Metropolitan Housing and Planning Council. Chicago: Center for Urban Studies, University of Chicago, August 1965.

Meyer, Eric W. *The Effect of Business Displacement Due to Urban Renewal: A Case Study of the Lindsay Park Urban Renewal Area in New York City.* Brooklyn, New York: Pratt Center for Community Improvement, Department of City and Regional Planning, Pratt Institute, 1967.

National Association of Housing and Redevelopment Officials. *Community Renewal Program Experience in Ten Cities: Report on a Conference Held at the Washington Center for Metropolitan Studies.* Washington, D. C.: by the author, 1964.

National Association of Housing and Redevelopment Officials. *Journal of Housing,* various issues.

National Association of Housing and Redevelopment Officials. *Selected References on Family and Business Relocation Caused by Urban Renewal and Other Public Improvements.* Chicago: by the author, 1961.

Niebanck, Paul L. *Relocation in Urban Planning: From Obstacle To Opportunity.* Philadelphia: University of Pennsylvania Press, 1968.

Parsons, Sandra. *Displacement Effects of Urban Renewal Upon Small Business: A Survey of the Literature.* Background Paper No. 2, Small Business Relocation Study. Chicago: Center for Urban Studies, University of Chicago, August 1966.

Philadelphia Housing Association. *Administrative Location of the Centralized Relocation Bureau.* Philadelphia: by the author, 1968.

Platt, Rutherford H. *Changing Congressional Provisions for Small Businesses Displaced by Urban Renewal.* Background Paper No. 1, Small Business Relocation Study. Chicago: Center for Urban Studies, University of Chicago, August 1966.

Rapkin, Chester (ed.). *Essays on the Problems Faced in the Relocation of Elderly Persons.* Philadelphia: Institute for Urban Studies, University of Pennsylvania, 1964.

Saperstein, Harriet. "The Dislocation of Small Business: Elmwood I," in *Studies in Change and Renewal in an Urban Community,* edited by Charles Lebeaux and Eleanor Wolf. 2 Volumes. Detroit: Wayne State University, 1965.

Slayton, William. "Urban Renewal: A Challenge to Businessmen," *Sears Urban Renewal Observer,* April 1962, p. 1.

U. S. Advisory Commission on Intergovernmental Relations. *Relocation: Unequal Treatment of People and Businesses Displaced by Governments.* A Commission Report. Washington, D. C.: U. S. Government Printing Office, 1965.

U. S. Attorney General. *Problems of Small Business Displacement under Programs of Public Investment: Report of the Attorney General Pursuant to Section 10 (c) of the Small Business Act of 1958, As Amended.* Washington, D. C.: Department of Justice, 1966.

U. S. Bureau of Public Roads. *Highway Relocation Assistance Study.* Washington, D. C., n.d.

U. S. Department of Housing and Urban Development. *HUD News,* various issues.

U. S. House of Representatives. Committee on Banking and Currency. *Basic Laws and Authorities on Housing and Urban Development.* Washington, D. C.: U. S. Government Printing Office, 1965.

U. S. House of Representatives. Committee on Banking and Currency. *Hearings before the Subcommittee on Housing (H. R. 9751).* Washington, D. C.: U. S. Government Printing Office, 1964.

U. S. House of Representatives. Committee on Banking and Currency. *Summary of the Housing and Urban Development Act of 1966 (H. R. 15890).* Washington, D. C.: U. S. Government Printing Office, June 25, 1966.

U. S. House of Representatives. Committee on Public Works. *Study of Compensation and Assistance for Persons Affected by Real Property Acquisition in Federal and Federally-Aided Programs.* 88th Congress, 2nd Session, 1965.

U. S. House of Representatives. District of Columbia Committee. *Authorized Payments of Relocation Costs Made Necessary by D. C. Government.* Washington, D. C.: U. S. Government Printing Office, September 1967.

U. S. House of Representatives. Select Committee on Small Business. *Small Business Problems in Urban Areas.* Hearings before Subcommittee Number 4. 88th Congress, 2nd Session, 1965.

U. S. House of Representatives. Select Committee on Small Business. *Small Business Problems in Urban Areas.* Hearings before Subcommittee Number 5. Volume II. 89th Congress, 1st Session, 1965.

U. S. House of Representatives. Select Committee on Small Business. *Small Business Problems in Urban Areas.* A Report of Subcommittee No. 5. H. R. 2343. Washington, D. C.: U. S. Government Printing Office, December 1966.

U. S. Senate. *Uniform Compensation for Relocation.* Hearings before the Subcommittee on Intergovernmental Relations of the Committee on Governmental Operations. Washington, D. C.: U. S. Government Printing Office, 1965.

U. S. Senate. Committee on Banking and Currency. *Housing Legislation of 1965: Hearing before a Subcommittee . . . on S. 1354.* Washington, D. C.: U. S. Government Printing Office, 1965.

U. S. Senate. Committee on Banking and Currency. *Housing Legislation of 1966: Hearings before a Subcommittee . . . on Proposed Housing Legislation for 1966.* 2 parts. Washington, D. C.: U. S. Government Printing Office, 1966.

U. S. Senate. Committee on Governmental Operations. *Uniform Compensation for Relocation: Hearings before the Subcommittee on Intergovernmental Relations . . . on S. 1201 and S. 1681.* Washington, D. C.: U. S. Government Printing Office, 1965.

U. S. Senate. Select Committee on Small Business. *Fifteenth Annual Report . . . Together with Minority and Additional Views.* Washington, D. C.: U. S. Government Printing Office, 1965.

U. S. Senate. Select Committee on Small Business. *Small Business Investment Act.* Washington, D. C., April 1, 1965.

U. S. Small Business Administration. *Lease Guarantee.* Washington, D. C.: U. S. Government Printing Office, December 1967.

U. S. Small Business Administration. *Lease Guarantee Program: Proposed Operating Plan.* Two Volumes. Washington, D. C.: by the author, January 31, 1967.

U. S. Small Business Administration. "SBA Loans for Displaced Business Concerns under Section 7 (6) of the Small Business Act," *SBA Notice,* July 1961.

U. S. Urban Renewal Administration. *Determining Local Relocation Standards.* Washington, D. C.: U. S. Government Printing Office, 1961.

U. S. Urban Renewal Administration. *Relocation from Urban Renewal Project Areas through December 1961.* Washington, D. C.: by the author, 1962.

U. S. Urban Renewal Administration. *Urban Renewal Notes,* various issues.

U. S. Urban Renewal Administration. *Urban Renewal Relocation of Business Concerns and Nonprofit Associations: A Fact Sheet.* Washington, D. C.: by the author, August 1965.

"Urban Renewal," Parts I and II, *Law and Contemporary Problems,* XXV and XXVI (Autumn 1960; Winter 1961), both issues devoted entirely to urban renewal programs.

Washington Housing Association. *Report on Re-examination of the Need for a Central Relocation Service.* Washington, D. C.: by the author, 1958.

Whitman, Edmund S. *Plant Relocation: A Case History.* New York: American Management Association, 1966.

Zimmer, Basil George. *Rebuilding Cities: The Effects of Displacement and Relocation on Small Business.* Chicago: Quadrangle Books, 1964.